GUNDAM
THE ORIGIN ™

GARMA

SECTION I

CREATED BY

HAJIME YATATE
YOSHIYUKI TOMINO

矢立肇・富野由悠季

MECHANICAL DESIGN

KUNIO OKAWARA

大河原邦男

PRESENTED BY

YOSHIKAZU
YASUHIKO

安彦良和

ASSISTANT: MASATO

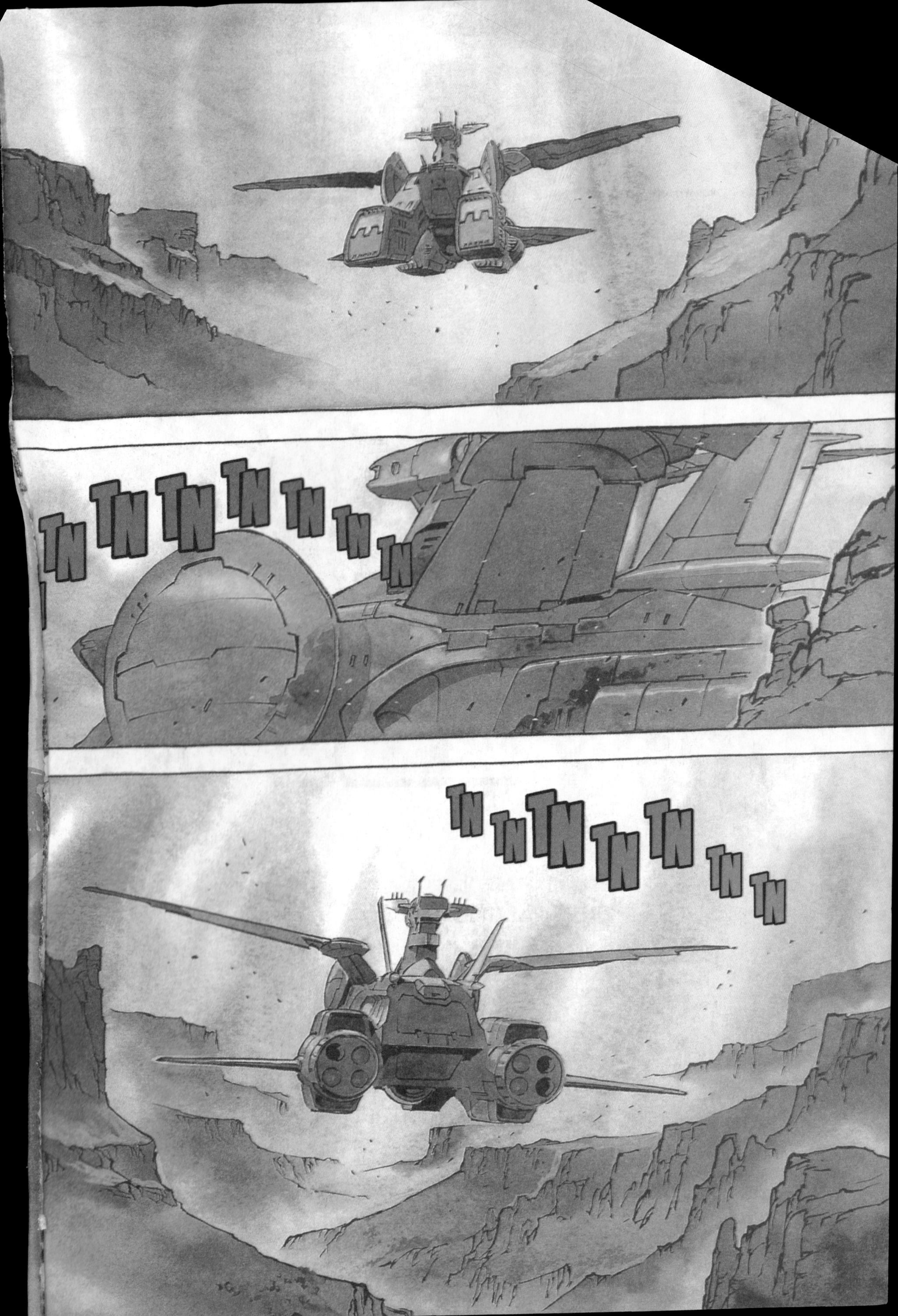
TN TN TN TN TN TN TN
TN TN TN TN TN TN TN

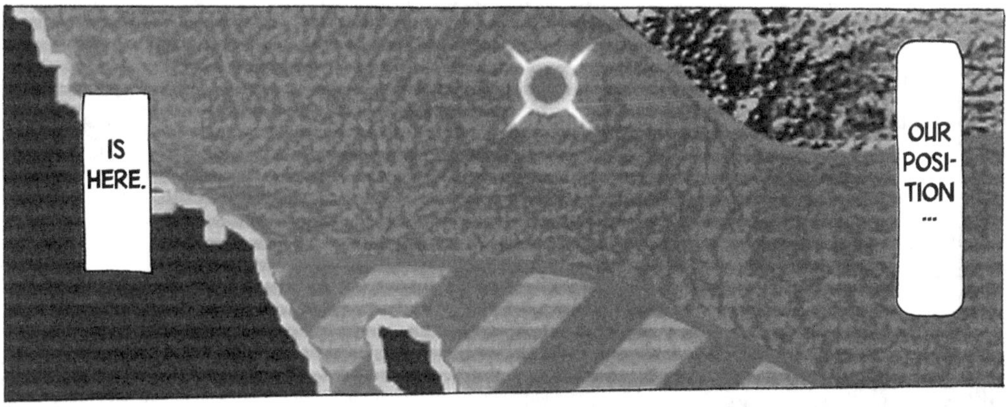
OUR POSI-TION ...
IS HERE.

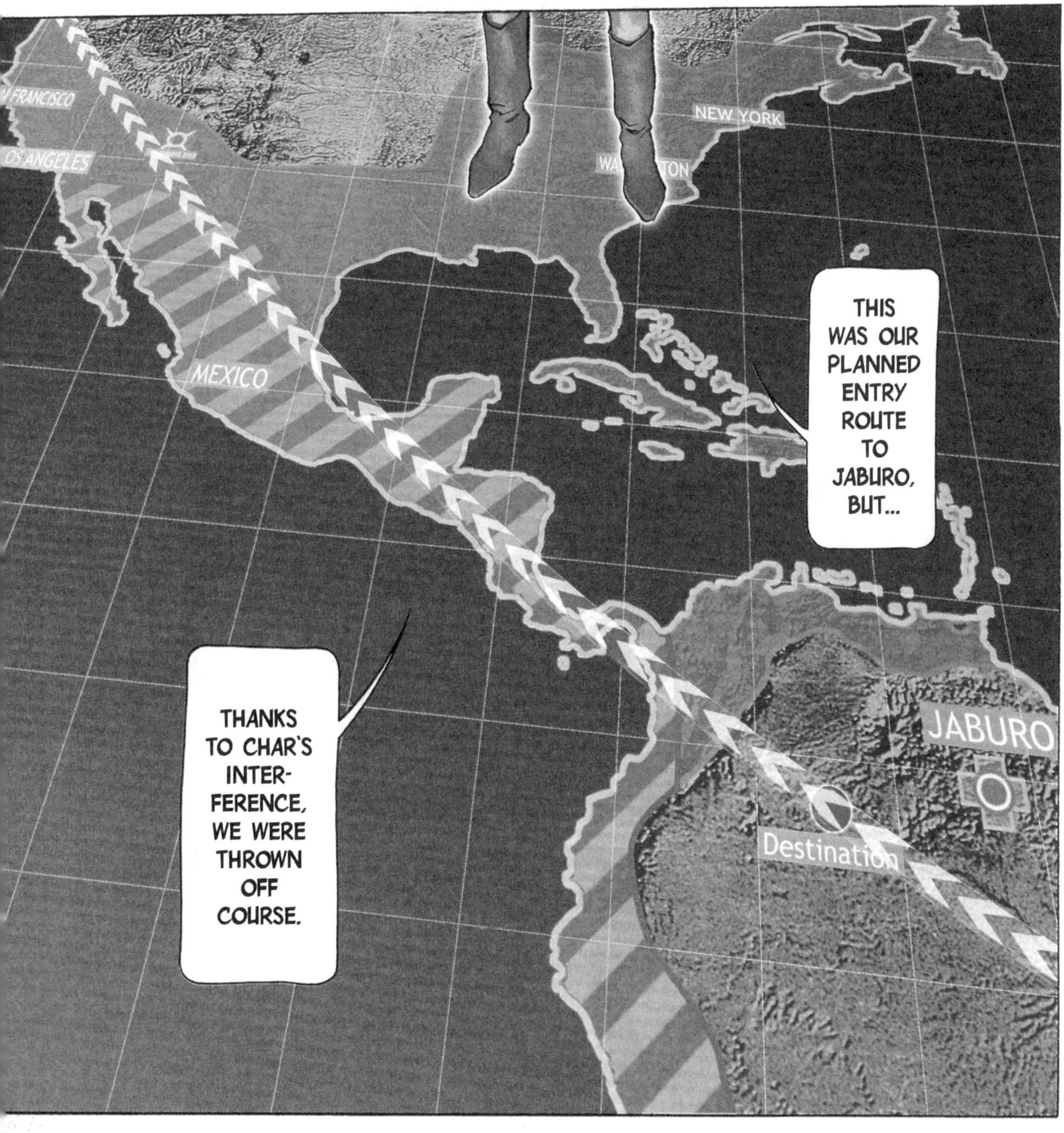
THIS WAS OUR PLANNED ENTRY ROUTE TO JABURO, BUT...
THANKS TO CHAR'S INTER-FERENCE, WE WERE THROWN OFF COURSE.
NEW YORK
MEXICO
JABURO
Destination

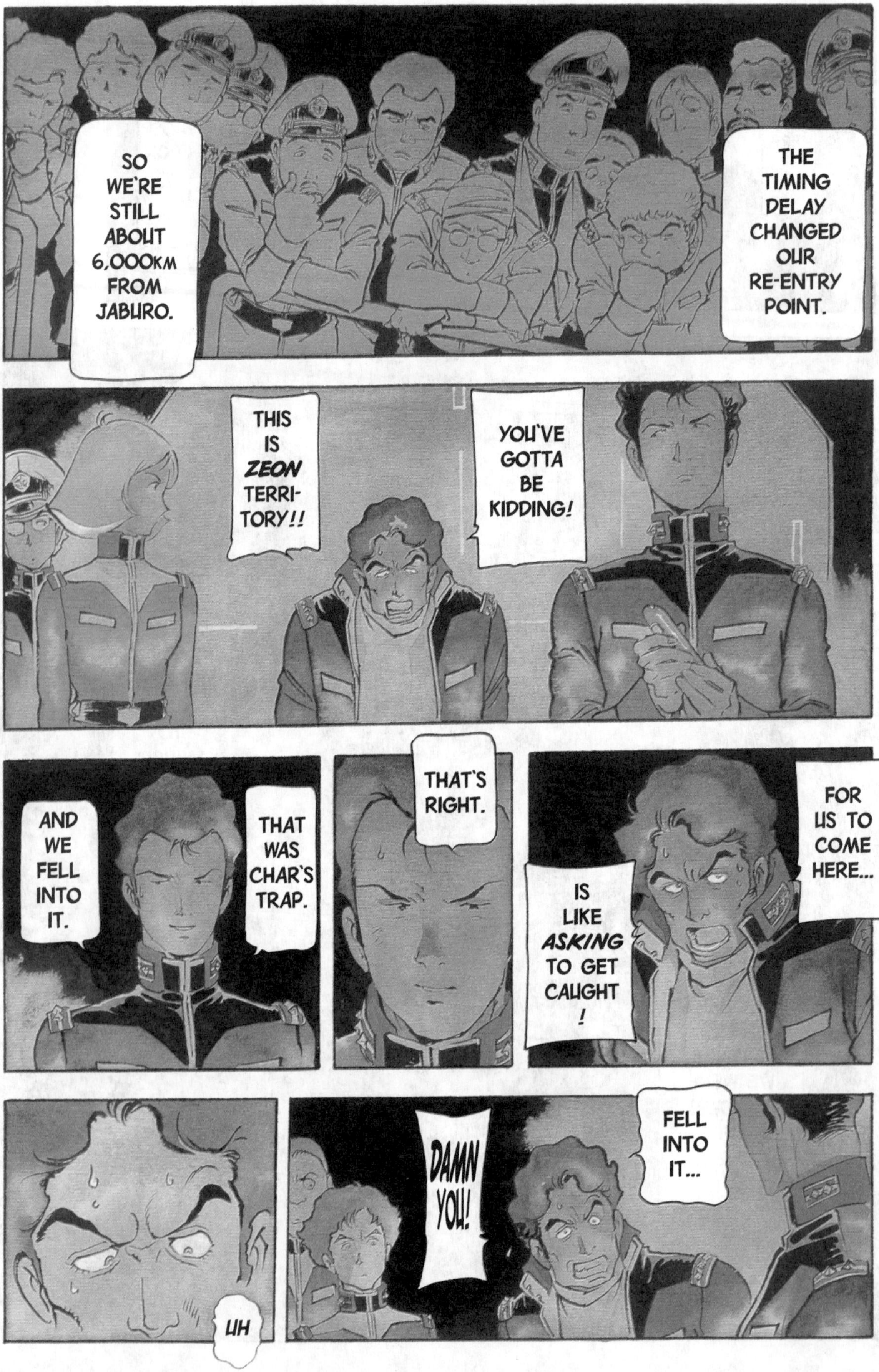
THE TIMING DELAY CHANGED OUR RE-ENTRY POINT.
SO WE'RE STILL ABOUT 6,000KM FROM JABURO.
YOU'VE GOTTA BE KIDDING!
THIS IS ZEON TERRITORY!!
FOR US TO COME HERE...
IS LIKE ASKING TO GET CAUGHT!
THAT'S RIGHT.
THAT WAS CHAR'S TRAP.
AND WE FELL INTO IT.
FELL INTO IT...
DAMN YOU!
UH

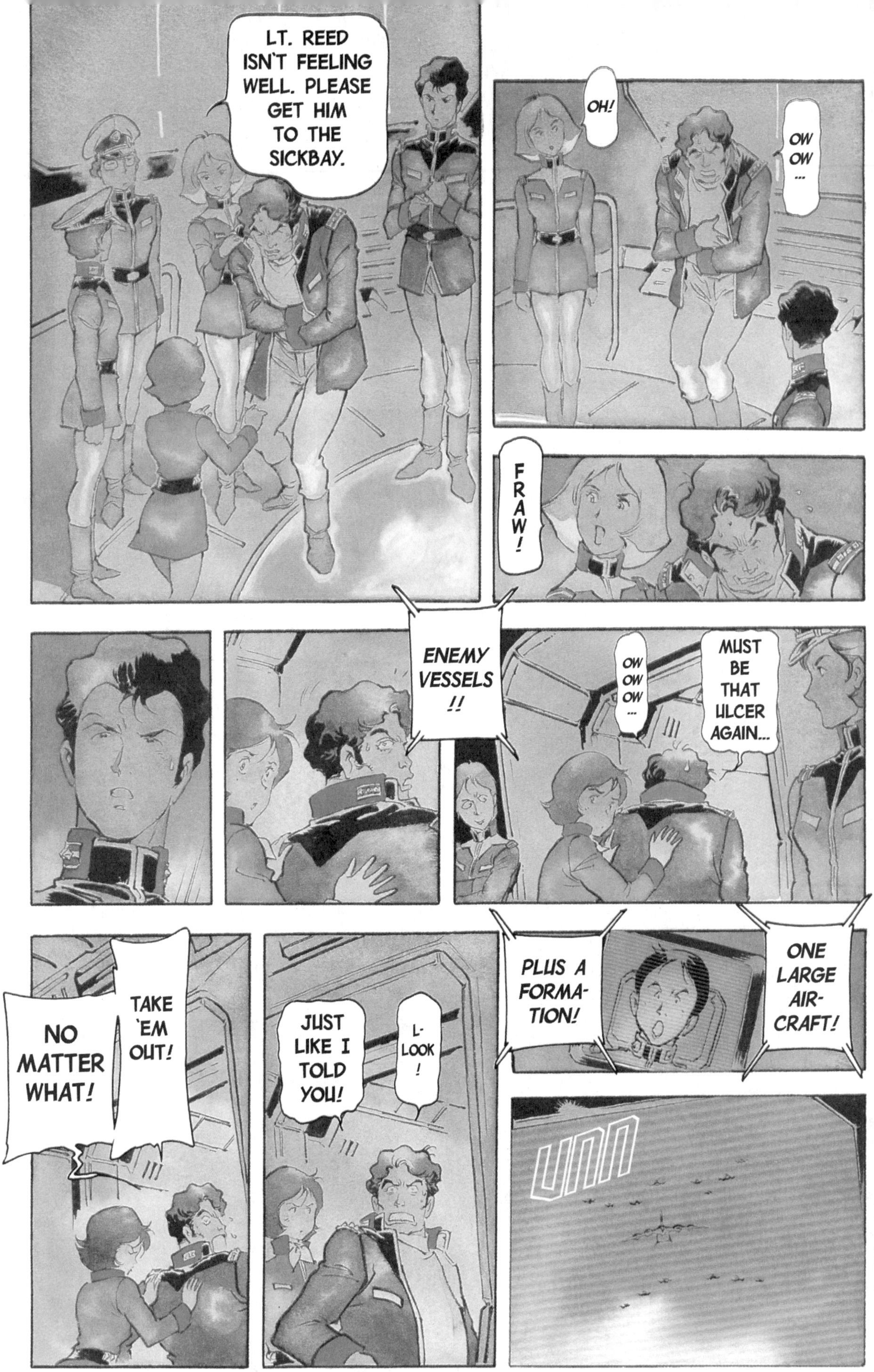
OH!
OW OW ...
FRAW!
LT. REED ISN'T FEELING WELL. PLEASE GET HIM TO THE SICKBAY.
MUST BE THAT ULCER AGAIN...
OW OW OW ...
ENEMY VESSELS !!
ONE LARGE AIR-CRAFT!
PLUS A FORMA-TION!
UNN
L-LOOK !
JUST LIKE I TOLD YOU!
TAKE 'EM OUT!
NO MATTER WHAT!

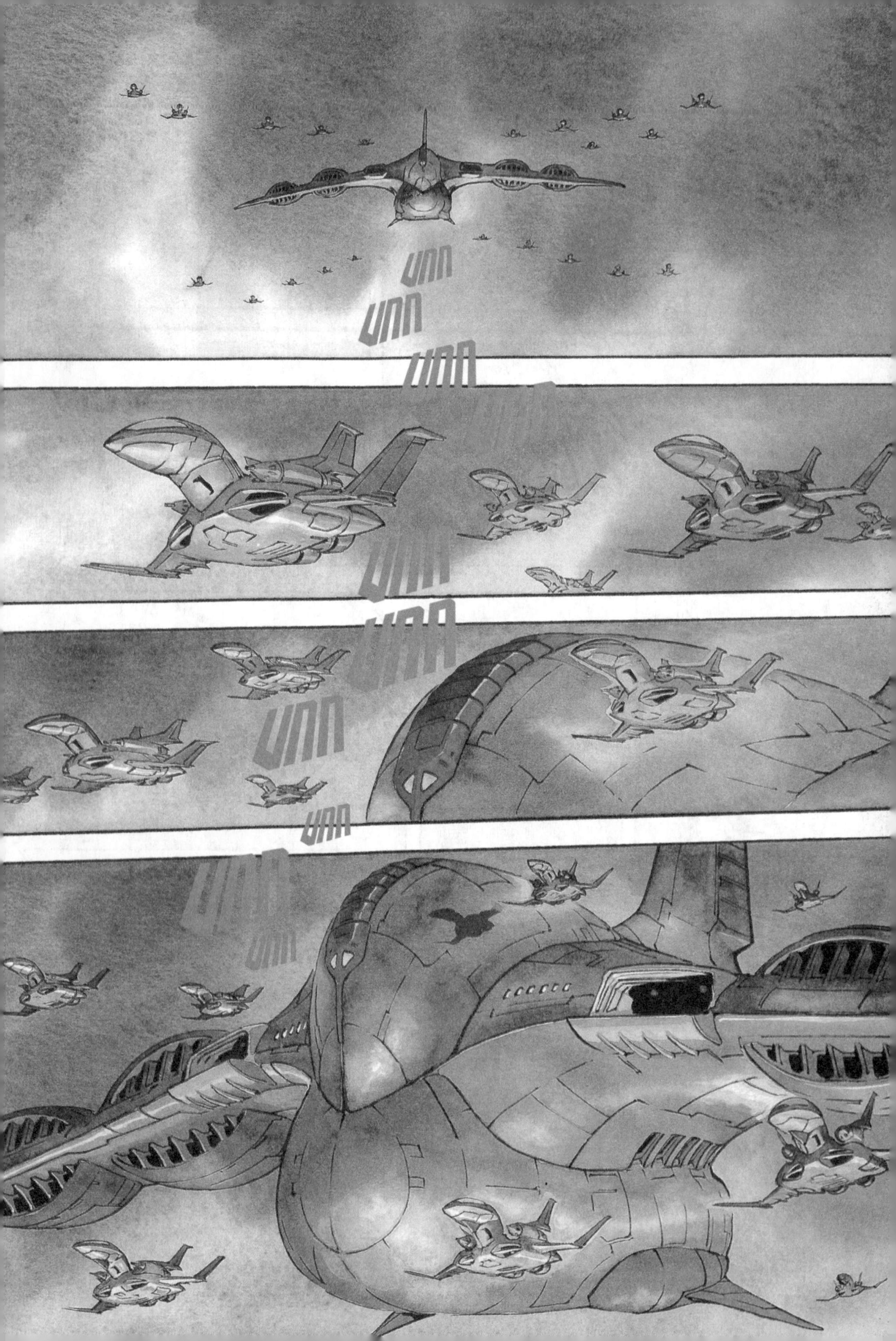
UNN
UNN
UNN
UNN
UNN
UNN
UNN
UNN

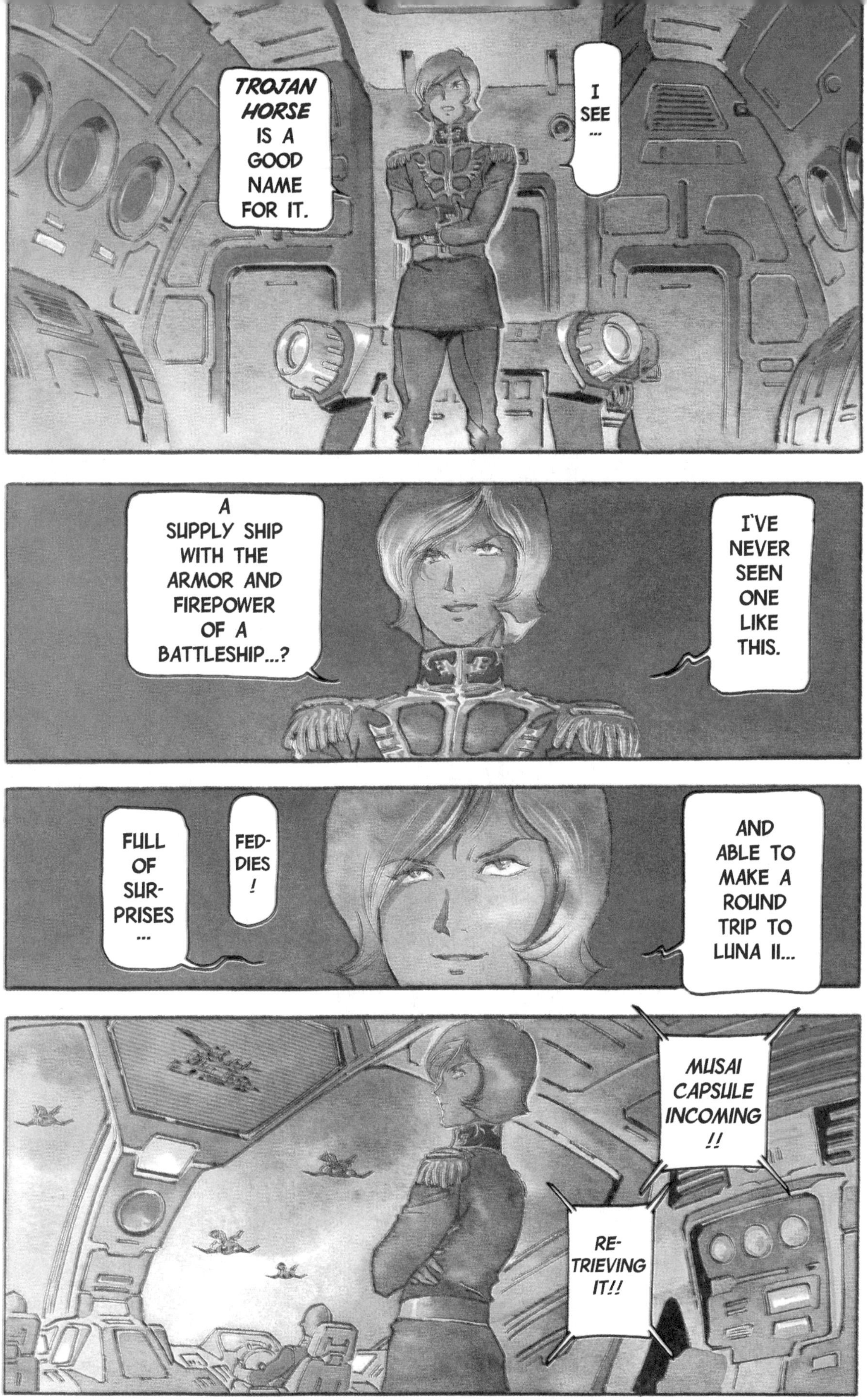
I SEE...
TROJAN HORSE IS A GOOD NAME FOR IT.
I'VE NEVER SEEN ONE LIKE THIS.
A SUPPLY SHIP WITH THE ARMOR AND FIREPOWER OF A BATTLESHIP...?
AND ABLE TO MAKE A ROUND TRIP TO LUNA II...
FED-DIES!
FULL OF SUR-PRISES...
MUSAI CAPSULE INCOMING!!
RE-TRIEVING IT!!

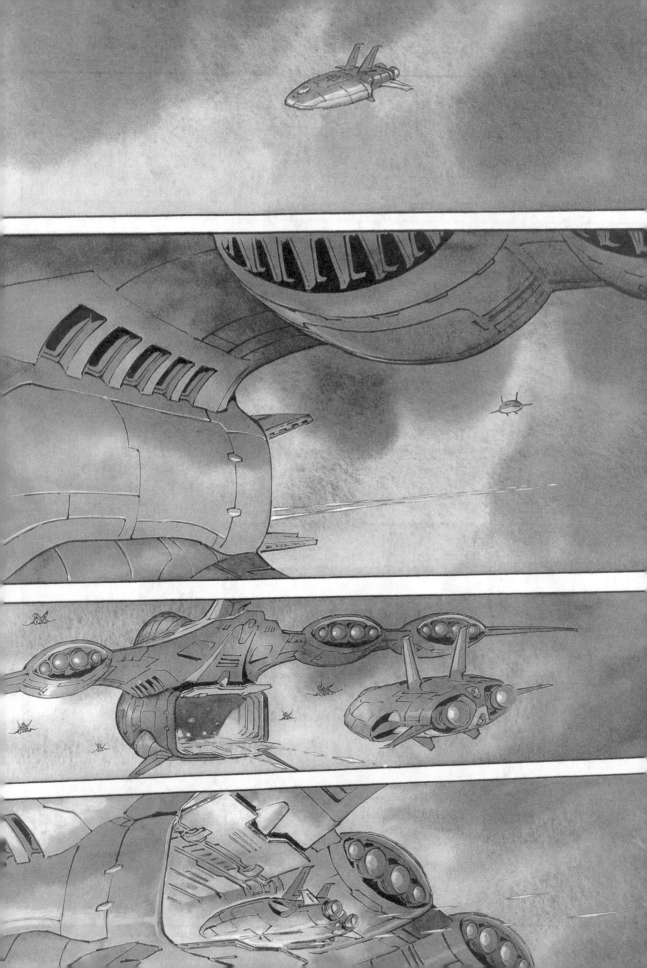

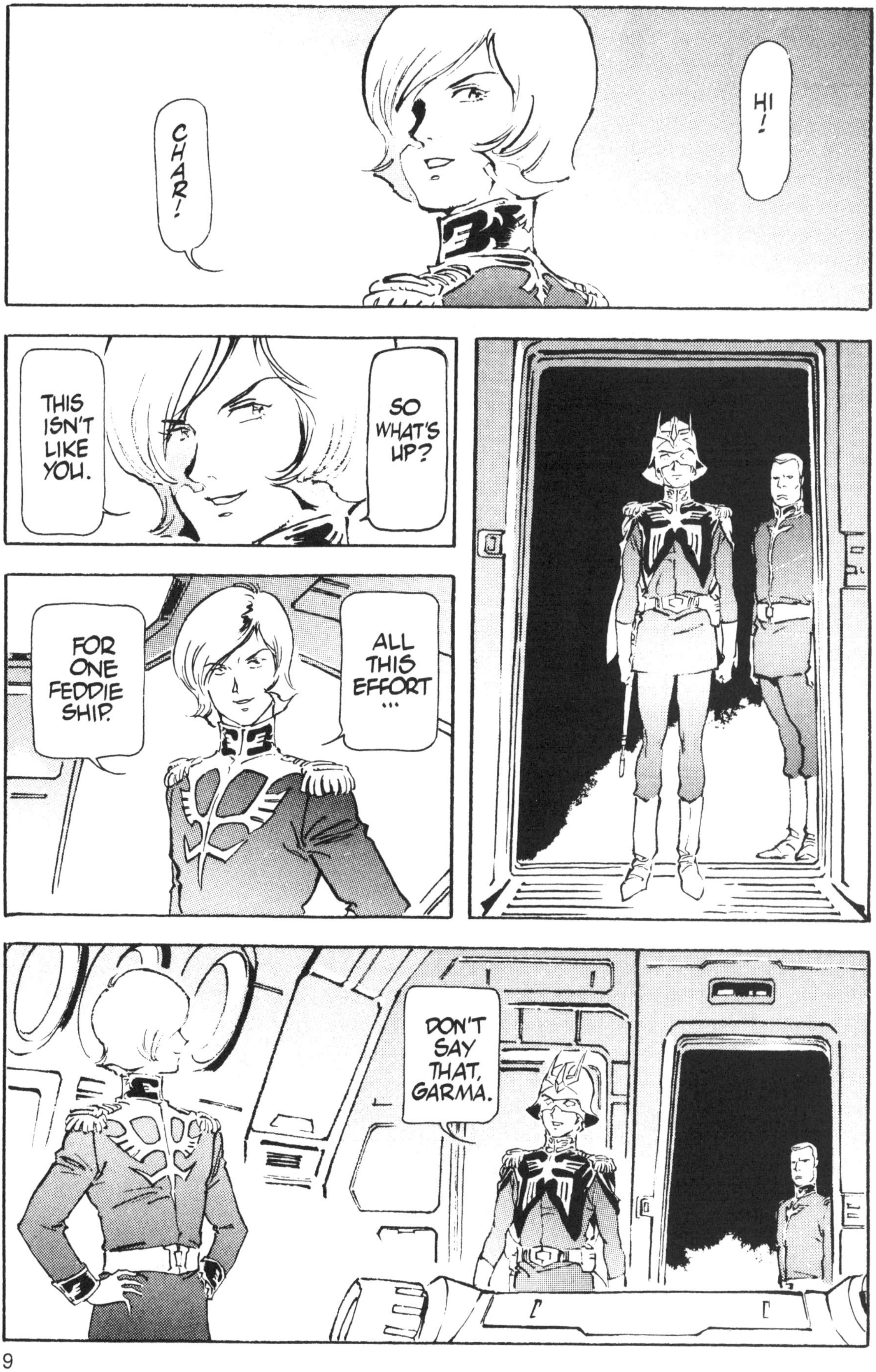
HI!
CHAR!
SO WHAT'S UP?
THIS ISN'T LIKE YOU.
ALL THIS EFFORT...
FOR ONE FEDDIE SHIP.
DON'T SAY THAT, GARMA.

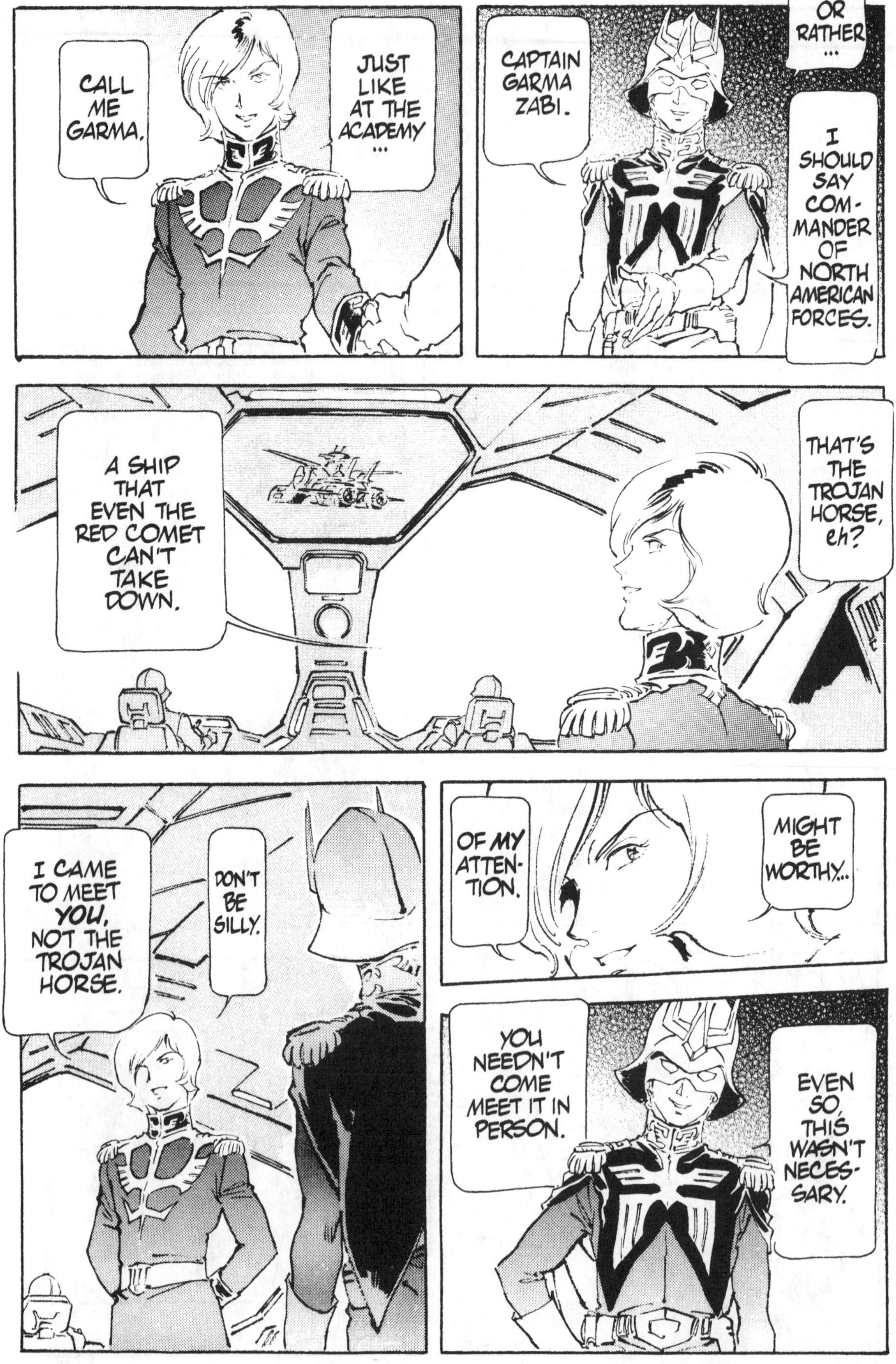
OR RATHER ...
I SHOULD SAY COMMANDER OF NORTH AMERICAN FORCES.
CAPTAIN GARMA ZABI.
JUST LIKE AT THE ACADEMY ...
CALL ME GARMA.
THAT'S THE TROJAN HORSE, eh?
A SHIP THAT EVEN THE RED COMET CAN'T TAKE DOWN.
MIGHT BE WORTHY...
OF MY ATTENTION.
EVEN SO, THIS WASN'T NECESSARY.
YOU NEEDN'T COME MEET IT IN PERSON.
DON'T BE SILLY.
I CAME TO MEET YOU, NOT THE TROJAN HORSE.

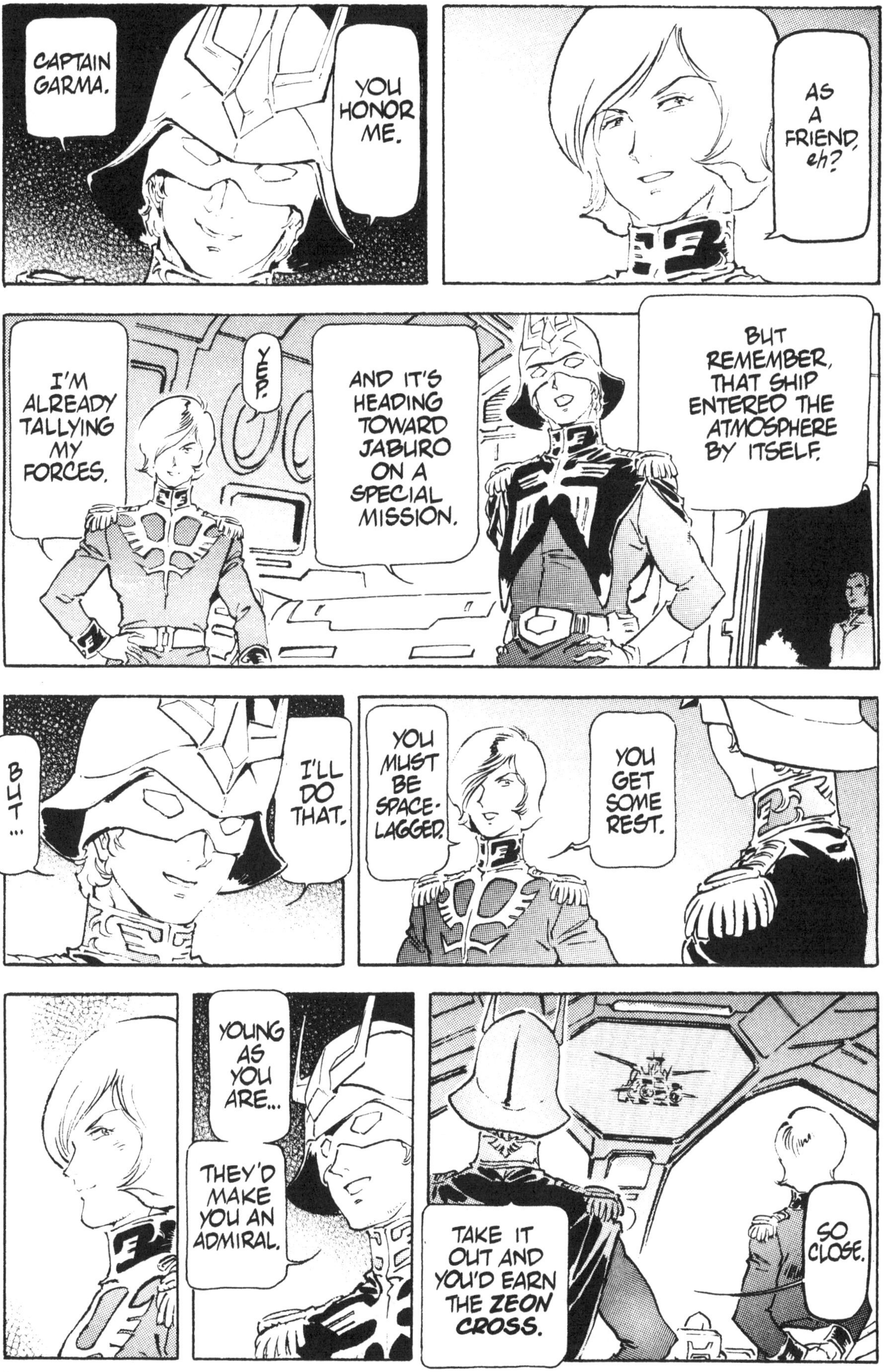
AS A FRIEND, eh?
YOU HONOR ME.
CAPTAIN GARMA.
BUT REMEMBER, THAT SHIP ENTERED THE ATMOSPHERE BY ITSELF.
AND IT'S HEADING TOWARD JABURO ON A SPECIAL MISSION.
YEP.
I'M ALREADY TALLYING MY FORCES.
YOU GET SOME REST.
YOU MUST BE SPACE-LAGGED.
I'LL DO THAT.
BUT...
SO CLOSE.
TAKE IT OUT AND YOU'D EARN THE **ZEON CROSS**.
YOUNG AS YOU ARE...
THEY'D MAKE YOU AN ADMIRAL.

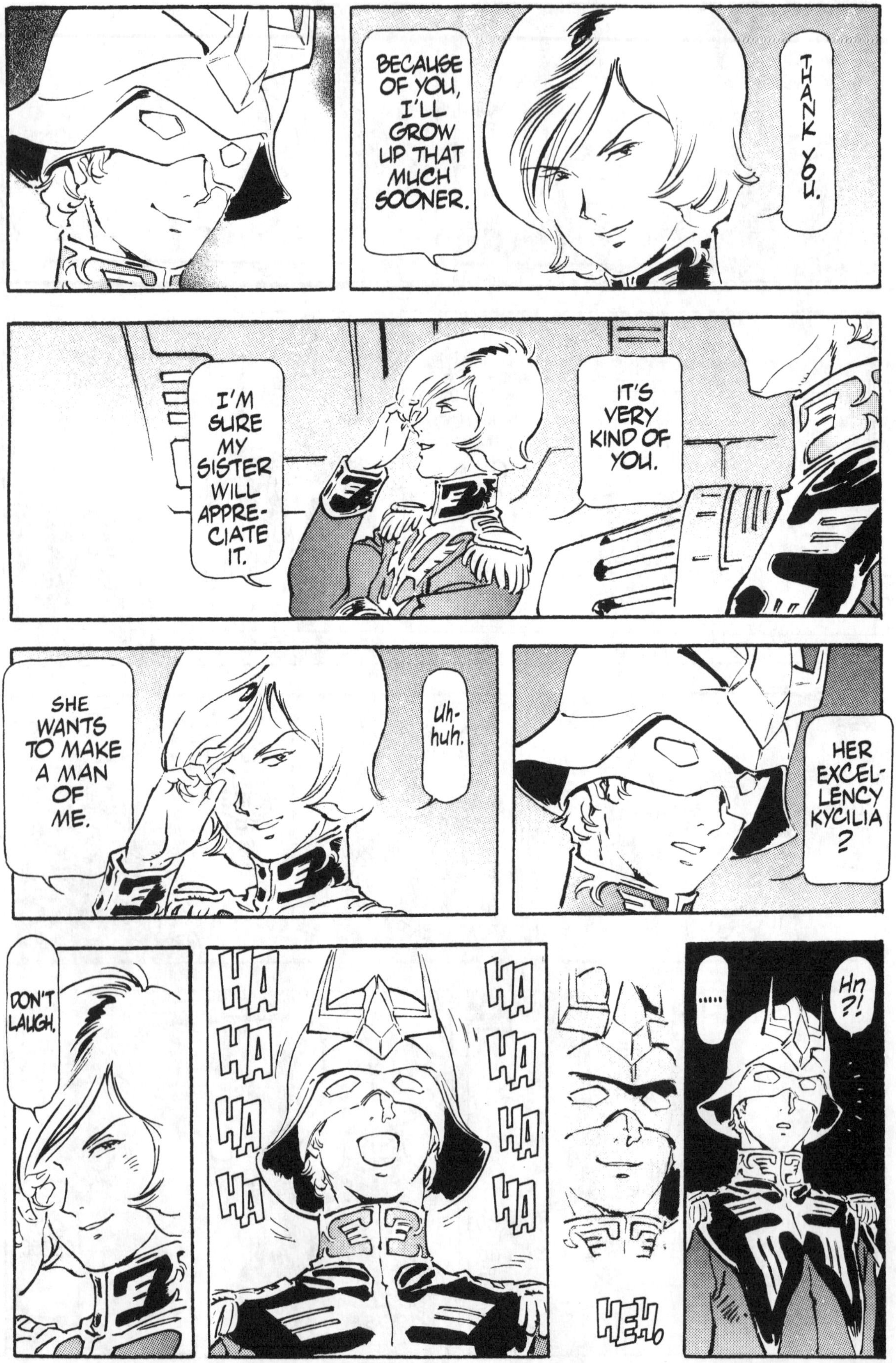
THANK YOU.
BECAUSE OF YOU, I'LL GROW UP THAT MUCH SOONER.
IT'S VERY KIND OF YOU.
I'M SURE MY SISTER WILL APPRECIATE IT.
HER EXCELLENCY KYCILIA?
Uh-huh.
SHE WANTS TO MAKE A MAN OF ME.
Hn?!
.....
HEH.
HA HA HA HA HA
HA HA HA HA
DON'T LAUGH.

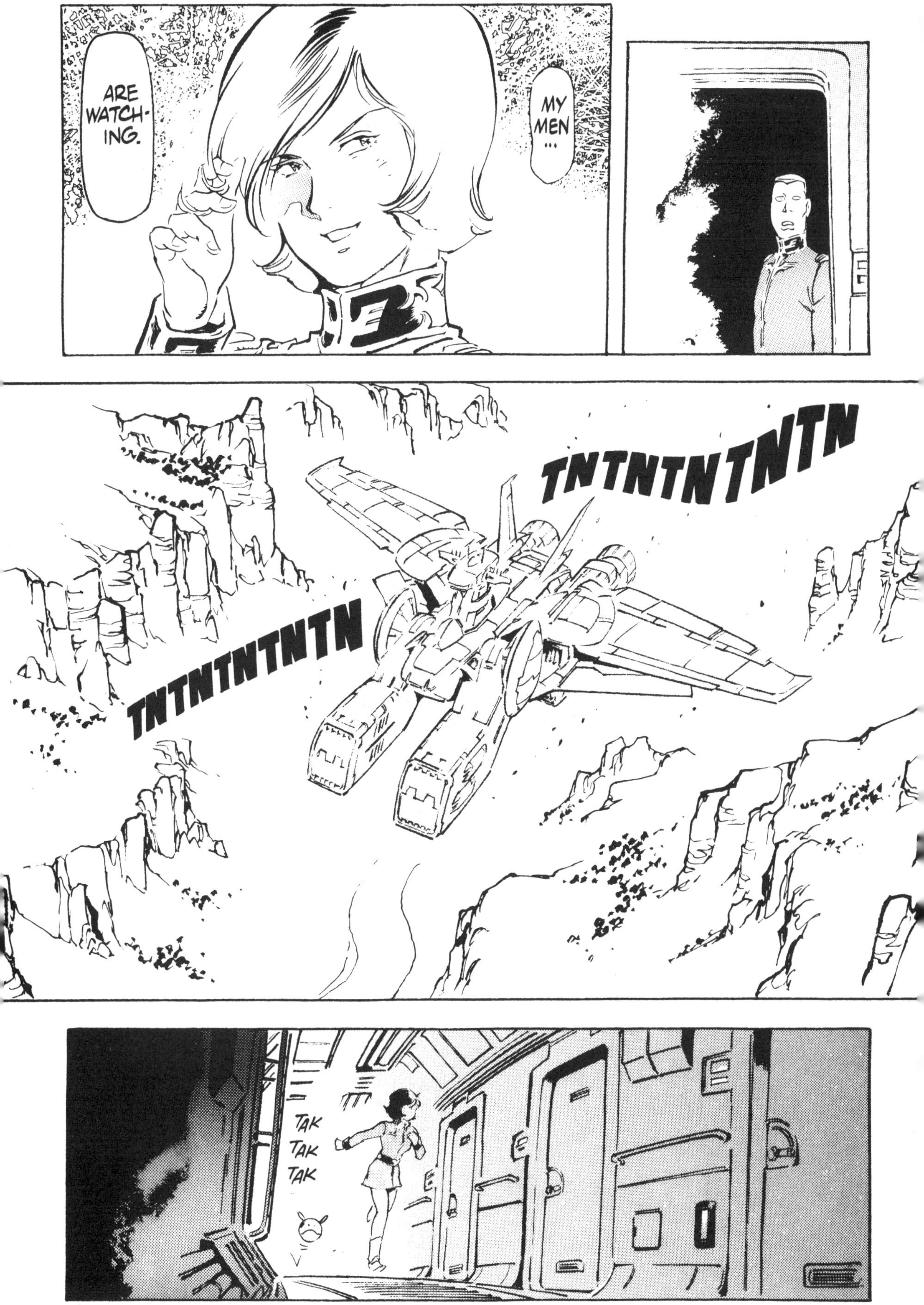
MY MEN ...
ARE WATCHING.
TNTNTNTNTN
TNTNTNTNTN
TAK TAK TAK

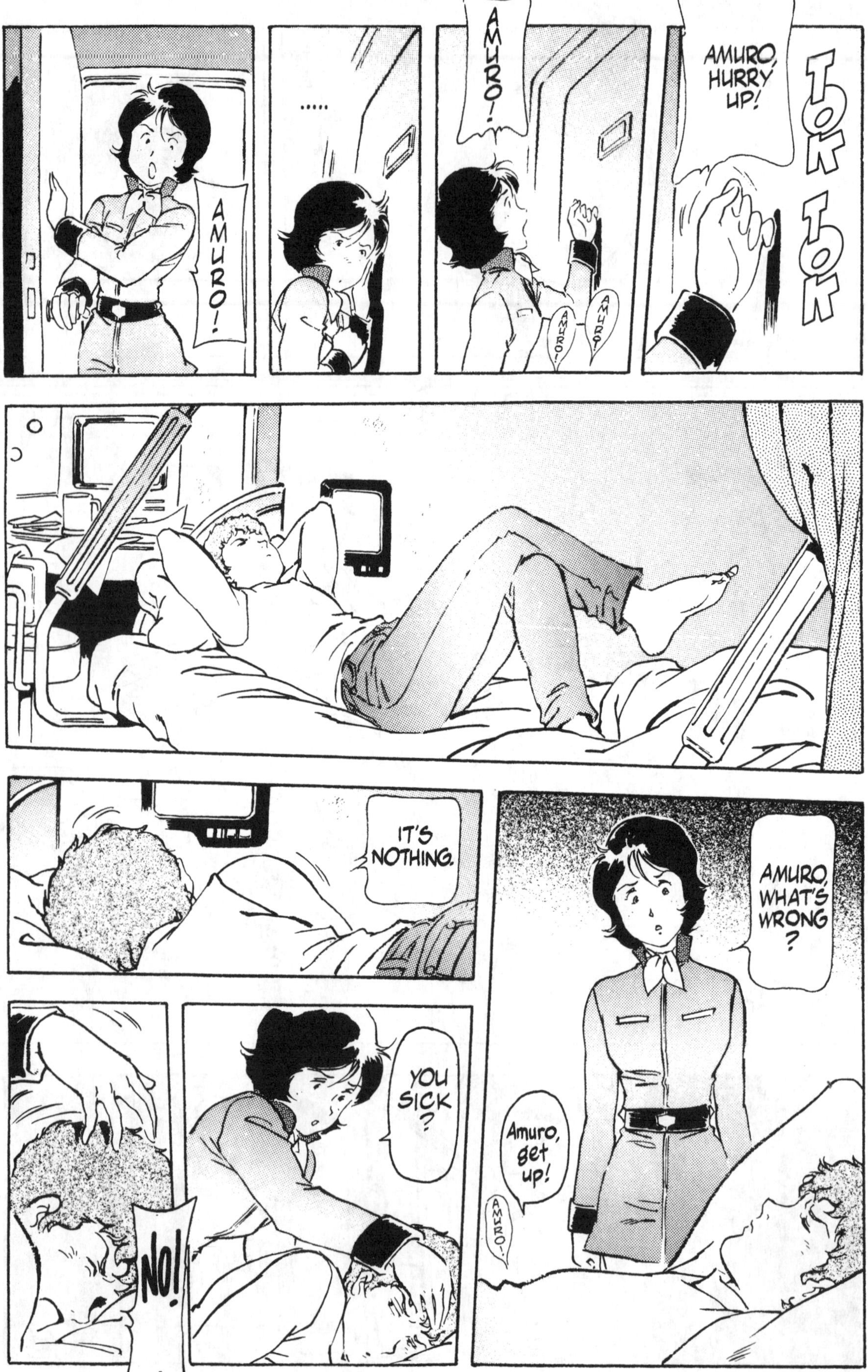
AMURO, HURRY UP!
TOK TOK
AMURO!
AMURO!
AMURO!
......
AMURO!
AMURO, WHAT'S WRONG?
Amuro, get up!
AMURO!
IT'S NOTHING.
YOU SICK?
NO!

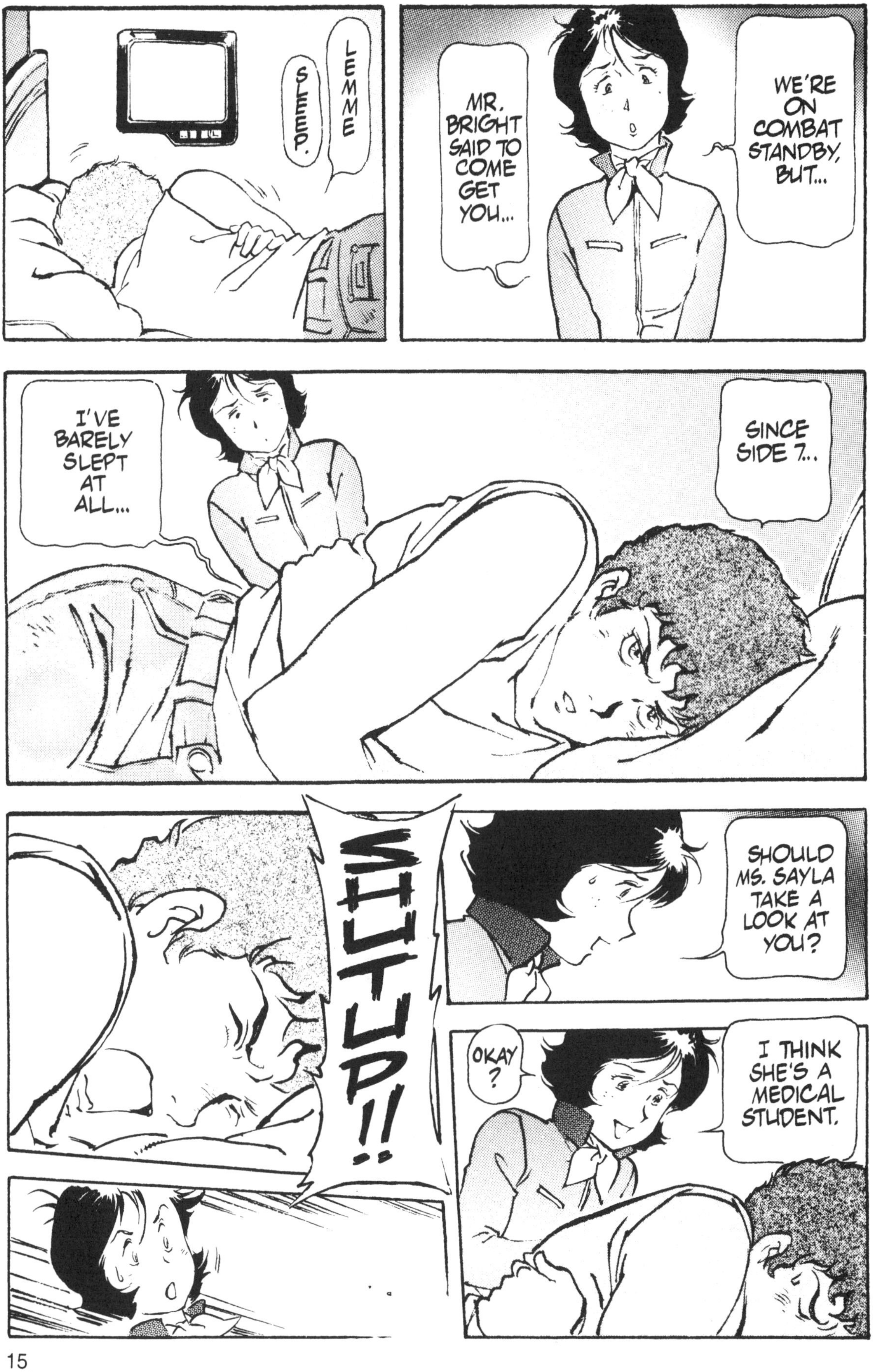
WE'RE ON COMBAT STANDBY, BUT...
MR. BRIGHT SAID TO COME GET YOU...
LEMME SLEEP.
SINCE SIDE 7...
I'VE BARELY SLEPT AT ALL...
SHOULD MS. SAYLA TAKE A LOOK AT YOU?
I THINK SHE'S A MEDICAL STUDENT.
OKAY?
SHUT UP!!

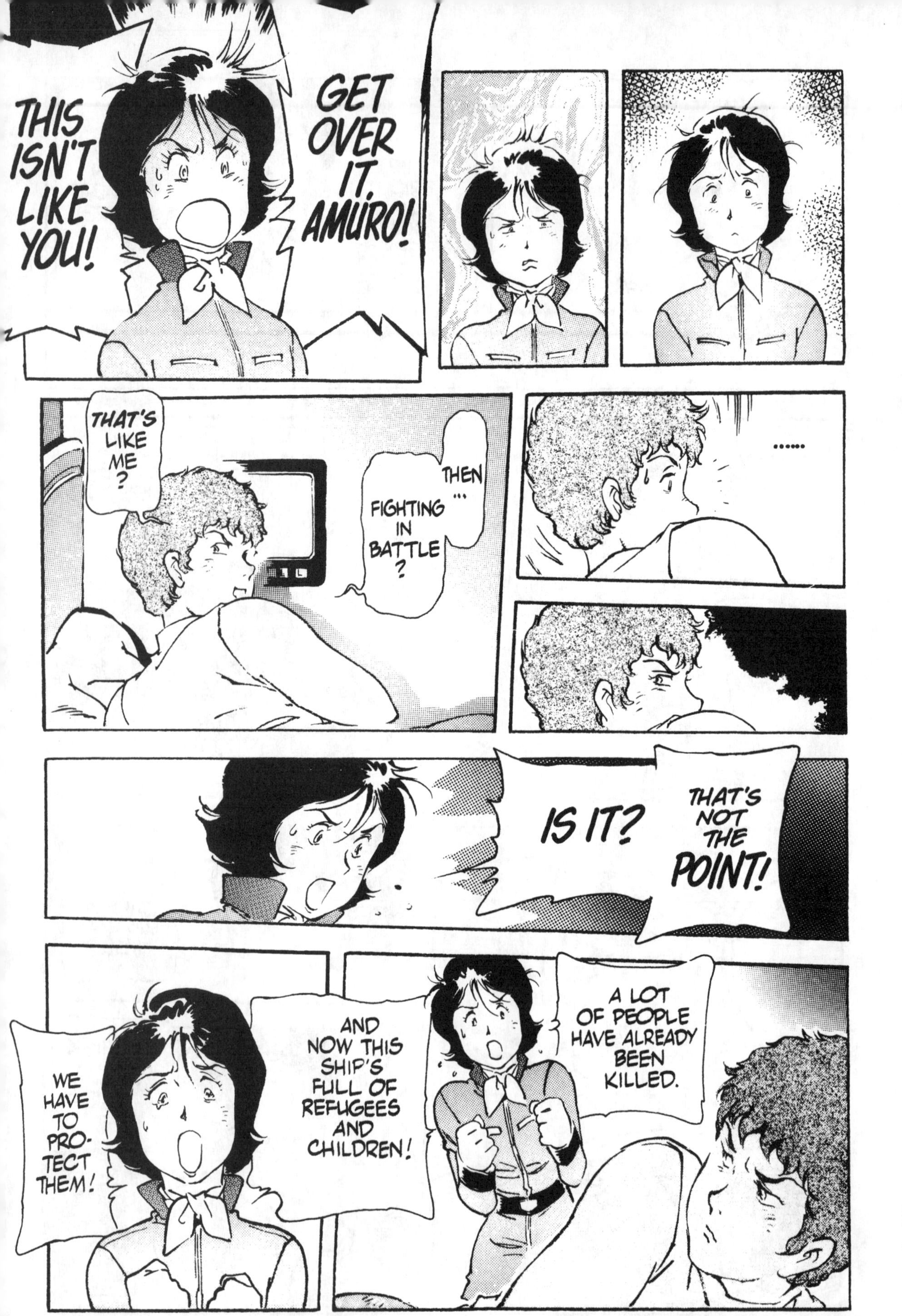
GET OVER IT, AMURO!
THIS ISN'T LIKE YOU!
......
THAT'S LIKE ME?
THEN... FIGHTING IN BATTLE?
THAT'S NOT THE POINT!
IS IT?
A LOT OF PEOPLE HAVE ALREADY BEEN KILLED.
AND NOW THIS SHIP'S FULL OF REFUGEES AND CHILDREN!
WE HAVE TO PROTECT THEM!

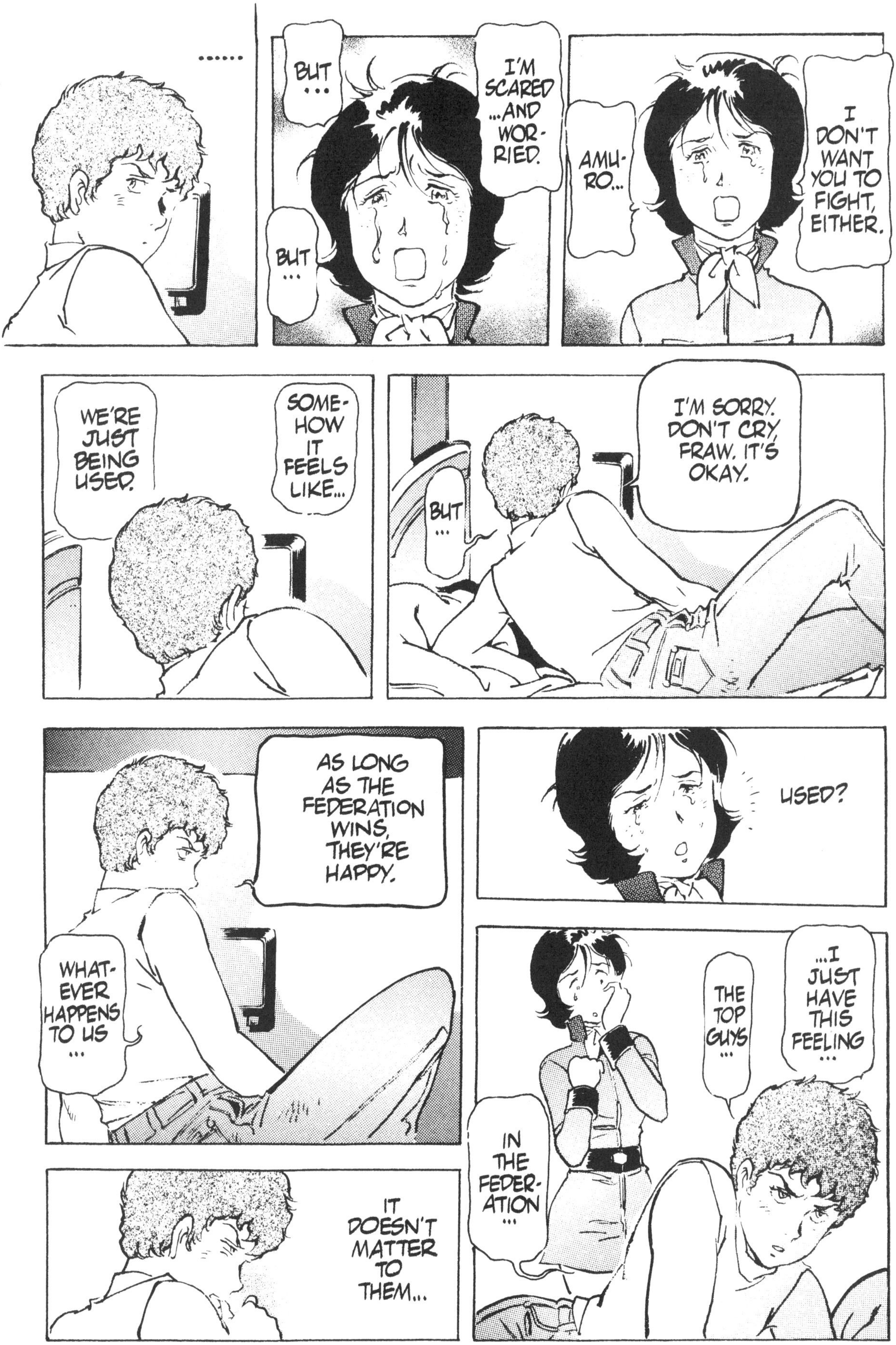
I DON'T WANT YOU TO FIGHT, EITHER.
AMU-RO...
I'M SCARED ...AND WOR-RIED.
BUT ...
BUT ...
......
I'M SORRY. DON'T CRY, FRAW. IT'S OKAY.
BUT ...
SOME-HOW IT FEELS LIKE...
WE'RE JUST BEING USED.
USED?
...I JUST HAVE THIS FEELING ...
THE TOP GUYS ...
IN THE FEDER-ATION ...
AS LONG AS THE FEDERATION WINS, THEY'RE HAPPY.
WHAT-EVER HAPPENS TO US ...
IT DOESN'T MATTER TO THEM...

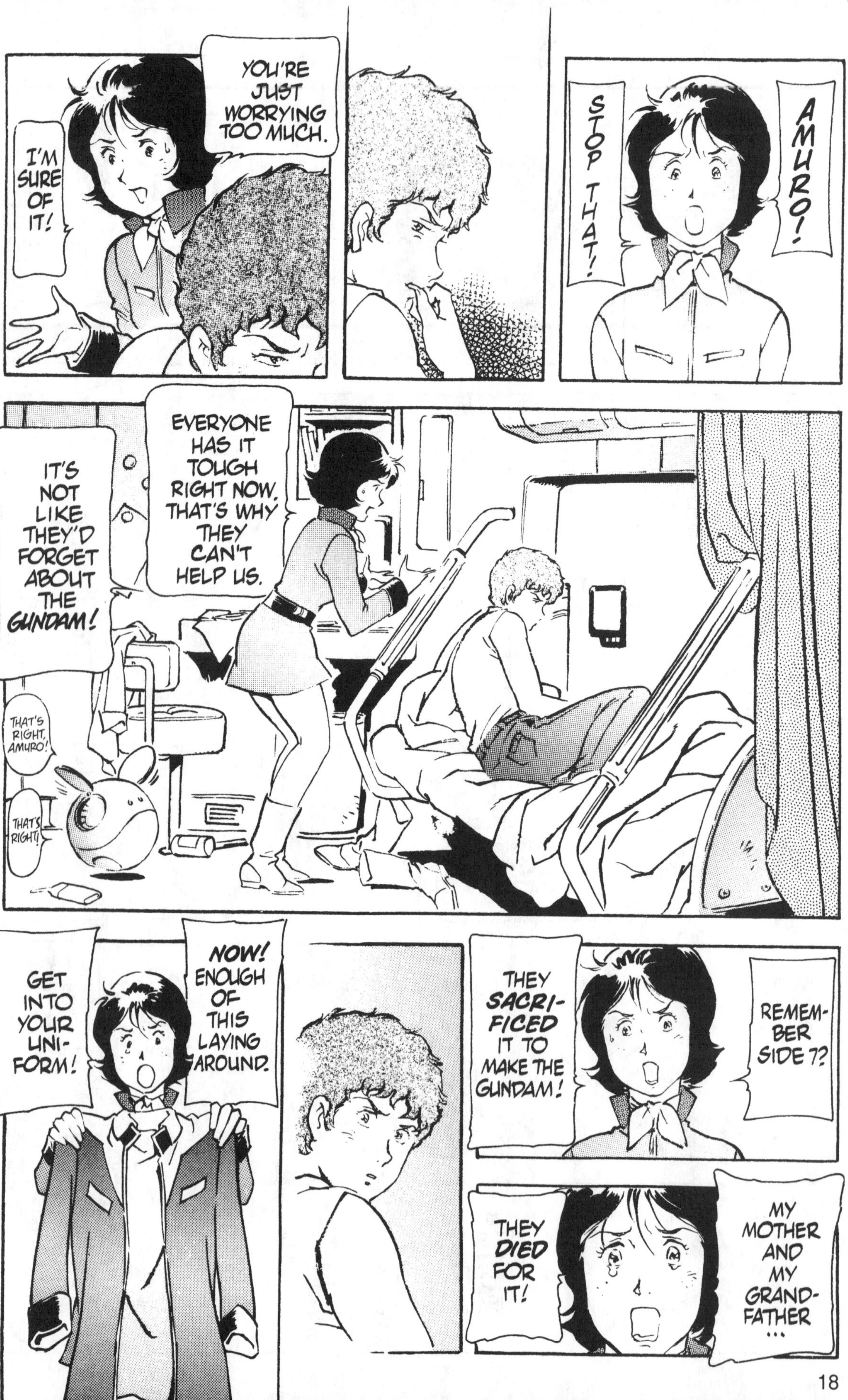
AMURO!
STOP THAT!
YOU'RE JUST WORRYING TOO MUCH.
I'M SURE OF IT!
EVERYONE HAS IT TOUGH RIGHT NOW. THAT'S WHY THEY CAN'T HELP US.
IT'S NOT LIKE THEY'D FORGET ABOUT THE GUNDAM!
THAT'S RIGHT, AMURO!
THAT'S RIGHT!
REMEMBER SIDE 7?
THEY SACRIFICED IT TO MAKE THE GUNDAM!
MY MOTHER AND MY GRANDFATHER...
THEY DIED FOR IT!
NOW! ENOUGH OF THIS LAYING AROUND.
GET INTO YOUR UNIFORM!

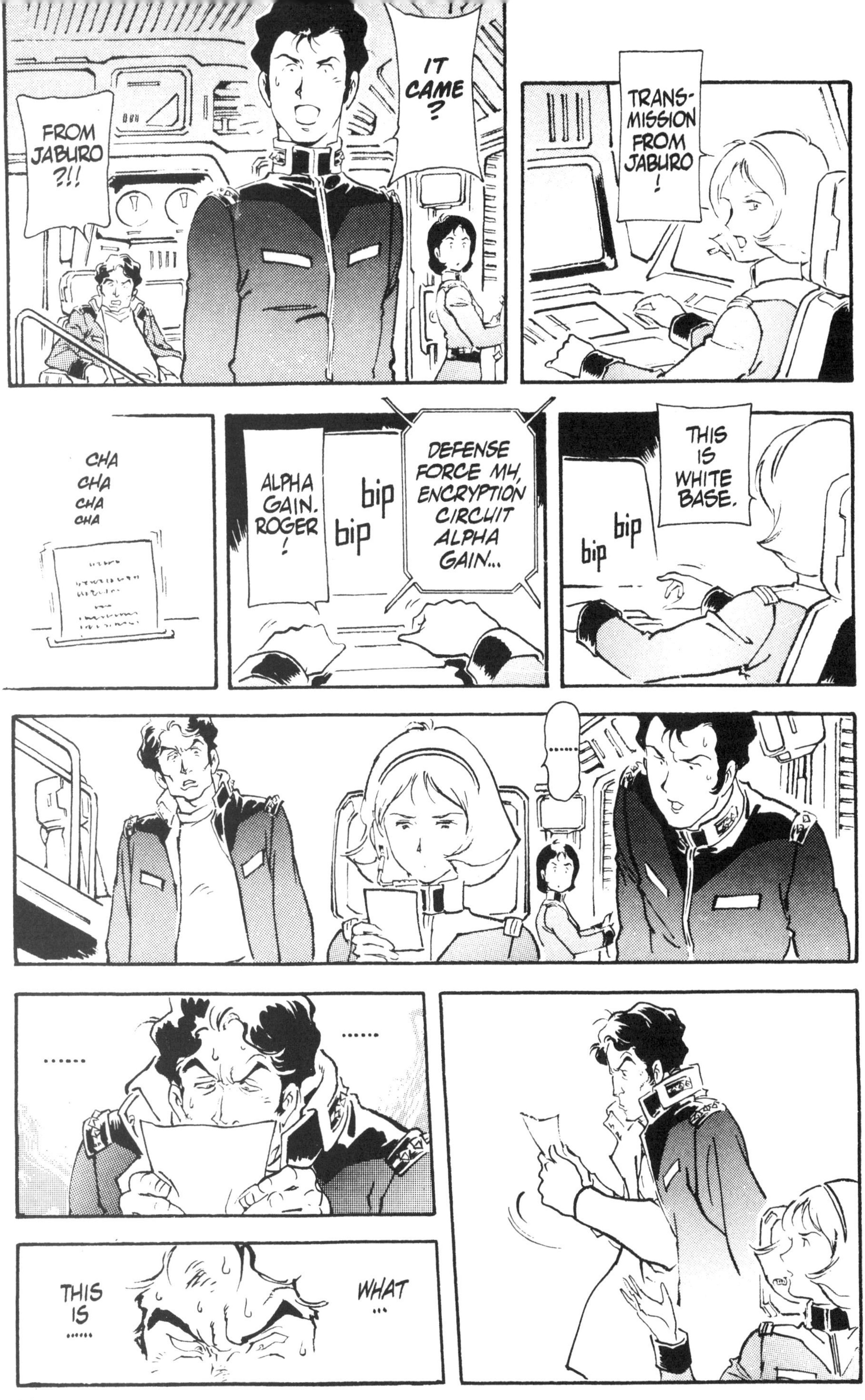

TRANS-MISSION FROM JABURO!
IT CAME?
FROM JABURO?!!
THIS IS WHITE BASE.
bip bip
DEFENSE FORCE M4, ENCRYPTION CIRCUIT ALPHA GAIN...
bip bip
ALPHA GAIN. ROGER!
CHA CHA CHA CHA
......
......
......
WHAT...
THIS IS......

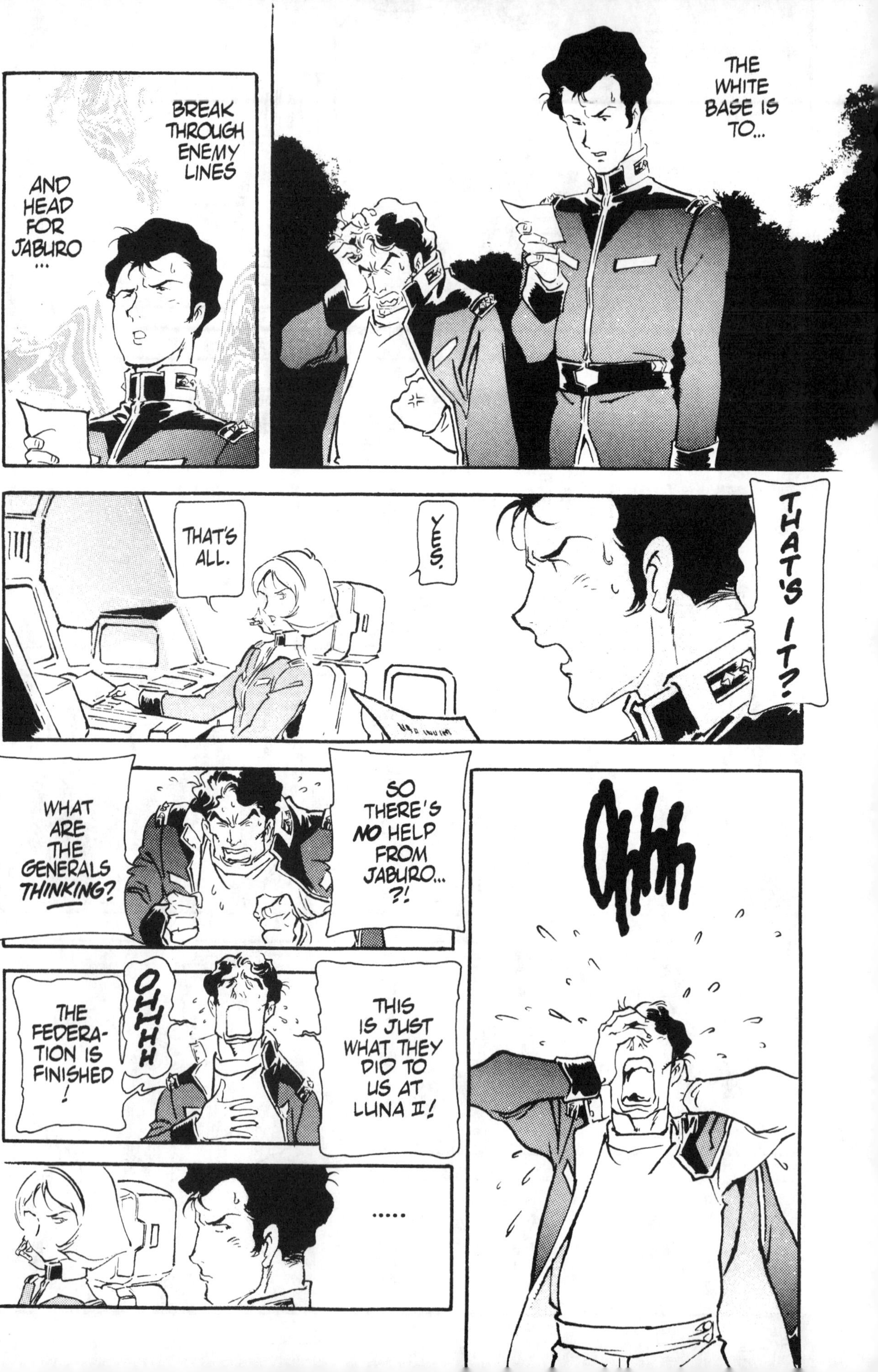
THE WHITE BASE IS TO...
BREAK THROUGH ENEMY LINES
AND HEAD FOR JABURO ...
THAT'S IT?
YES.
THAT'S ALL.
Ohhh
SO THERE'S NO HELP FROM JABURO... ?!
WHAT ARE THE GENERALS THINKING?
THIS IS JUST WHAT THEY DID TO US AT LUNA II!
OHHHH
THE FEDERATION IS FINISHED!
.....

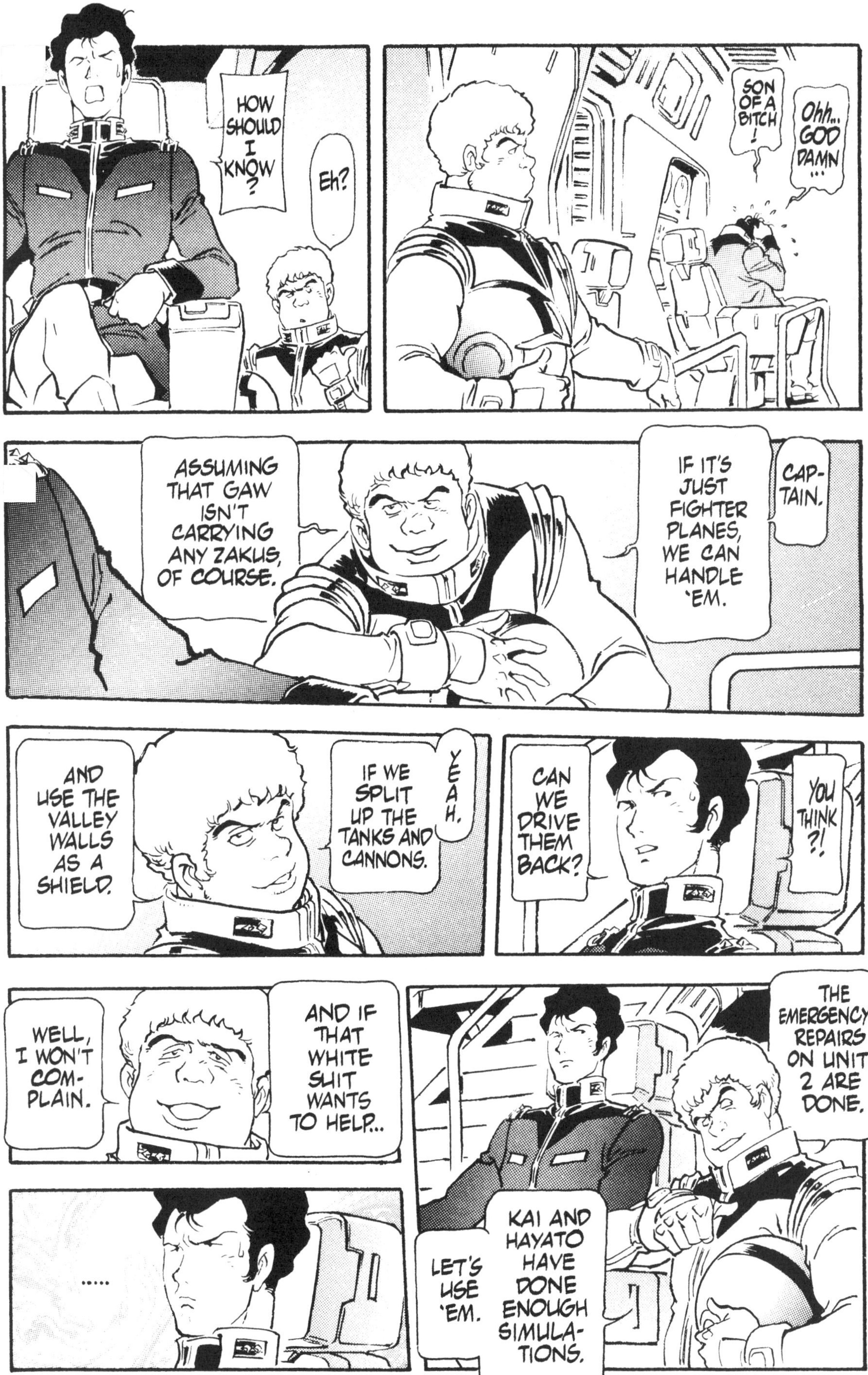
Ohh... GOD DAMN...
SON OF A BITCH!
Eh?
HOW SHOULD I KNOW?
CAP-TAIN.
IF IT'S JUST FIGHTER PLANES, WE CAN HANDLE 'EM.
ASSUMING THAT GAW ISN'T CARRYING ANY ZAKUS, OF COURSE.
YOU THINK?!
CAN WE DRIVE THEM BACK?
YEAH.
IF WE SPLIT UP THE TANKS AND CANNONS.
AND USE THE VALLEY WALLS AS A SHIELD.
THE EMERGENCY REPAIRS ON UNIT 2 ARE DONE.
KAI AND HAYATO HAVE DONE ENOUGH SIMULATIONS.
LET'S USE 'EM.
AND IF THAT WHITE SUIT WANTS TO HELP...
WELL, I WON'T COMPLAIN.
.....

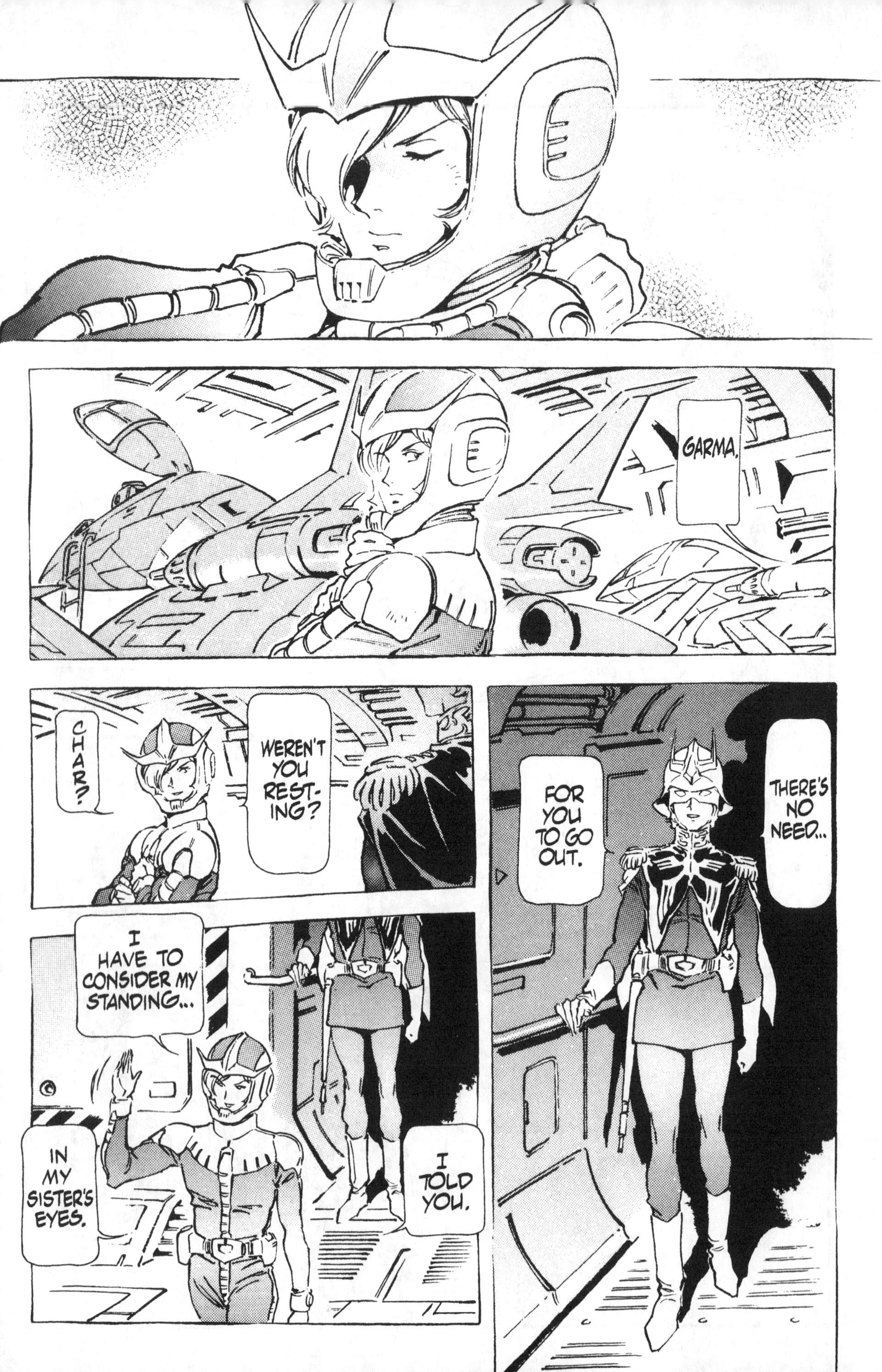
GARMA.
THERE'S NO NEED...
FOR YOU TO GO OUT.
WEREN'T YOU REST-ING?
CHAR?
I HAVE TO CONSIDER MY STANDING...
IN MY SISTER'S EYES.
I TOLD YOU.

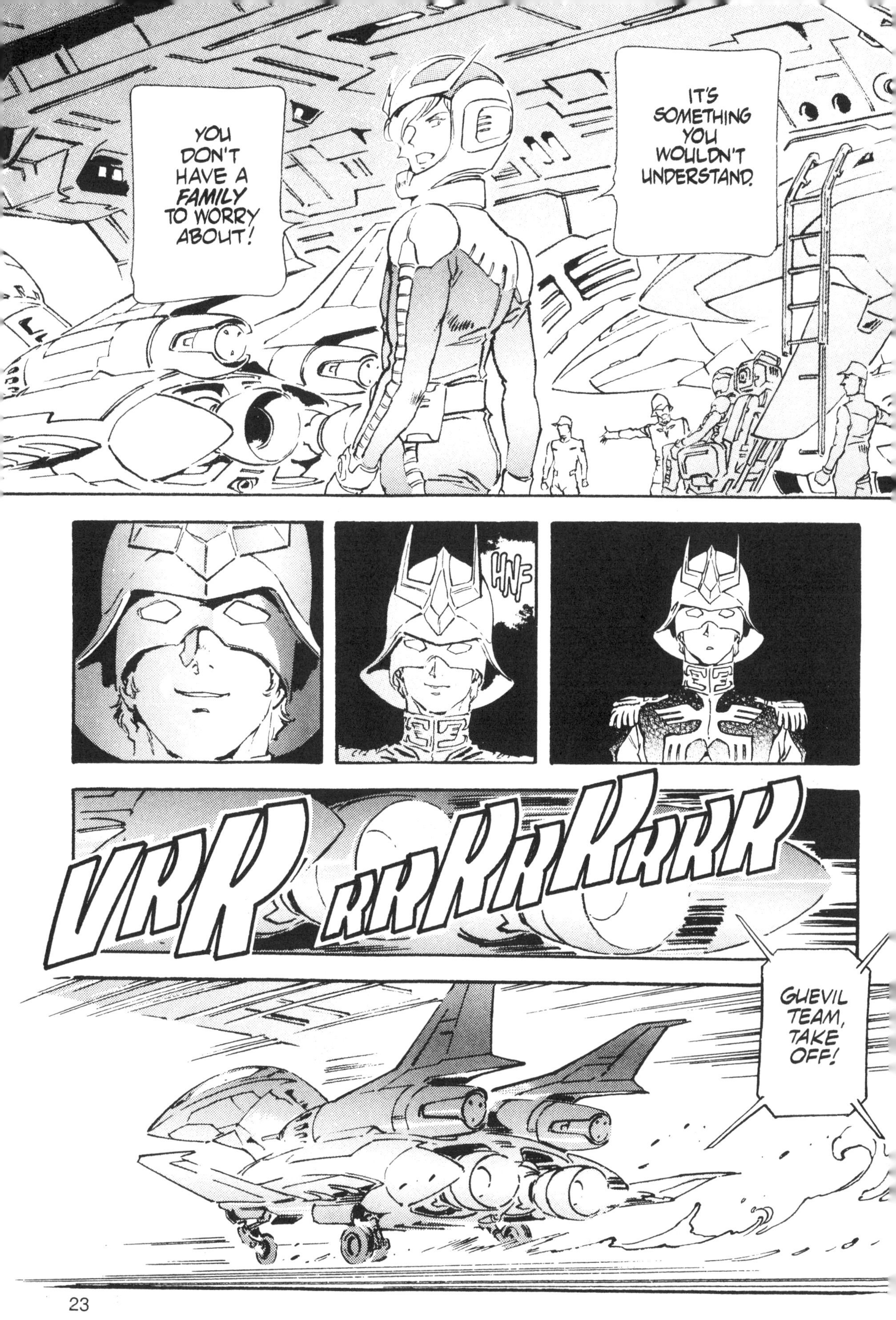
IT'S SOMETHING YOU WOULDN'T UNDERSTAND.
YOU DON'T HAVE A FAMILY TO WORRY ABOUT!
HNF
URR RRRRRRRRRR
GUEVIL TEAM, TAKE OFF!

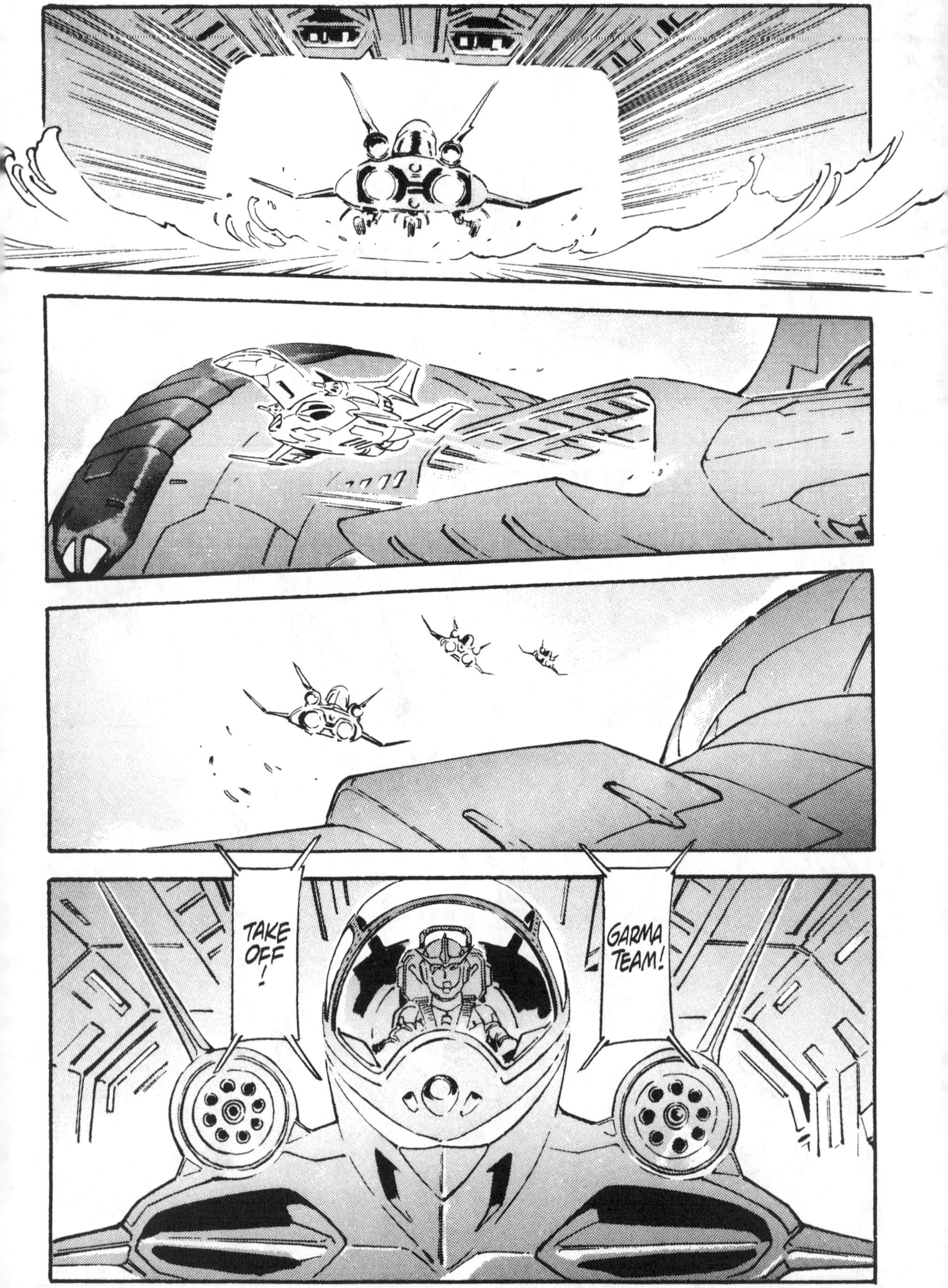
GARMA TEAM!
TAKE OFF!

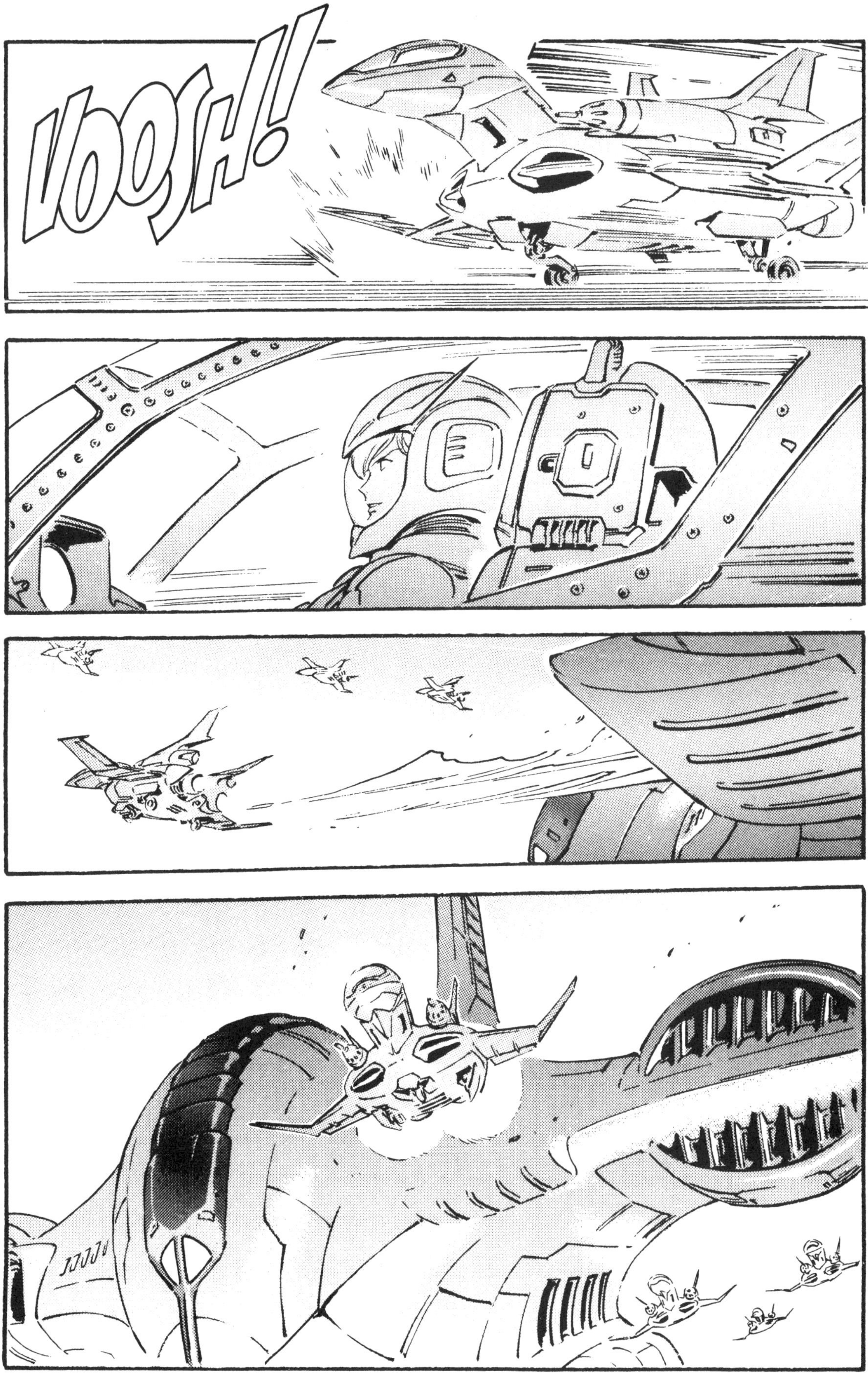
VOOSH!

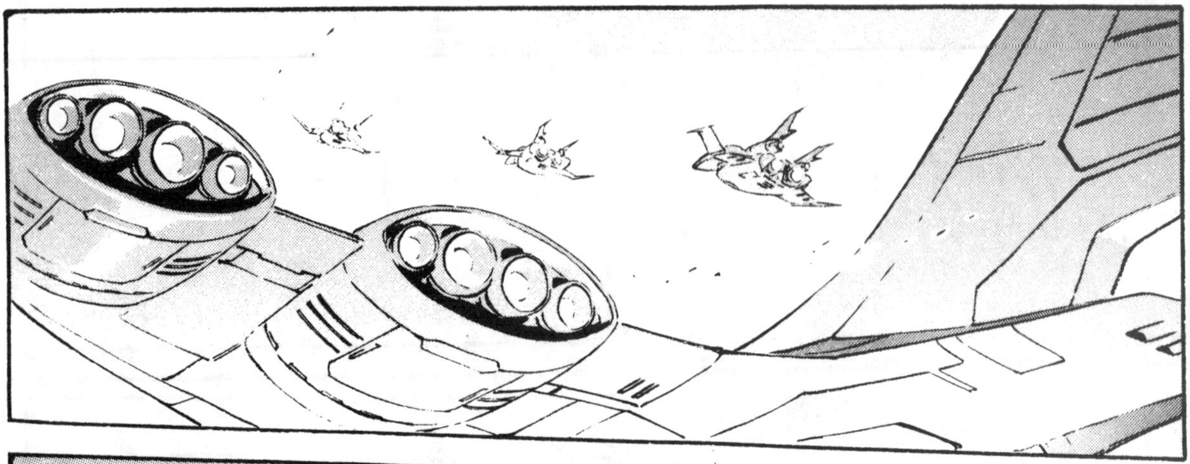
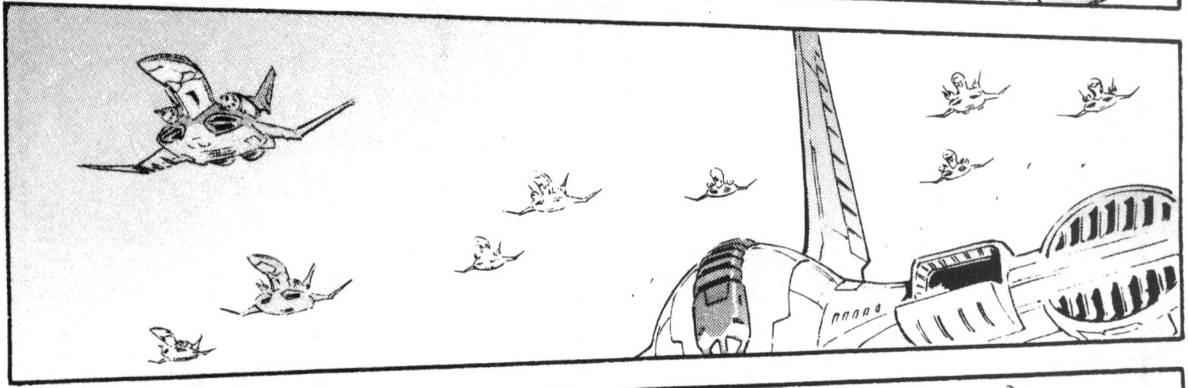
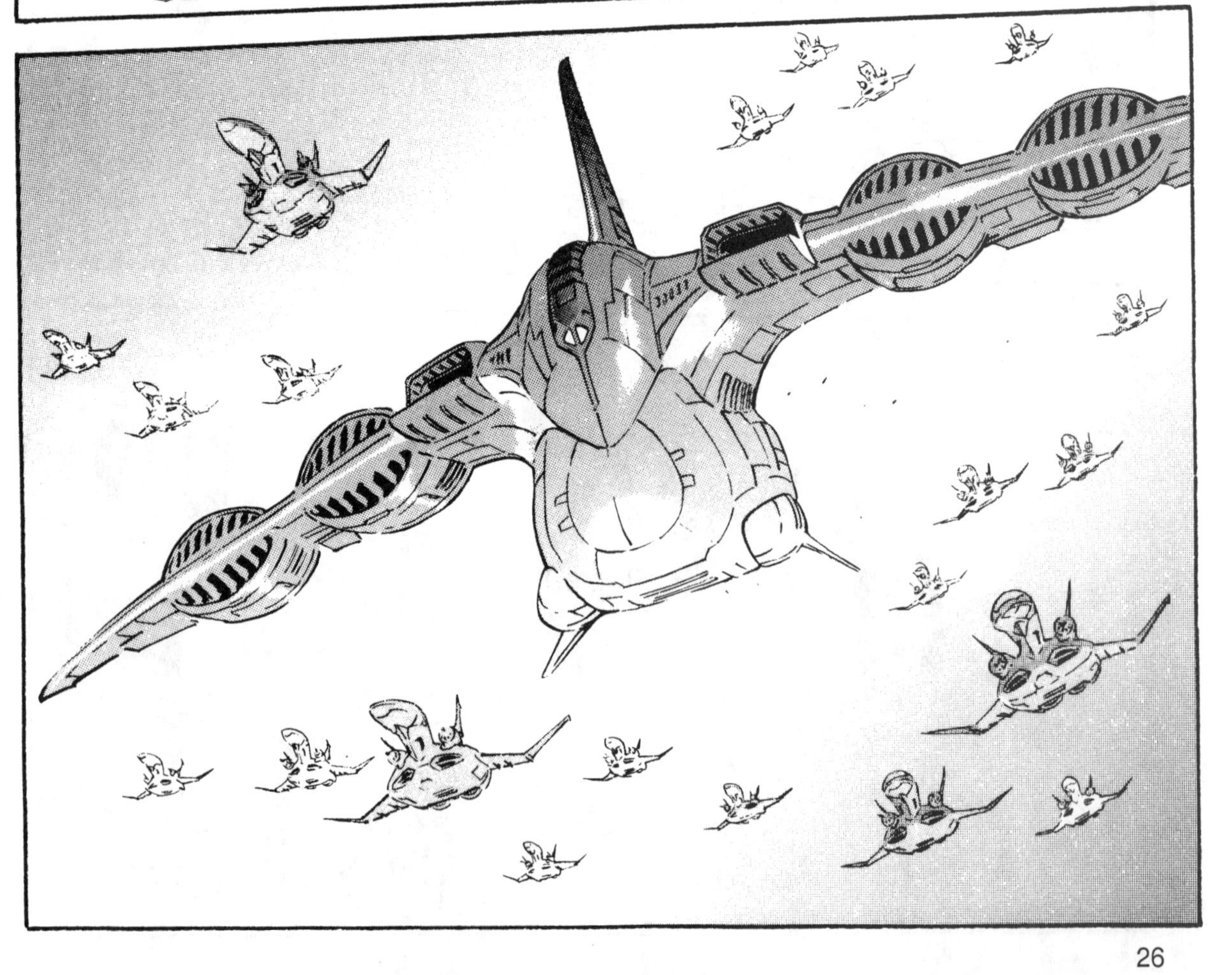

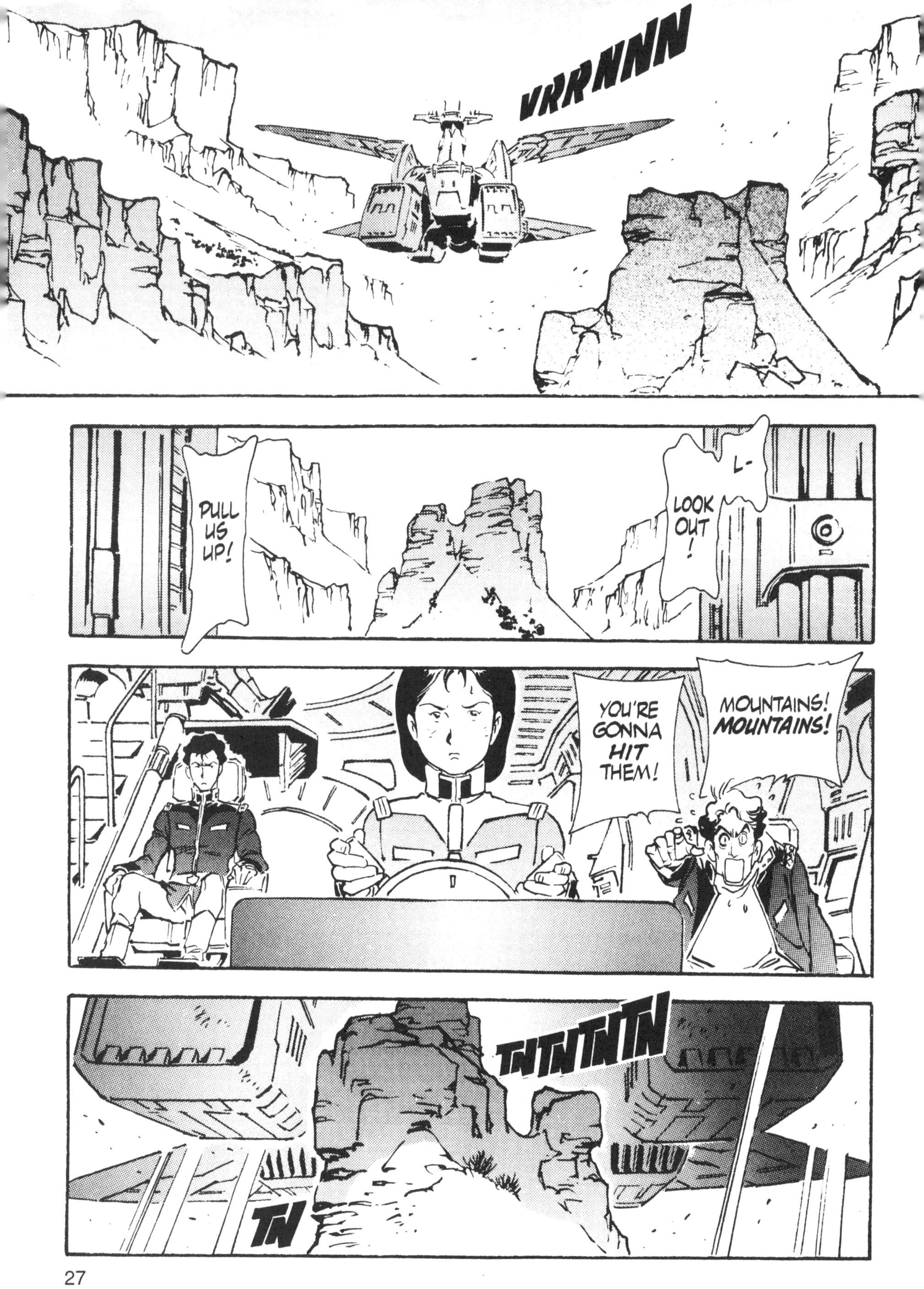
VRRNNN
L-
LOOK OUT!
PULL US UP!
MOUNTAINS! MOUNTAINS!
YOU'RE GONNA HIT THEM!
TNTNTNTN
TN

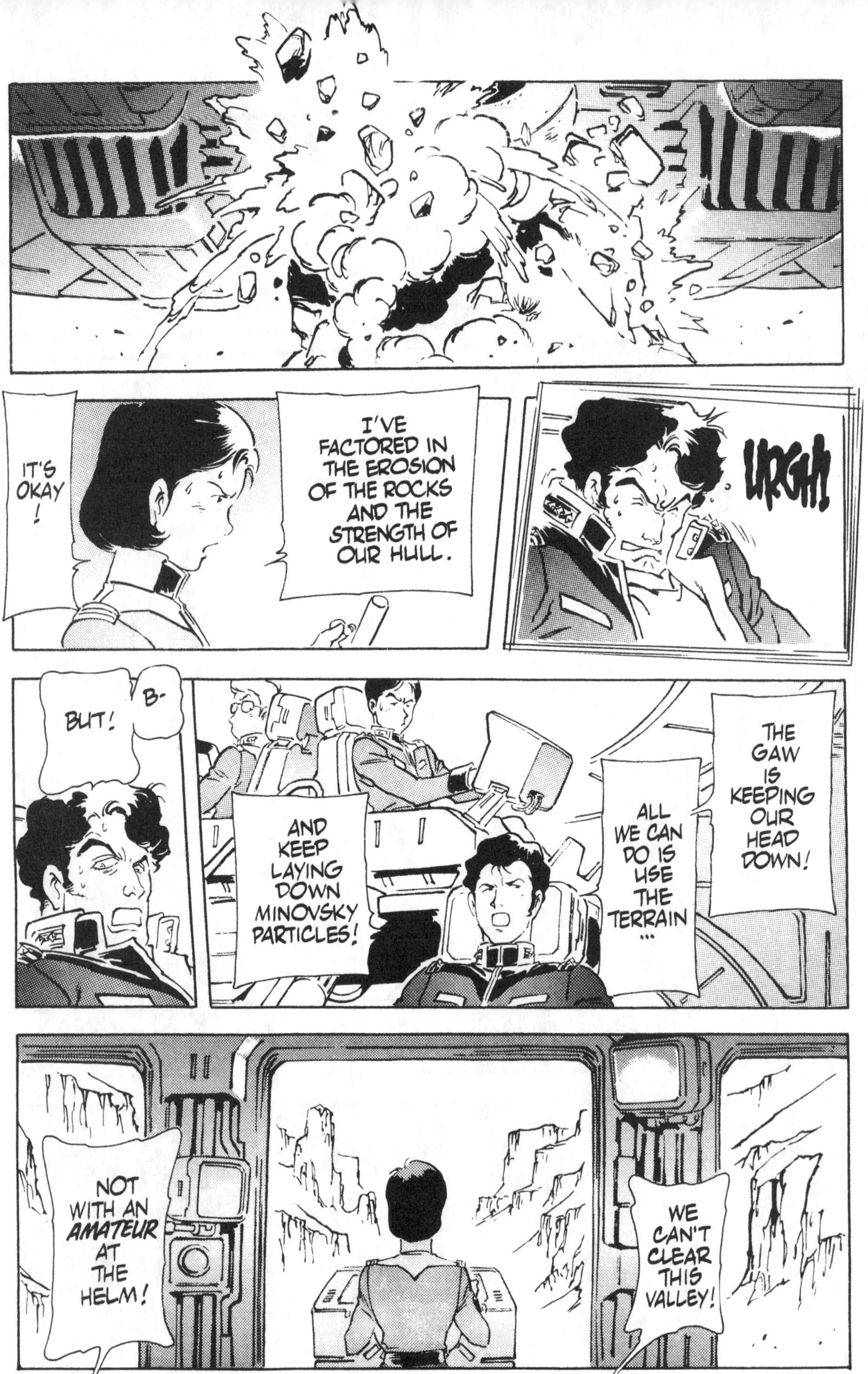

IT'S OKAY!
I'VE FACTORED IN THE EROSION OF THE ROCKS AND THE STRENGTH OF OUR HULL.
URGH!
B- BUT!
AND KEEP LAYING DOWN MINOVSKY PARTICLES!
ALL WE CAN DO IS USE THE TERRAIN...
THE GAW IS KEEPING OUR HEAD DOWN!
NOT WITH AN *AMATEUR* AT THE HELM!
WE CAN'T CLEAR THIS VALLEY!

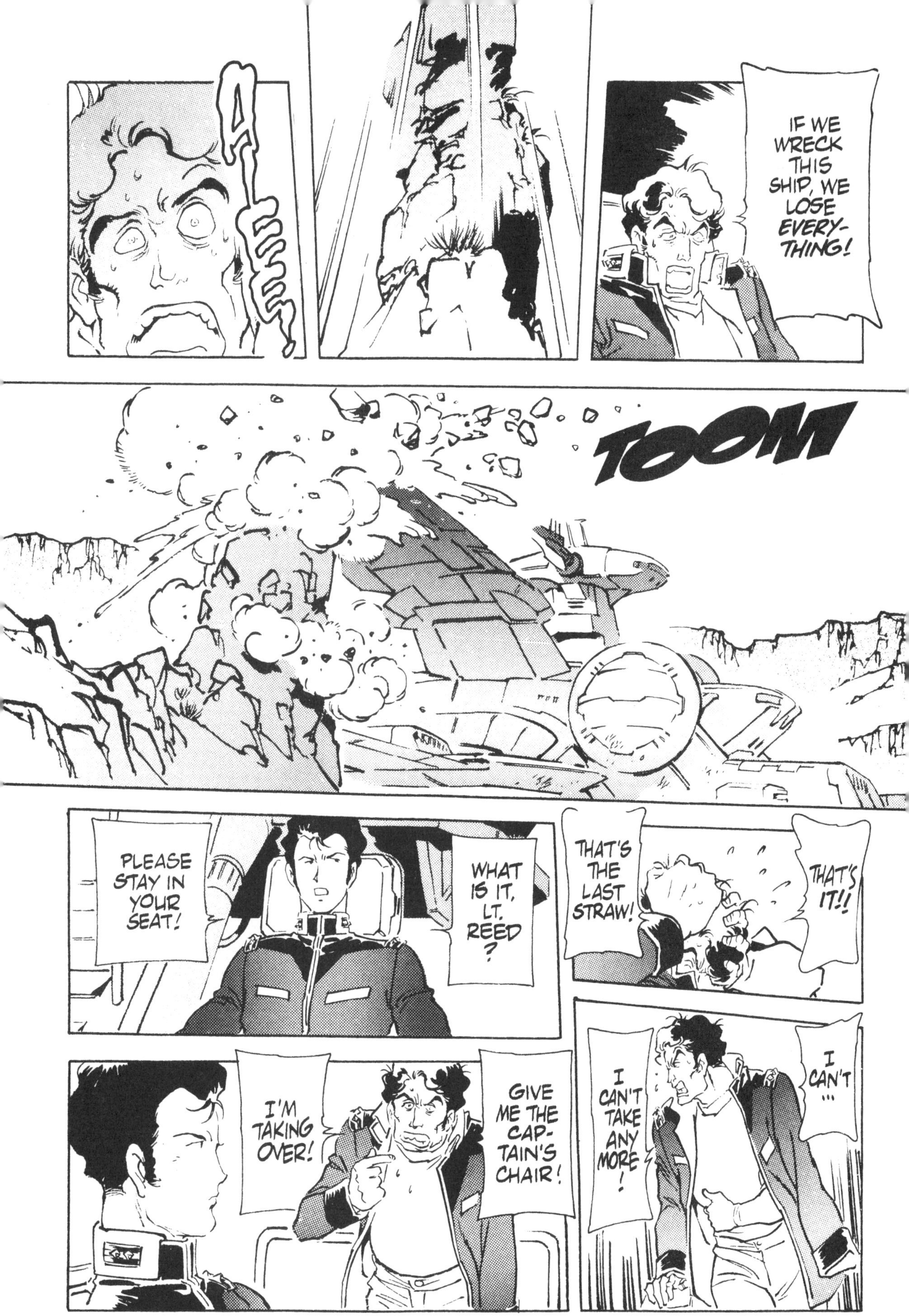
IF WE WRECK THIS SHIP, WE LOSE EVERY-THING!
A
TOOM
THAT'S IT!!
THAT'S THE LAST STRAW!
WHAT IS IT, LT. REED?
PLEASE STAY IN YOUR SEAT!
I CAN'T ...
I CAN'T TAKE ANY MORE!
GIVE ME THE CAP-TAIN'S CHAIR!
I'M TAKING OVER!

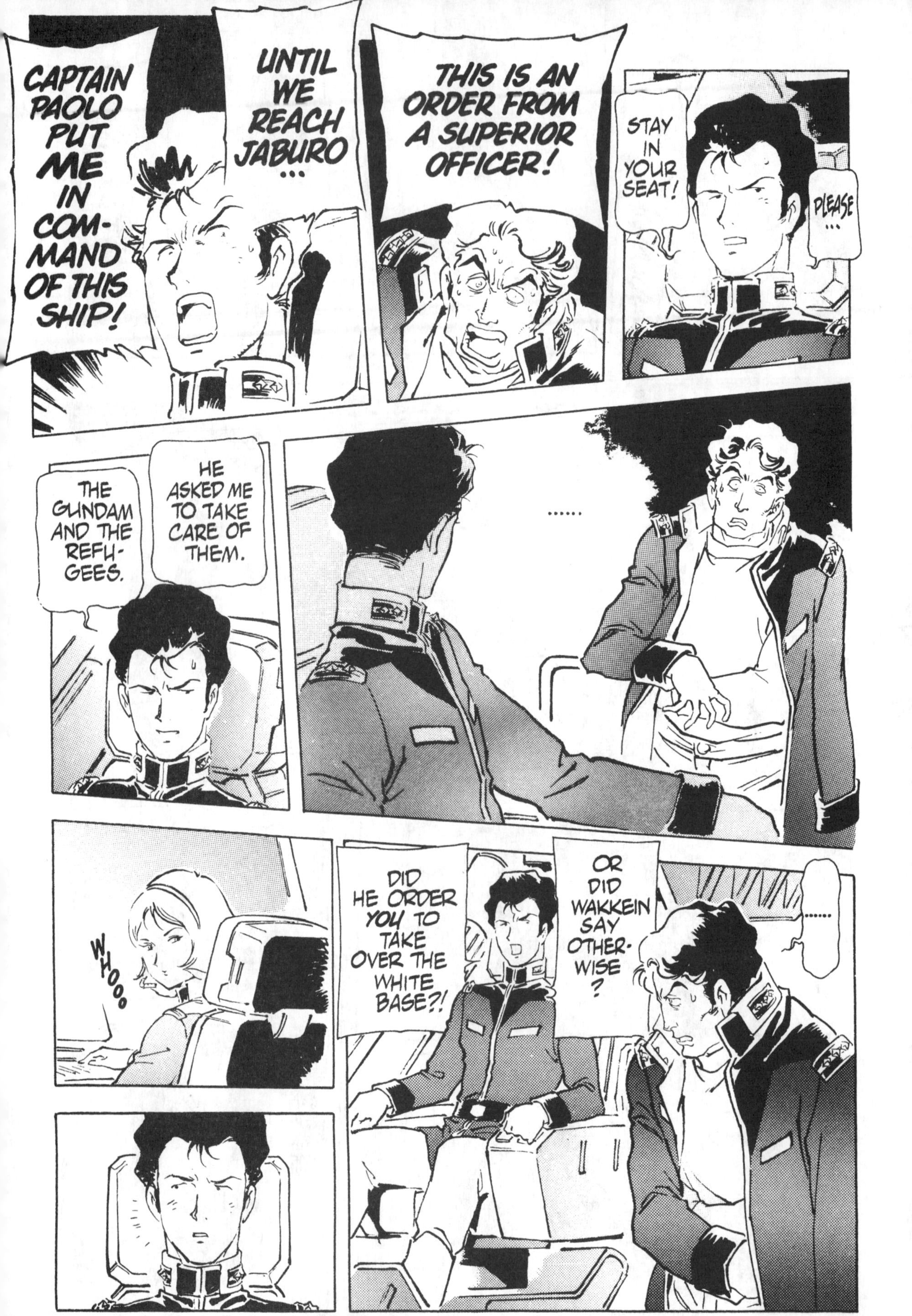

STAY IN YOUR SEAT!
PLEASE ...
THIS IS AN ORDER FROM A SUPERIOR OFFICER!
UNTIL WE REACH JABURO ...
CAPTAIN PAOLO PUT ME IN COMMAND OF THIS SHIP!
......
HE ASKED ME TO TAKE CARE OF THEM.
THE GUNDAM AND THE REFUGEES.
......
OR DID WAKKEIN SAY OTHERWISE?
DID HE ORDER YOU TO TAKE OVER THE WHITE BASE?!
WHOOO

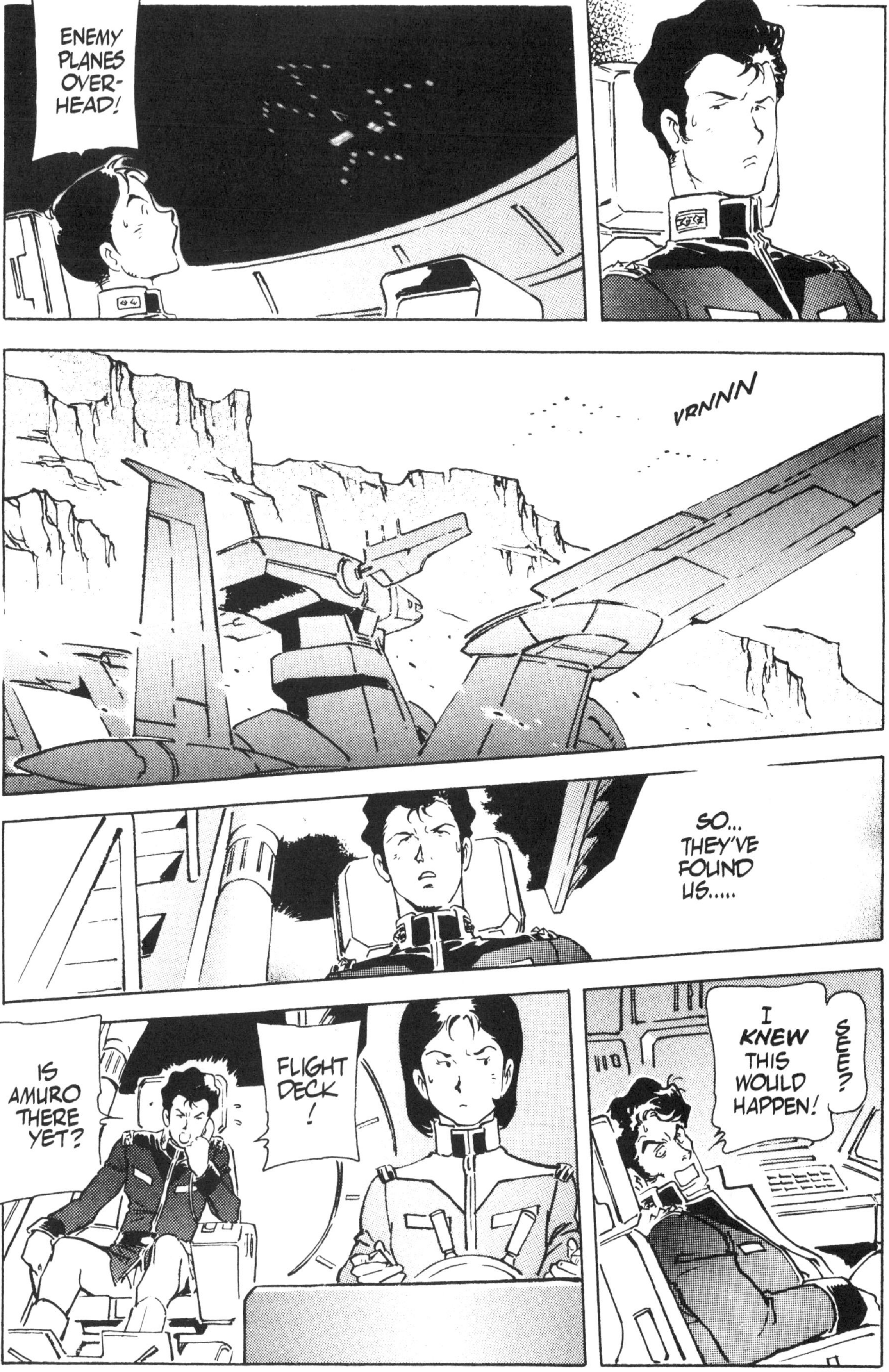
ENEMY PLANES OVER-HEAD!
VRNNN
SO... THEY'VE FOUND US.....
SEE?
I KNEW THIS WOULD HAPPEN!
FLIGHT DECK!
IS AMURO THERE YET?

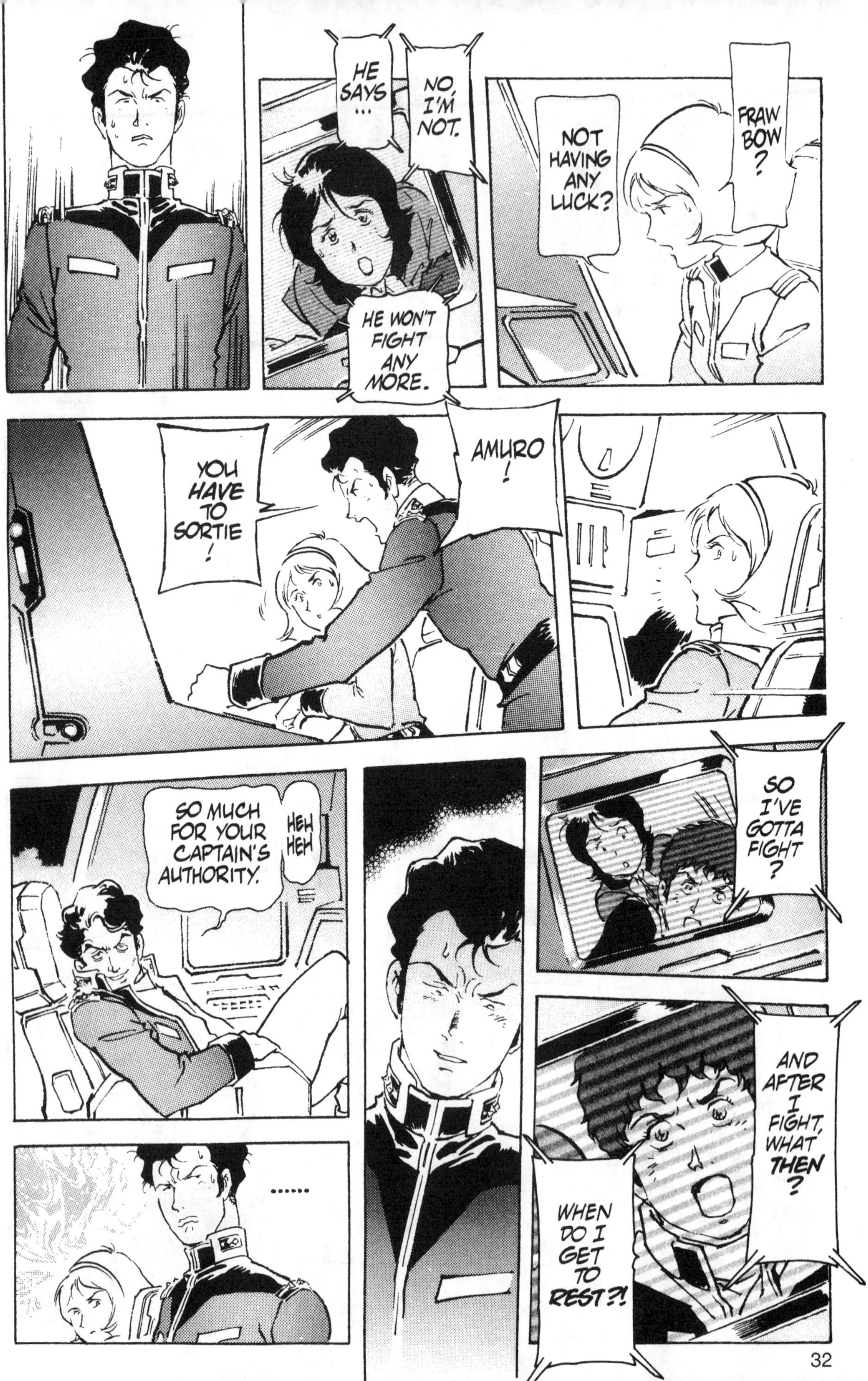
FRAW BOW?
NOT HAVING ANY LUCK?
NO, I'M NOT.
HE SAYS...
HE WON'T FIGHT ANY MORE.
AMURO!
YOU HAVE TO SORTIE!
SO I'VE GOTTA FIGHT?
AND AFTER I FIGHT, WHAT THEN?
WHEN DO I GET TO REST?!
HEH HEH
SO MUCH FOR YOUR CAPTAIN'S AUTHORITY.
......

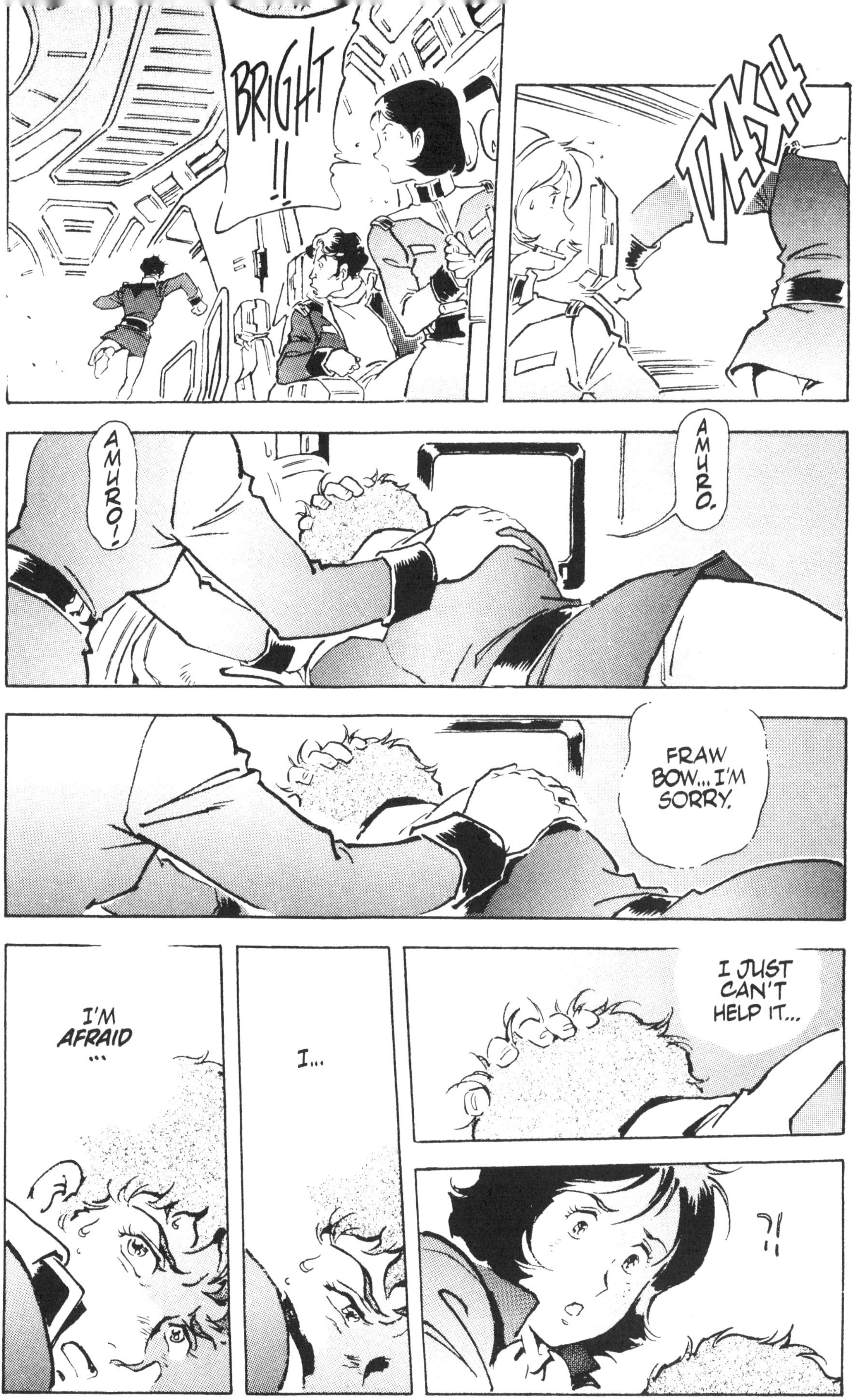
DASH
BRIGHT!!
AMURO.
AMURO!
FRAW BOW... I'M SORRY.
I JUST CAN'T HELP IT...
?!
I...
I'M AFRAID ...

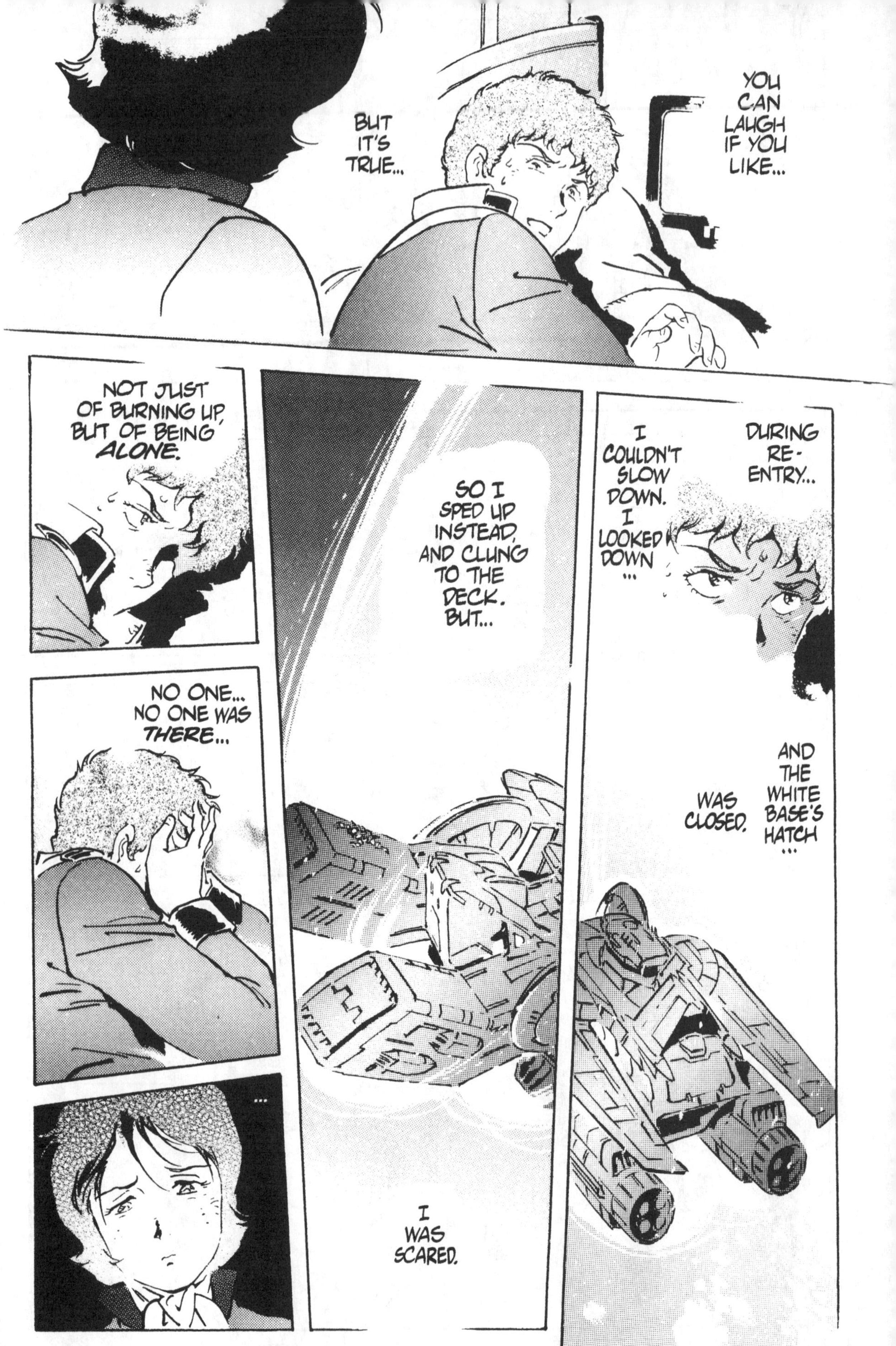
YOU CAN LAUGH IF YOU LIKE...
BUT IT'S TRUE...
DURING RE-ENTRY...
I COULDN'T SLOW DOWN. I LOOKED DOWN...
AND THE WHITE BASE'S HATCH...
WAS CLOSED.
SO I SPED UP INSTEAD, AND CLUNG TO THE DECK. BUT...
I WAS SCARED.
NOT JUST OF BURNING UP, BUT OF BEING *ALONE*.
NO ONE... NO ONE WAS *THERE*...
...

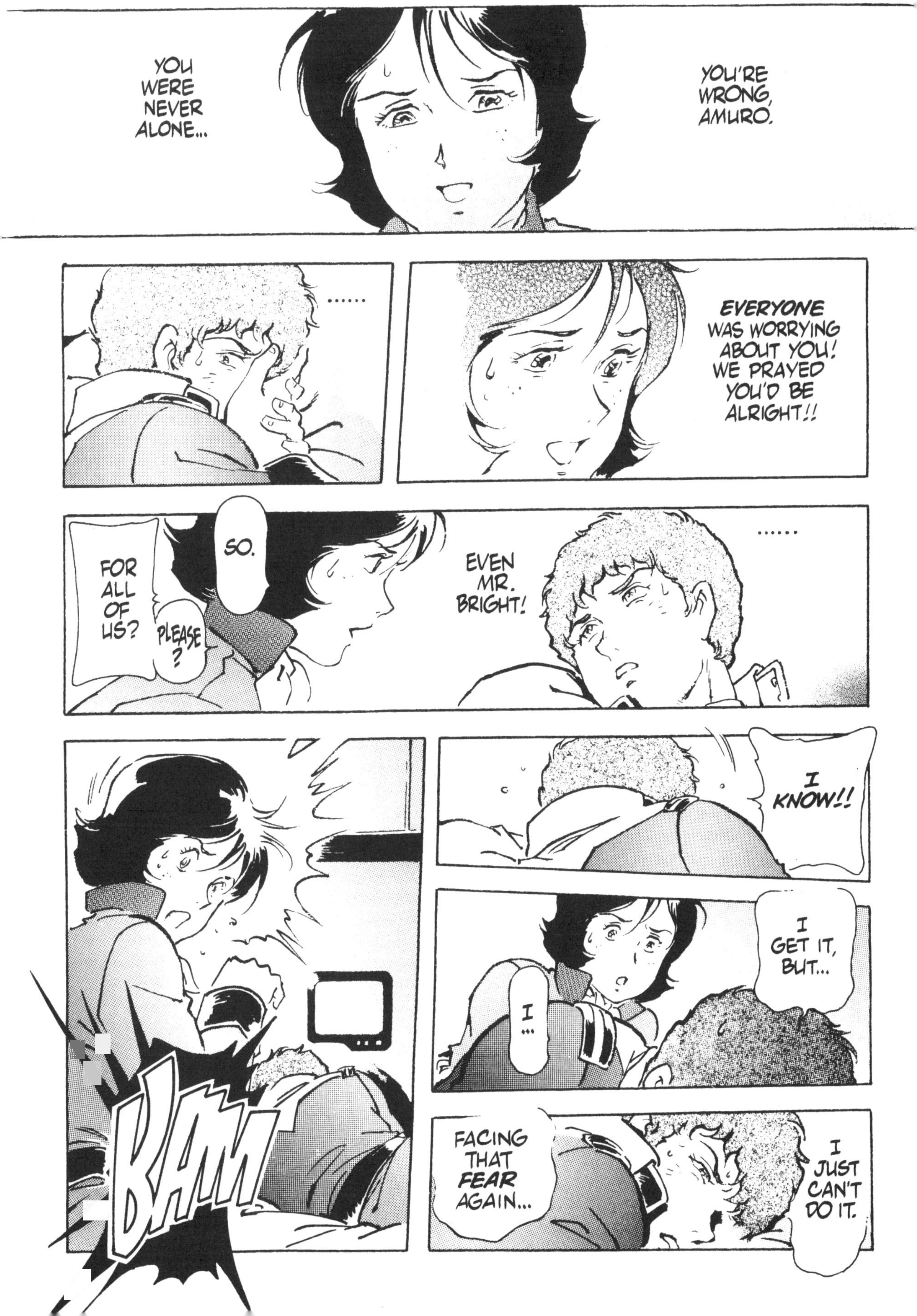
YOU'RE WRONG, AMURO.
YOU WERE NEVER ALONE...
EVERYONE WAS WORRYING ABOUT YOU! WE PRAYED YOU'D BE ALRIGHT!!
......
......
EVEN MR. BRIGHT!
SO.
PLEASE?
FOR ALL OF US?
I KNOW!!
I GET IT, BUT...
I...
I JUST CAN'T DO IT.
FACING THAT FEAR AGAIN...
BAM

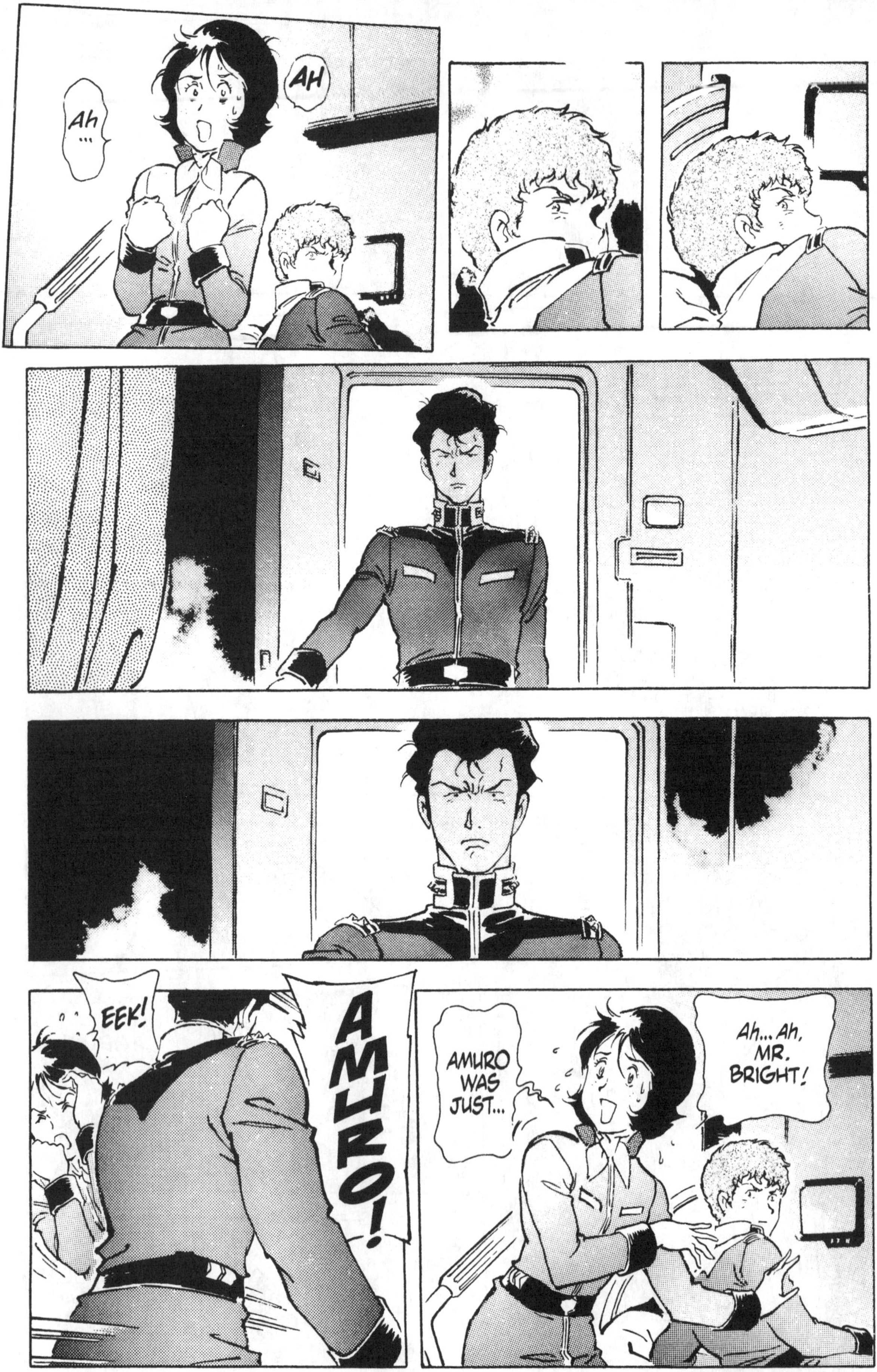
AH
Ah ...
Ah... Ah, MR. BRIGHT!
AMURO WAS JUST...
AMURO!
EEK!

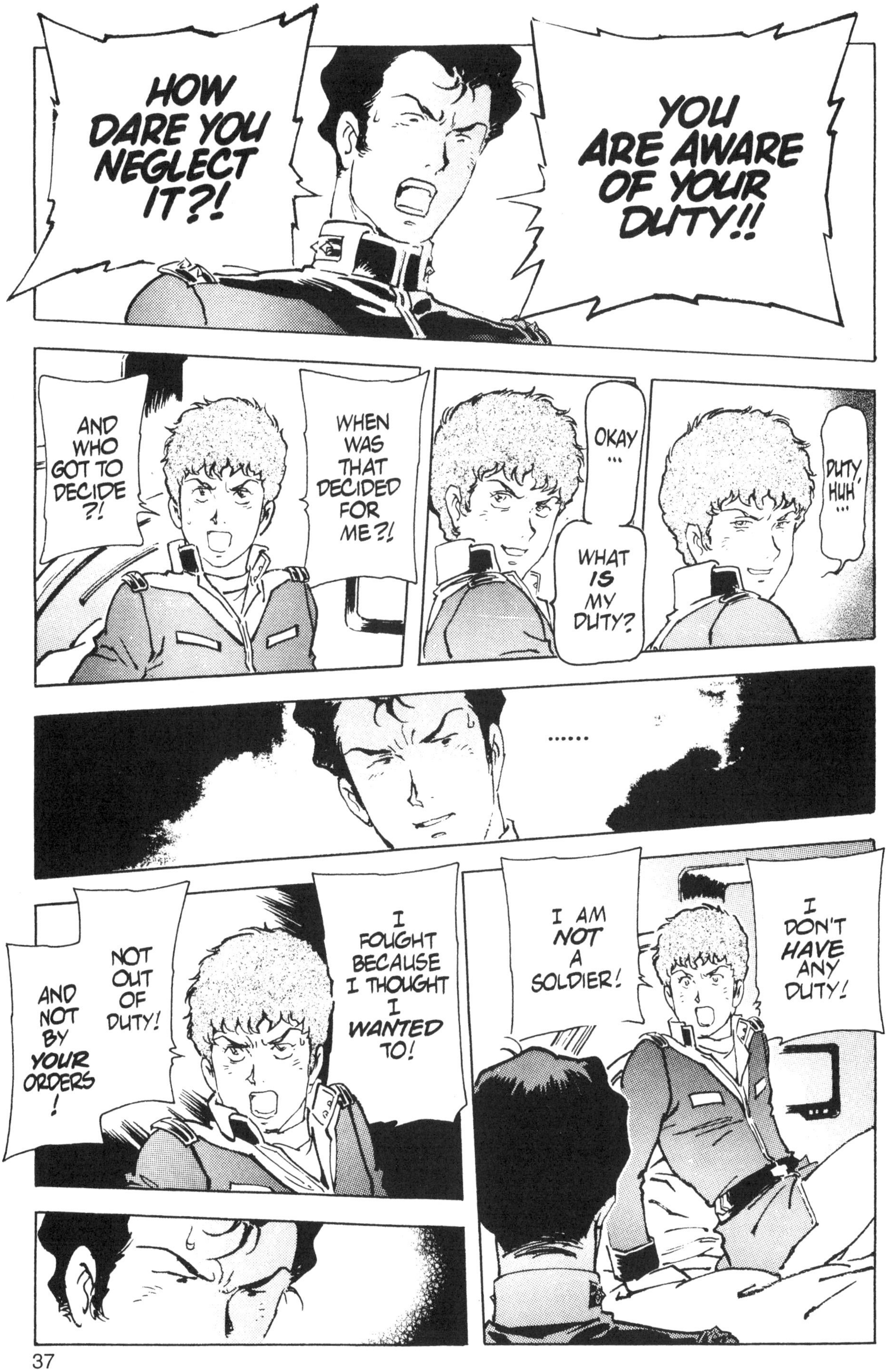
YOU ARE AWARE OF YOUR DUTY!!
HOW DARE YOU NEGLECT IT?!
DUTY, HUH ...
OKAY ...
WHAT IS MY DUTY?
WHEN WAS THAT DECIDED FOR ME?!
AND WHO GOT TO DECIDE?!
......
I DON'T HAVE ANY DUTY!
I AM NOT A SOLDIER!
I FOUGHT BECAUSE I THOUGHT I WANTED TO!
NOT OUT OF DUTY!
AND NOT BY YOUR ORDERS!

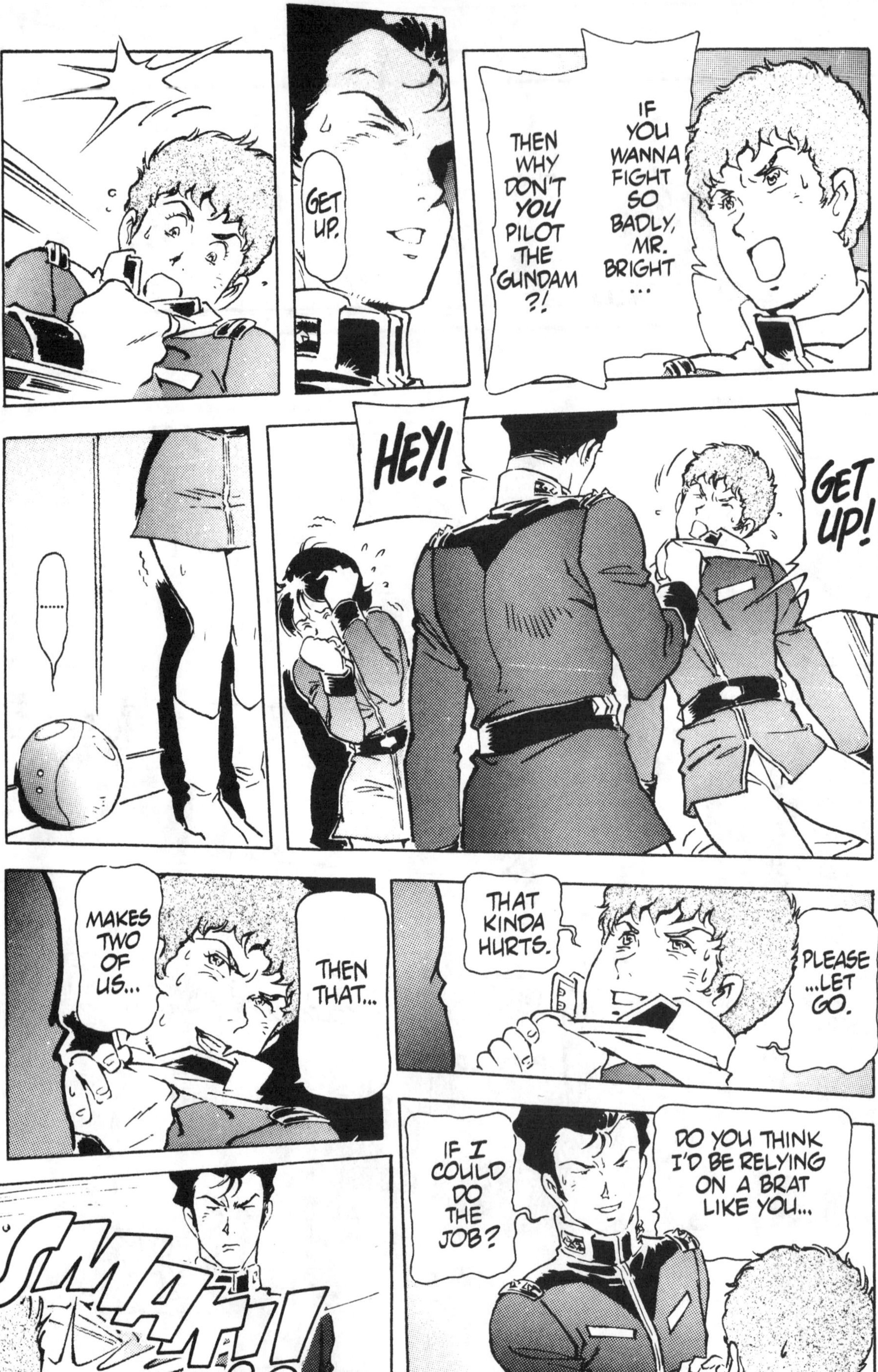
IF YOU WANNA FIGHT SO BADLY, MR. BRIGHT...
THEN WHY DON'T YOU PILOT THE GUNDAM?!
GET UP.
GET UP!
HEY!
......
PLEASE ...LET GO.
THAT KINDA HURTS.
THEN THAT...
MAKES TWO OF US...
DO YOU THINK I'D BE RELYING ON A BRAT LIKE YOU...
IF I COULD DO THE JOB?
SMAK!!

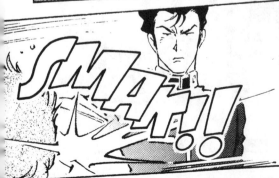

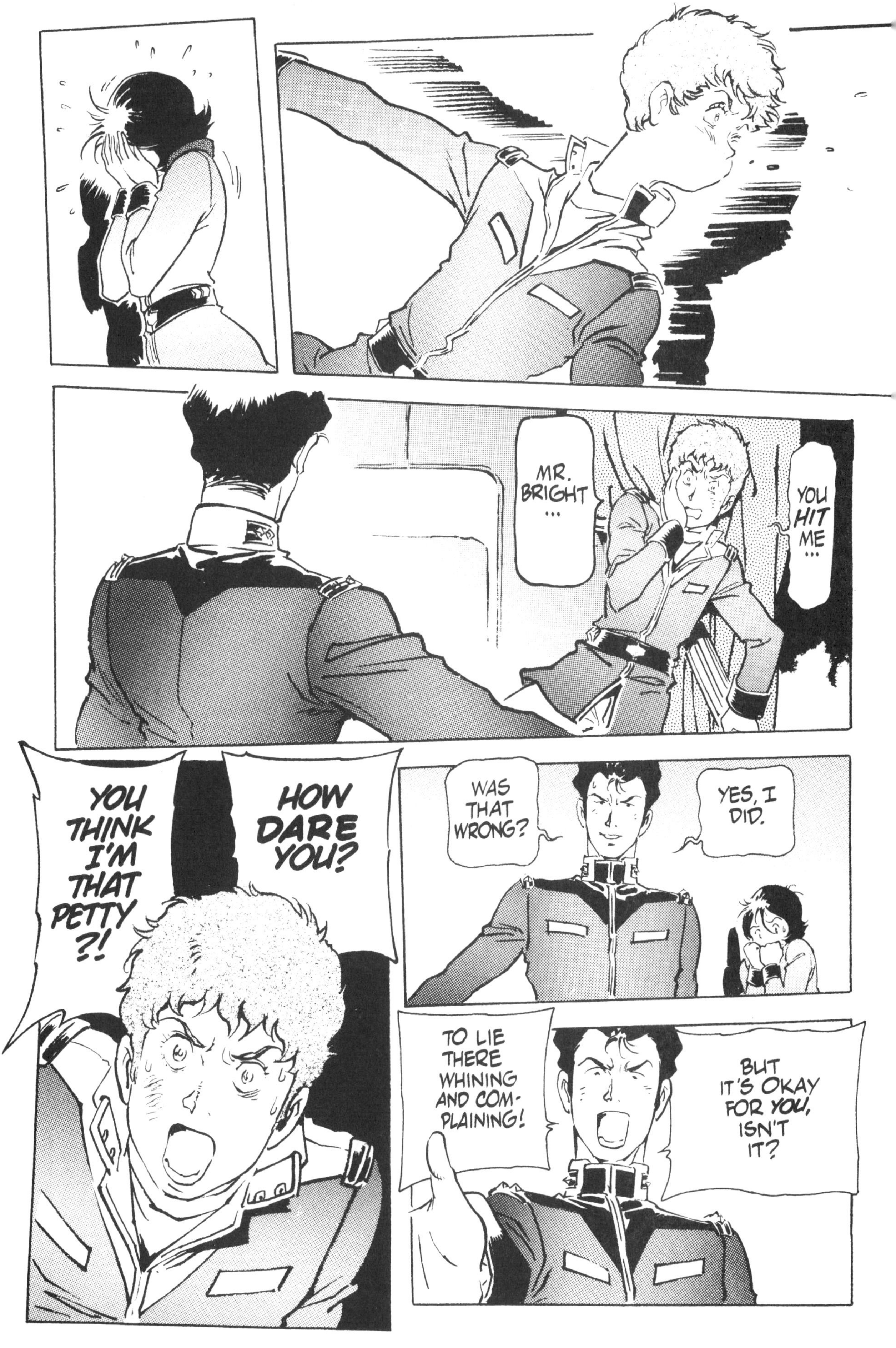
YOU HIT ME ...
MR. BRIGHT ...
YES, I DID.
WAS THAT WRONG?
BUT IT'S OKAY FOR YOU, ISN'T IT?
TO LIE THERE WHINING AND COM-PLAINING!
HOW DARE YOU?
YOU THINK I'M THAT PETTY?!

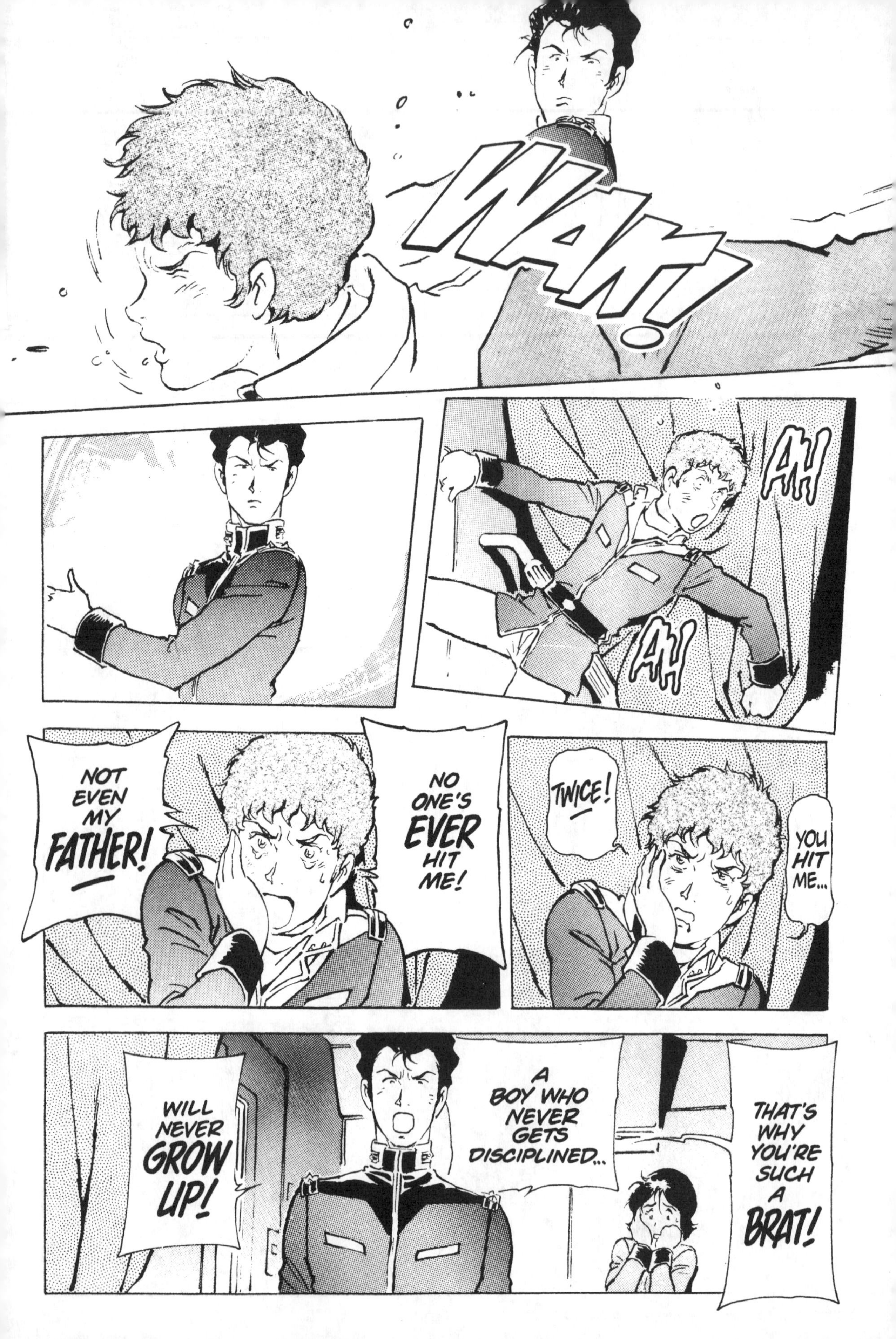
WHAM!
AH
AH
YOU HIT ME...
TWICE!
NO ONE'S EVER HIT ME!
NOT EVEN MY FATHER!
THAT'S WHY YOU'RE SUCH A BRAT!
A BOY WHO NEVER GETS DISCIPLINED...
WILL NEVER GROW UP!

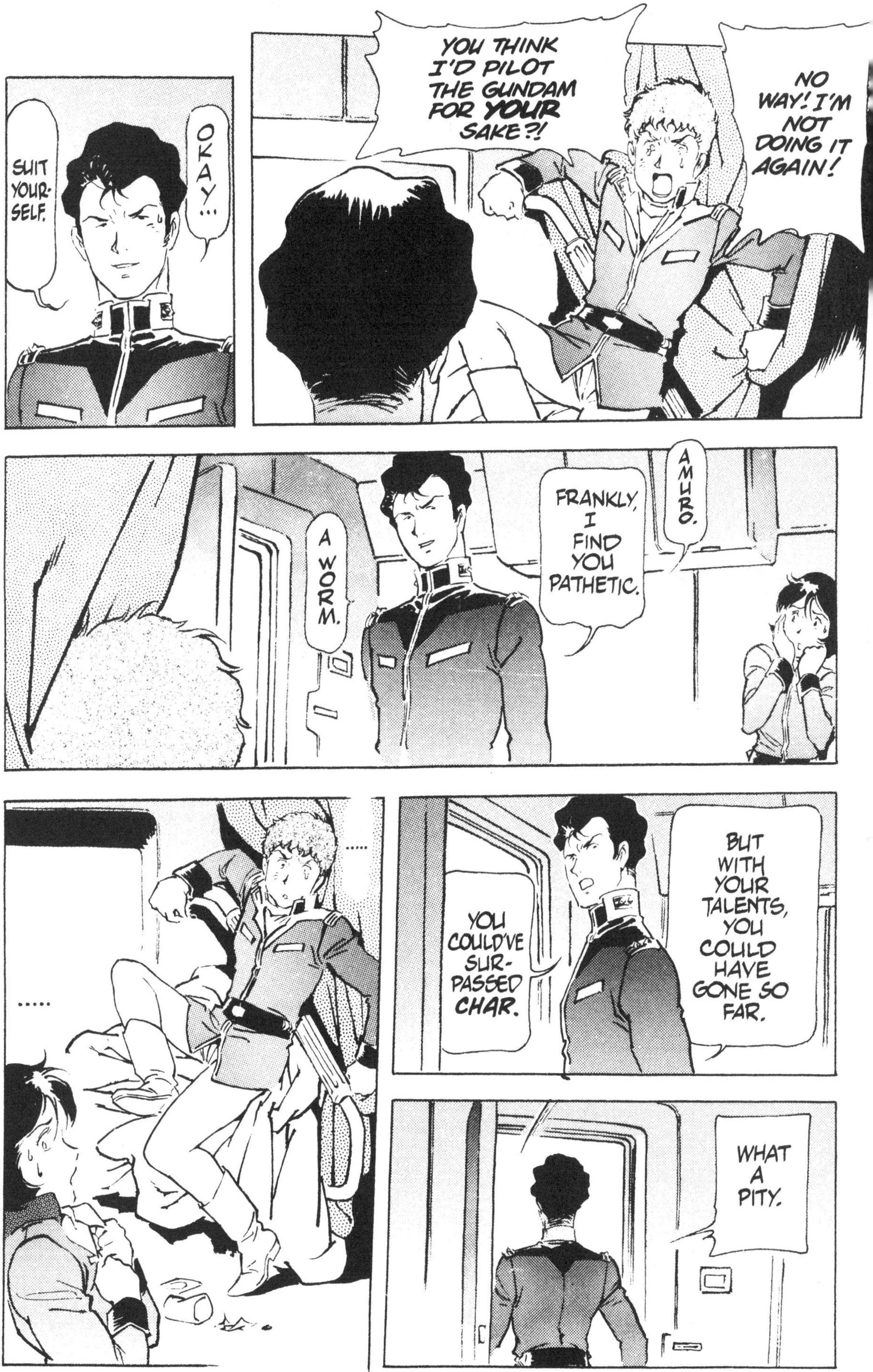
OKAY...
SUIT YOURSELF.
YOU THINK I'D PILOT THE GUNDAM FOR YOUR SAKE?!
NO WAY! I'M NOT DOING IT AGAIN!
AMURO.
FRANKLY, I FIND YOU PATHETIC.
A WORM.
.....
.....
BUT WITH YOUR TALENTS, YOU COULD HAVE GONE SO FAR.
YOU COULD'VE SURPASSED CHAR.
WHAT A PITY.

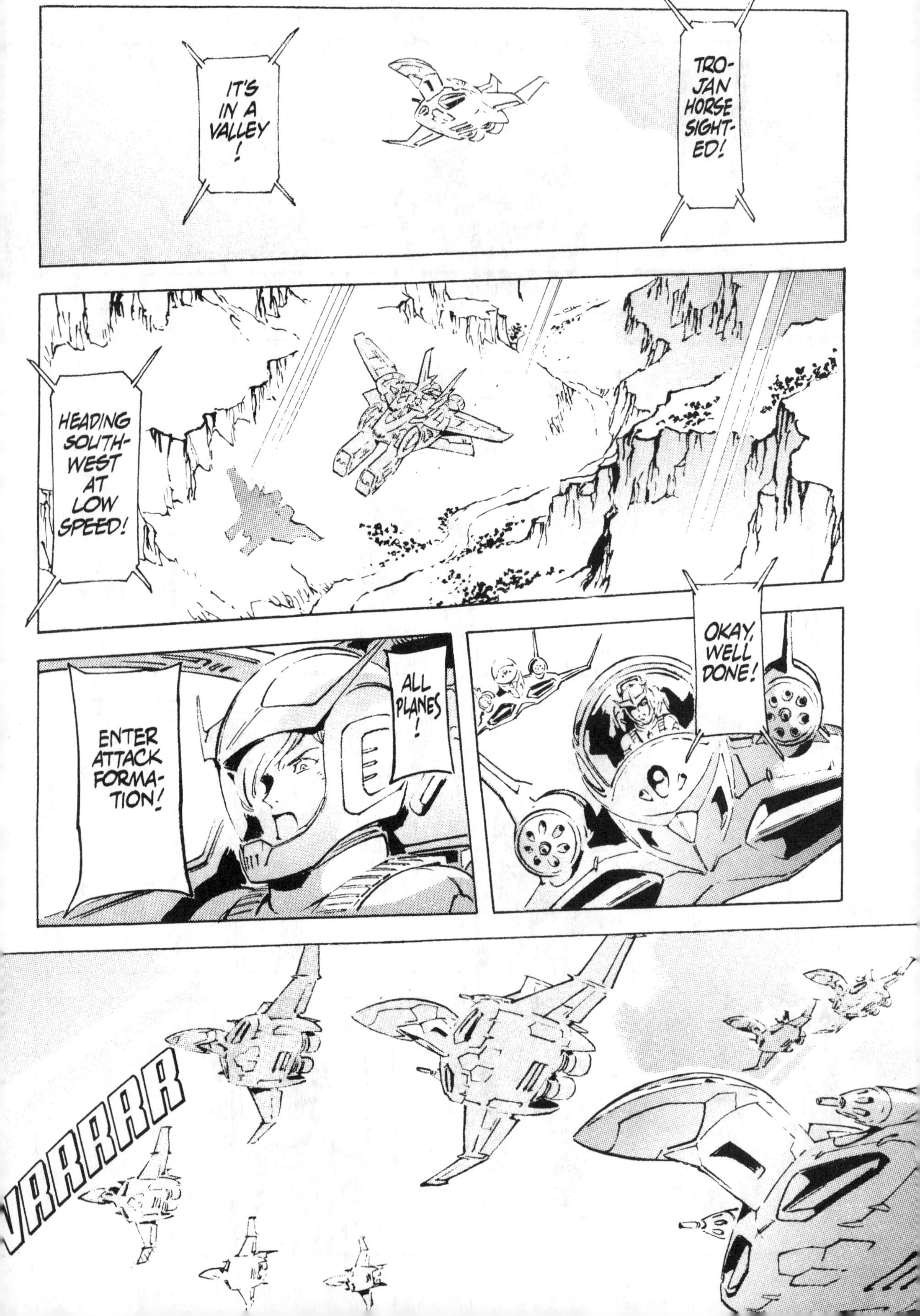
TRO-JAN HORSE SIGHT-ED!
IT'S IN A VALLEY!
HEADING SOUTH-WEST AT LOW SPEED!
OKAY, WELL DONE!
ALL PLANES!
ENTER ATTACK FORMA-TION!
VRRRRR

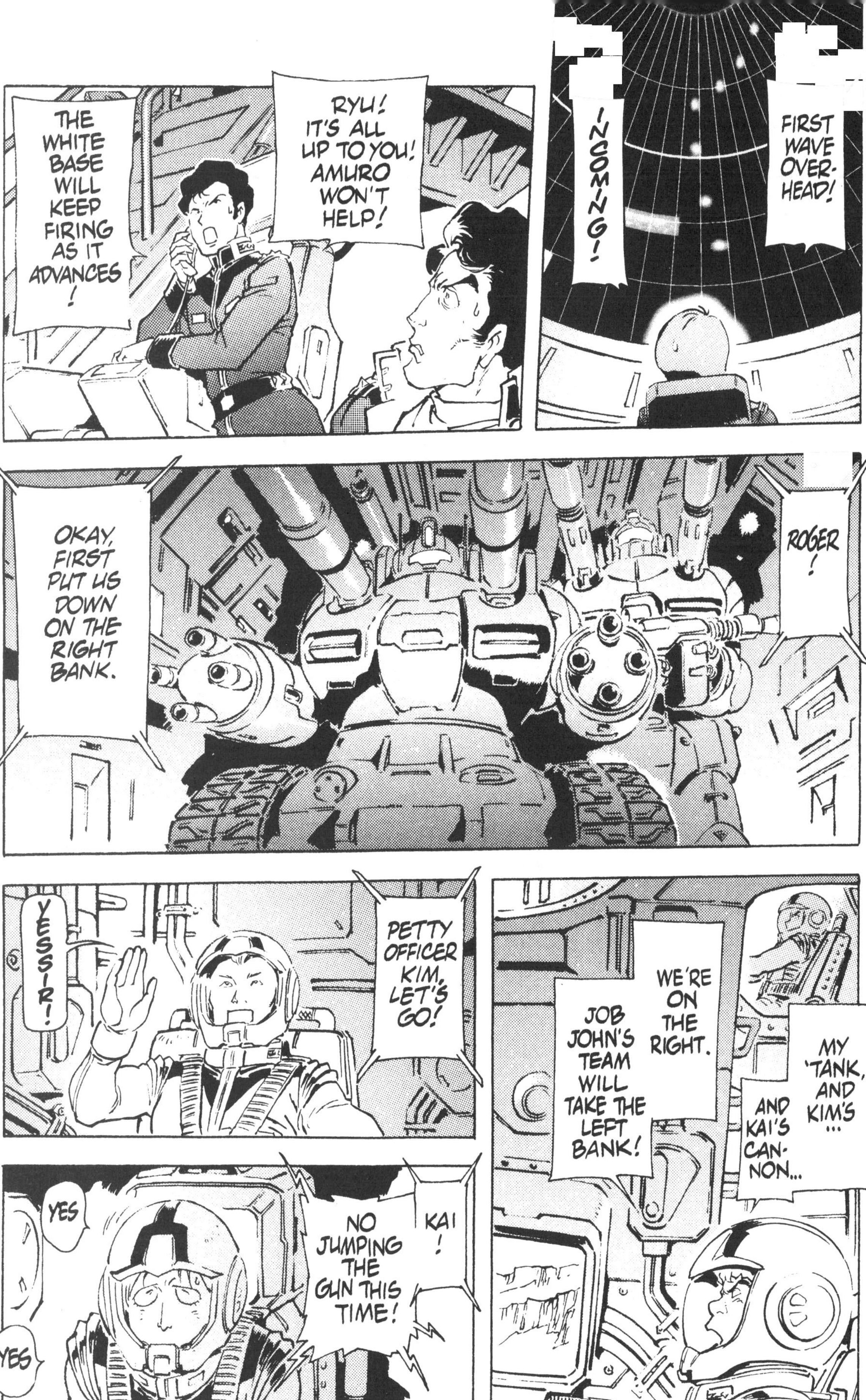
FIRST WAVE OVER-HEAD!
INCOMING!
RYU! IT'S ALL UP TO YOU! AMURO WON'T HELP!
THE WHITE BASE WILL KEEP FIRING AS IT ADVANCES!
ROGER!
OKAY, FIRST PUT US DOWN ON THE RIGHT BANK.
MY 'TANK, AND KIM'S...
AND KAI'S CAN-NON...
WE'RE ON THE RIGHT.
JOB JOHN'S TEAM WILL TAKE THE LEFT BANK!
PETTY OFFICER KIM, LET'S GO!
YESSIR!
KAI!
NO JUMPING THE GUN THIS TIME!
YES
YES

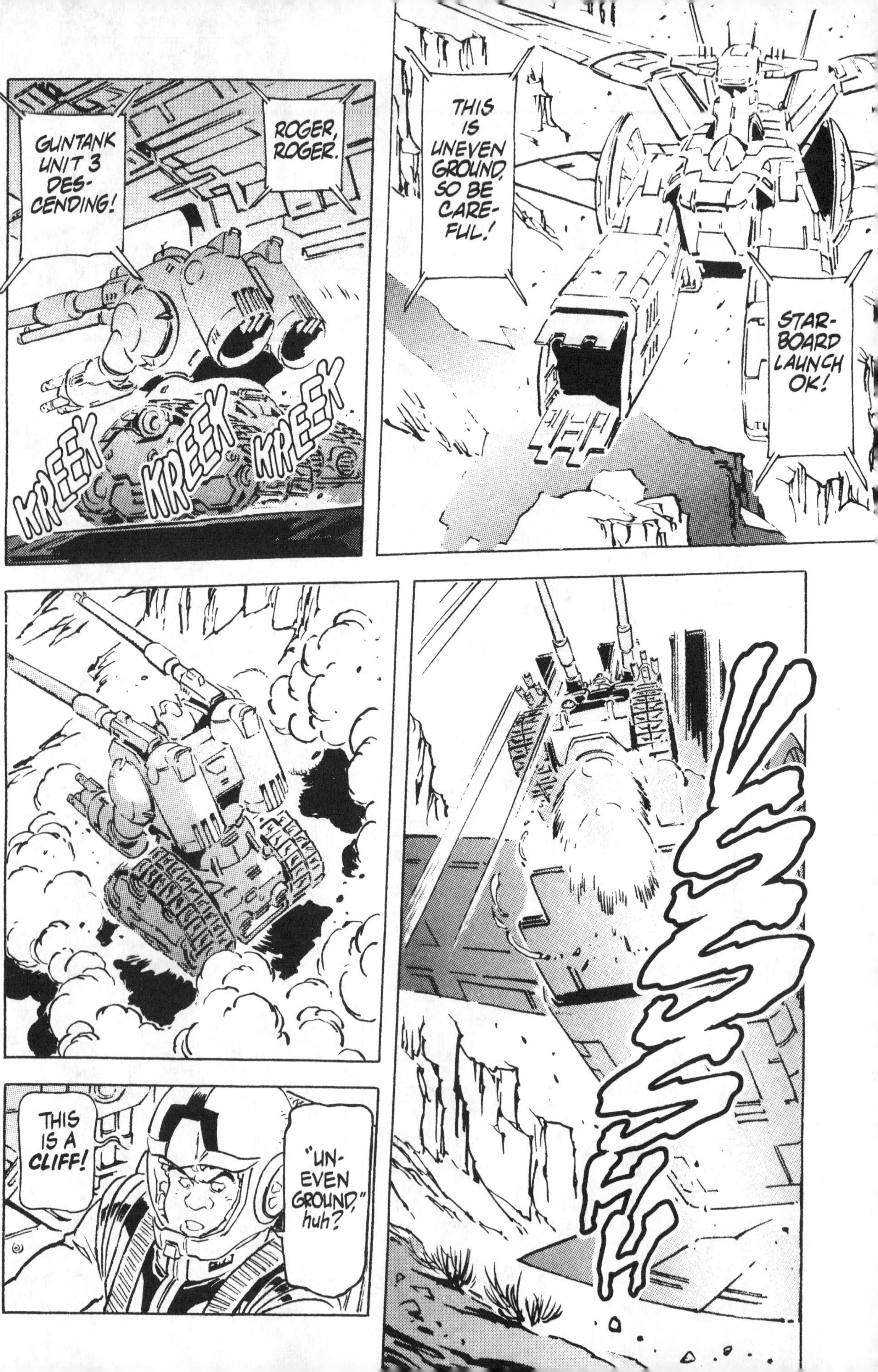

STAR-BOARD LAUNCH OK!
THIS IS UNEVEN GROUND, SO BE CARE-FUL!
GUNTANK UNIT 3 DES-CENDING!
ROGER, ROGER.
KREEK KREEK KREEK
"UN-EVEN GROUND," huh?
THIS IS A **CLIFF**!

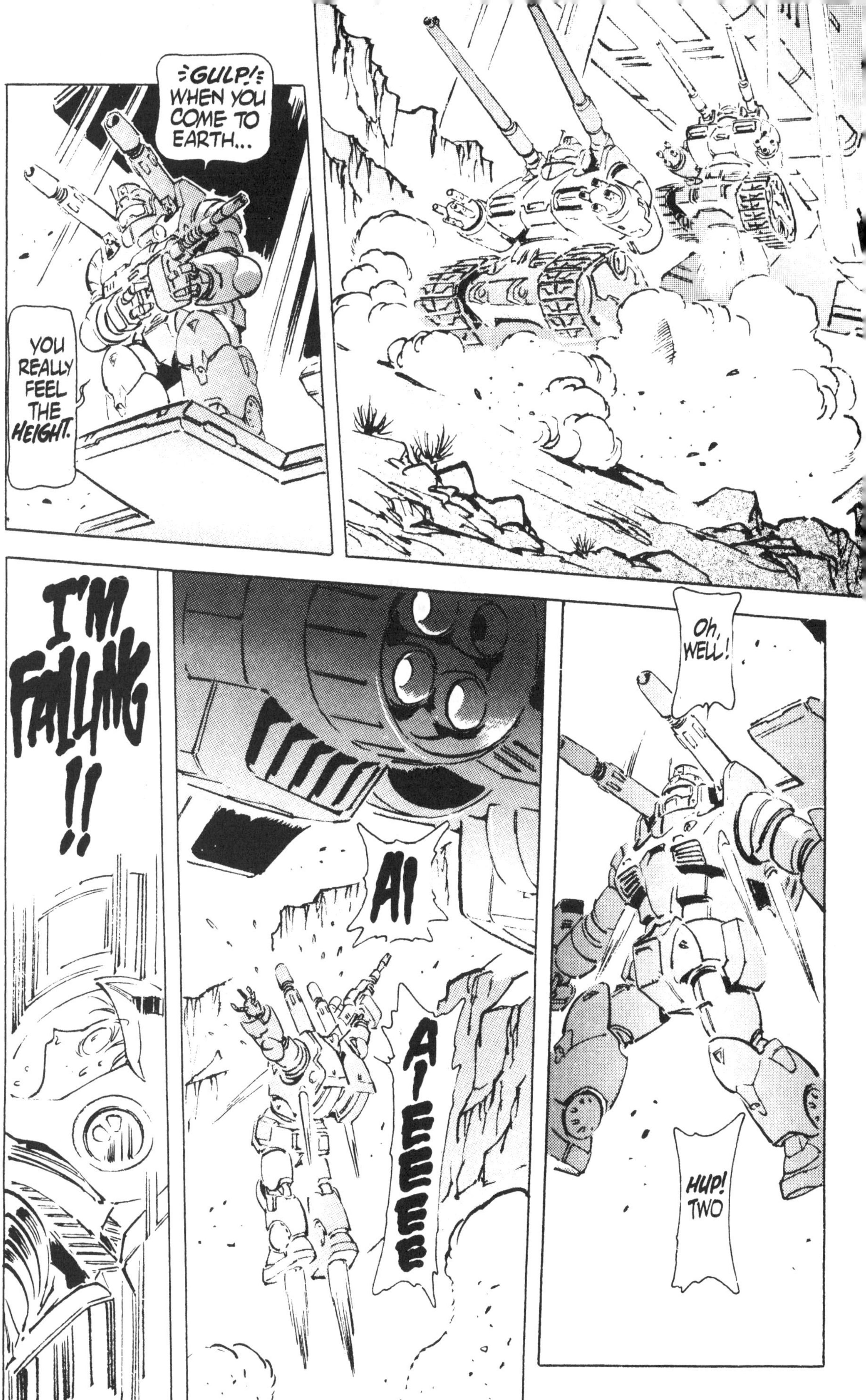
GULP! WHEN YOU COME TO EARTH...
YOU REALLY FEEL THE HEIGHT.
I'M FALLING!!
AI
AIEEEEE
Oh, WELL!
HUP! TWO

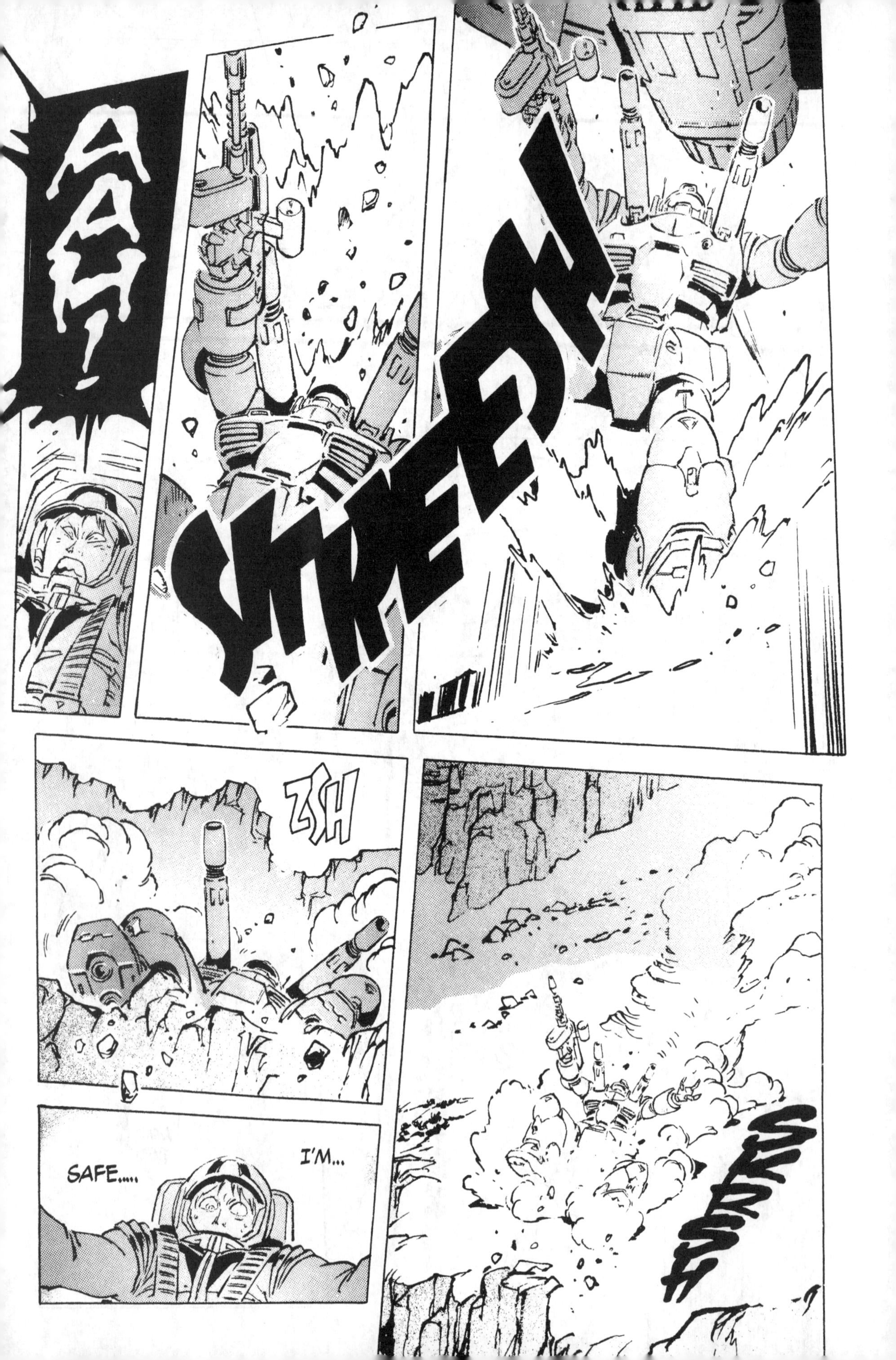
SKREEE!
AAH!
ZSH
I'M...
SAFE.....

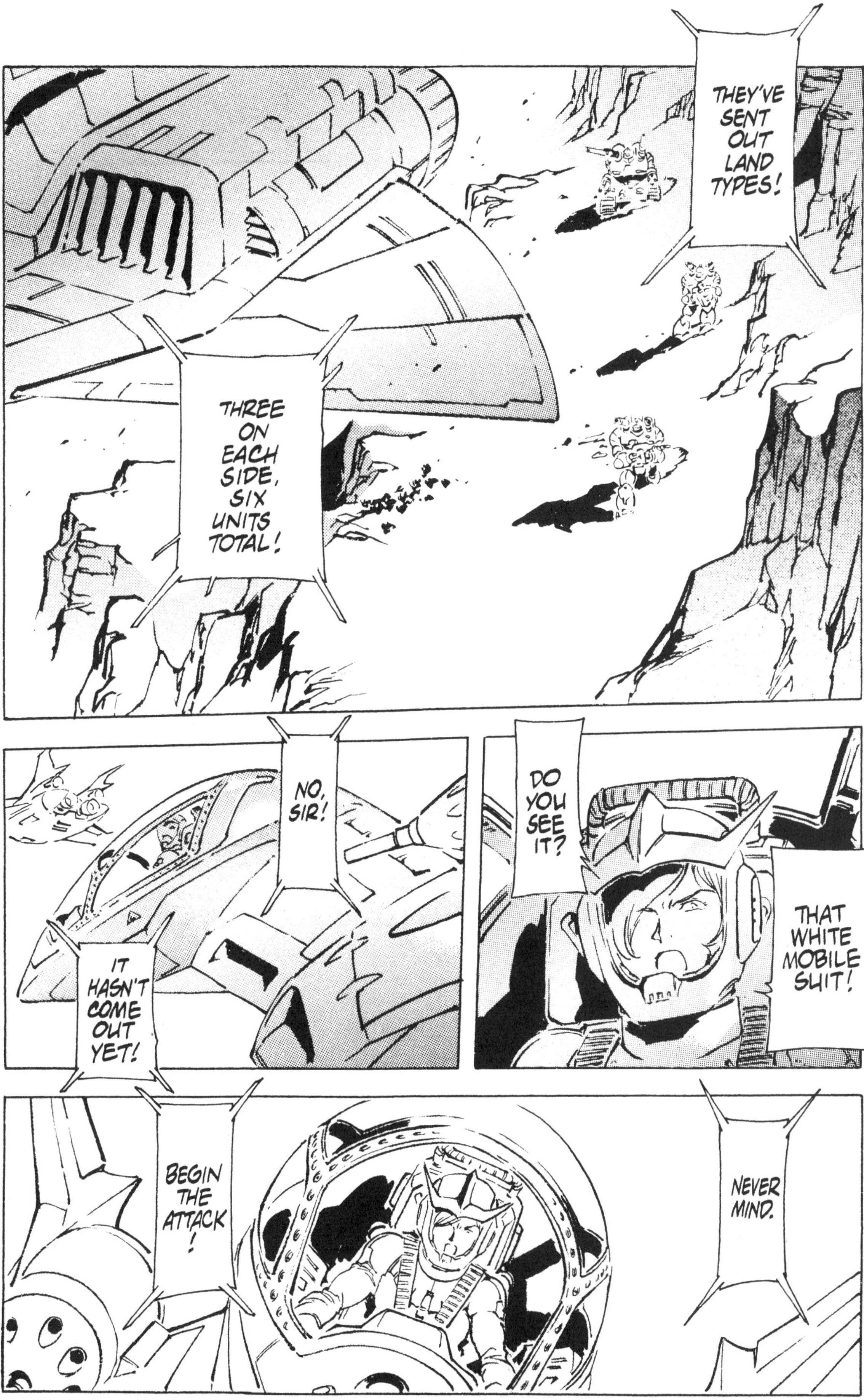
THEY'VE SENT OUT LAND TYPES!
THREE ON EACH SIDE, SIX UNITS TOTAL!
DO YOU SEE IT?
THAT WHITE MOBILE SUIT!
NO, SIR!
IT HASN'T COME OUT YET!
NEVER MIND.
BEGIN THE ATTACK!

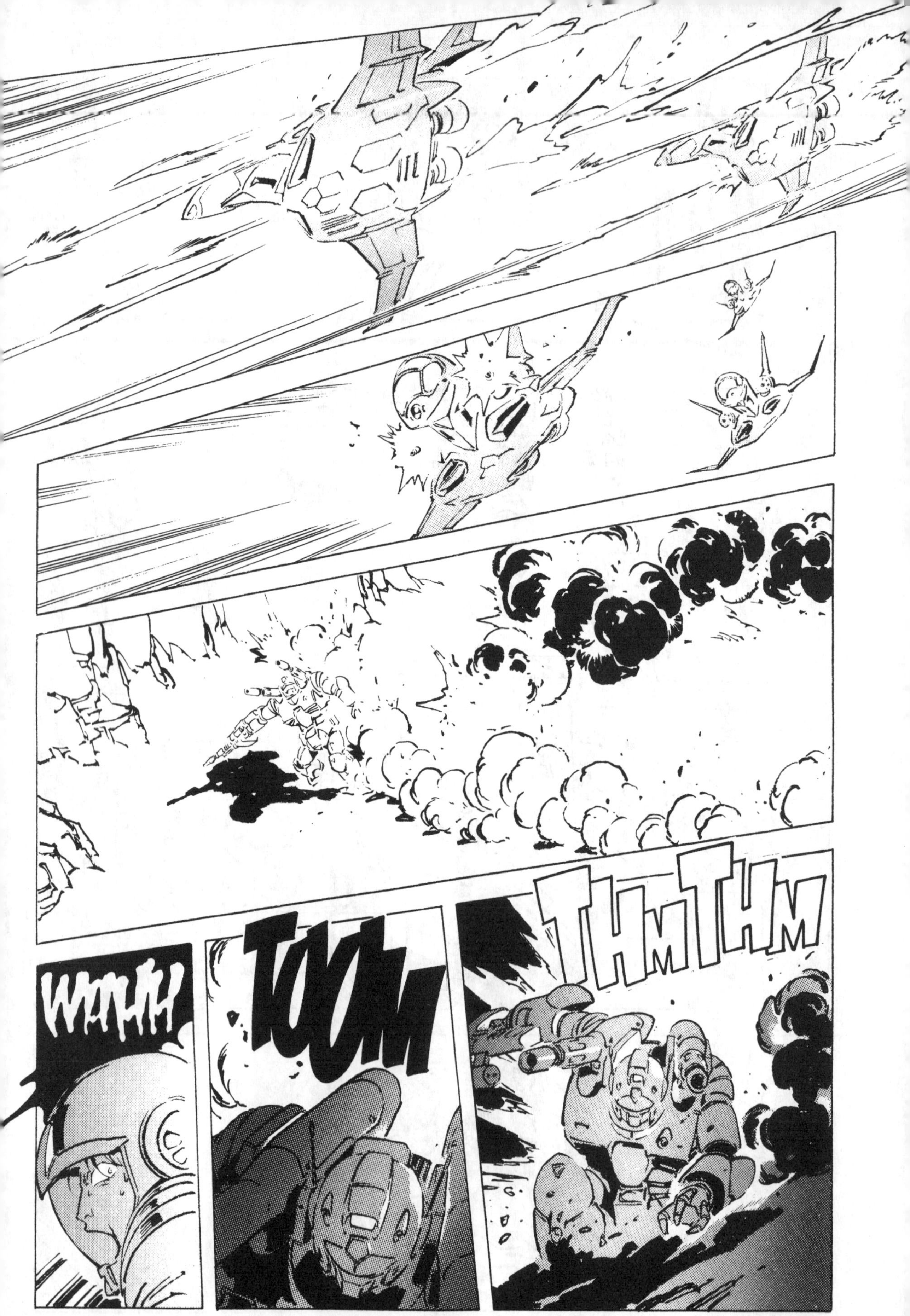
THMTHM
TOOM
WAHH

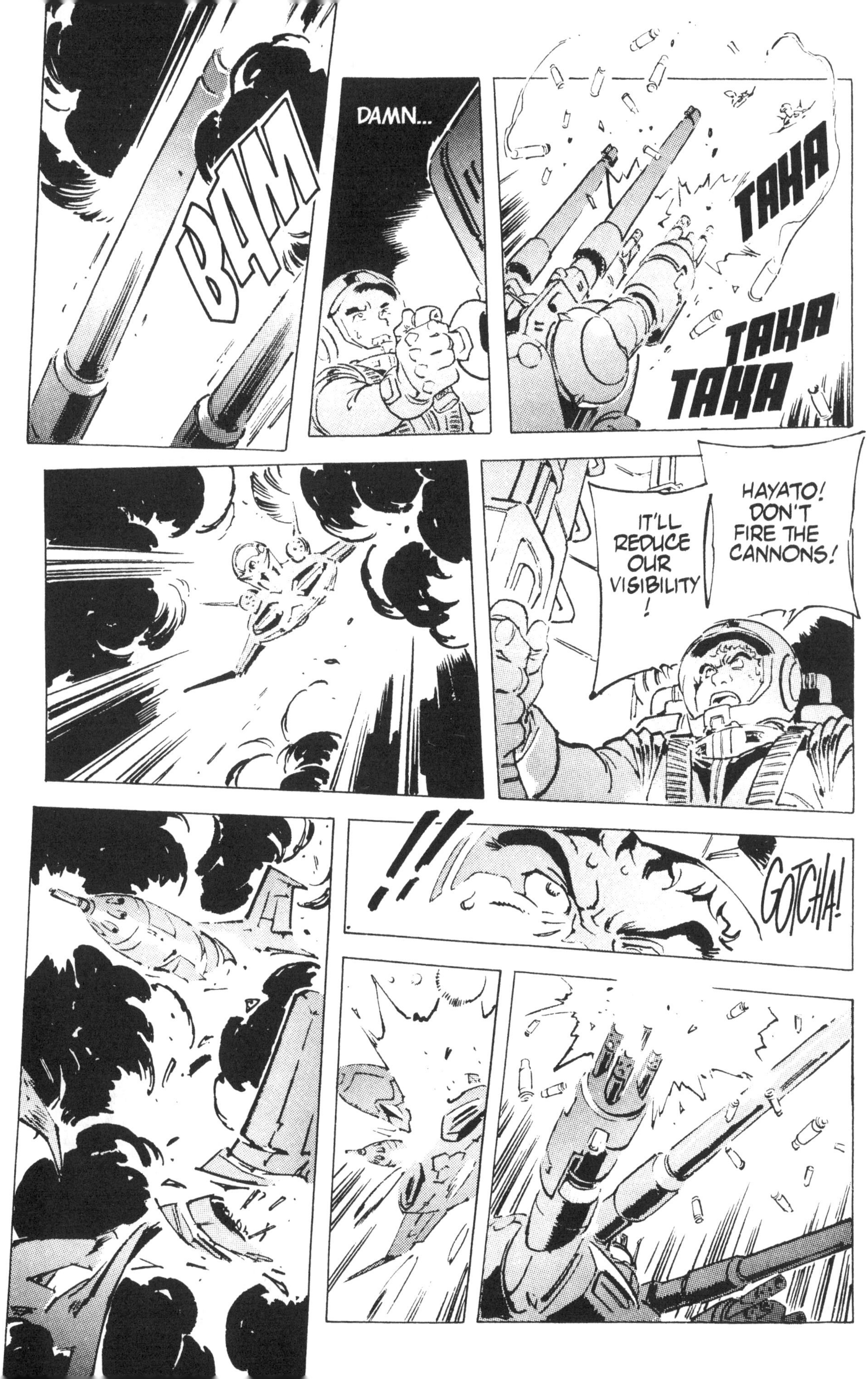
TAKA
TAKA
TAKA
DAMN...
BAM
HAYATO! DON'T FIRE THE CANNONS!
IT'LL REDUCE OUR VISIBILITY!
GOTCHA!
!!

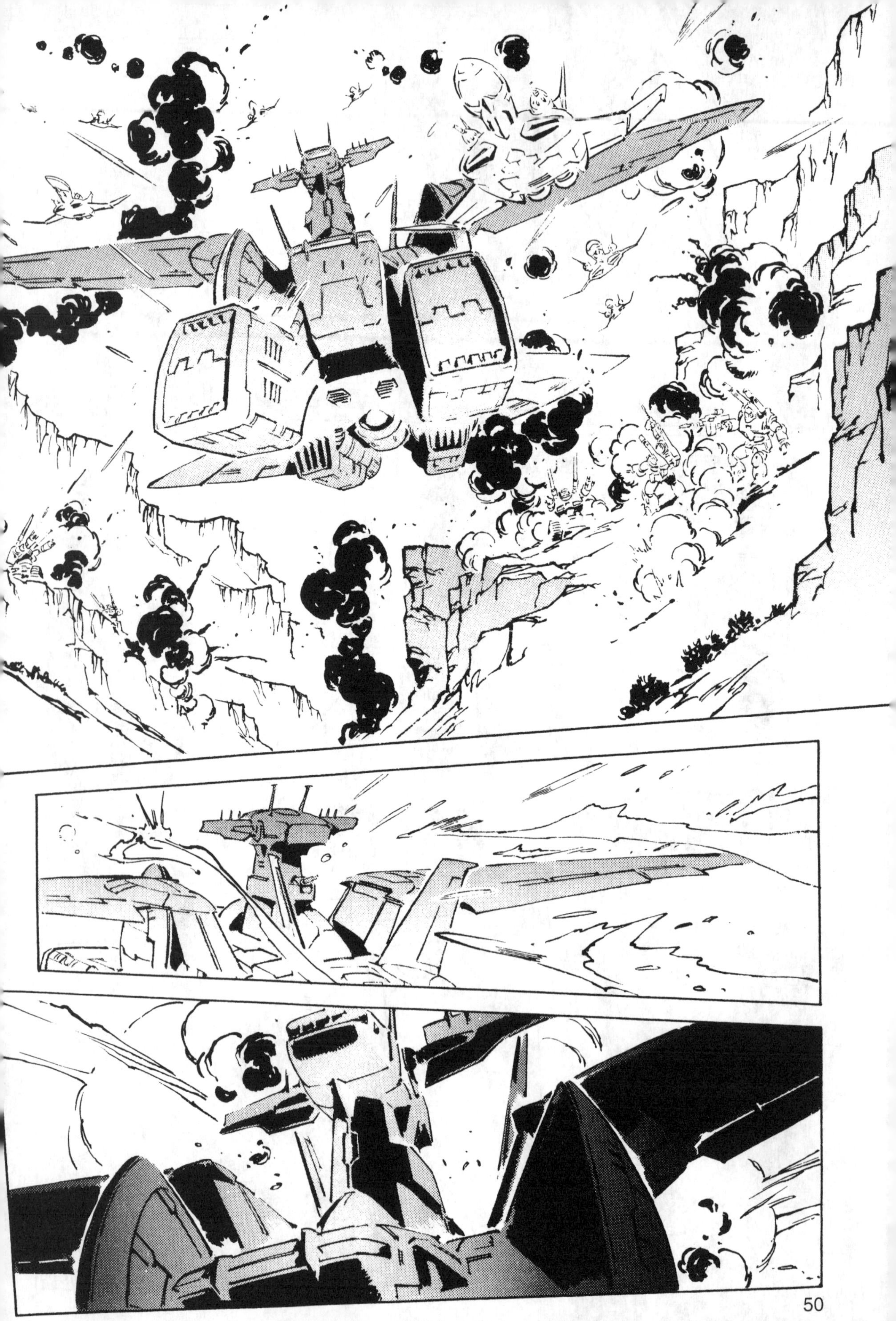

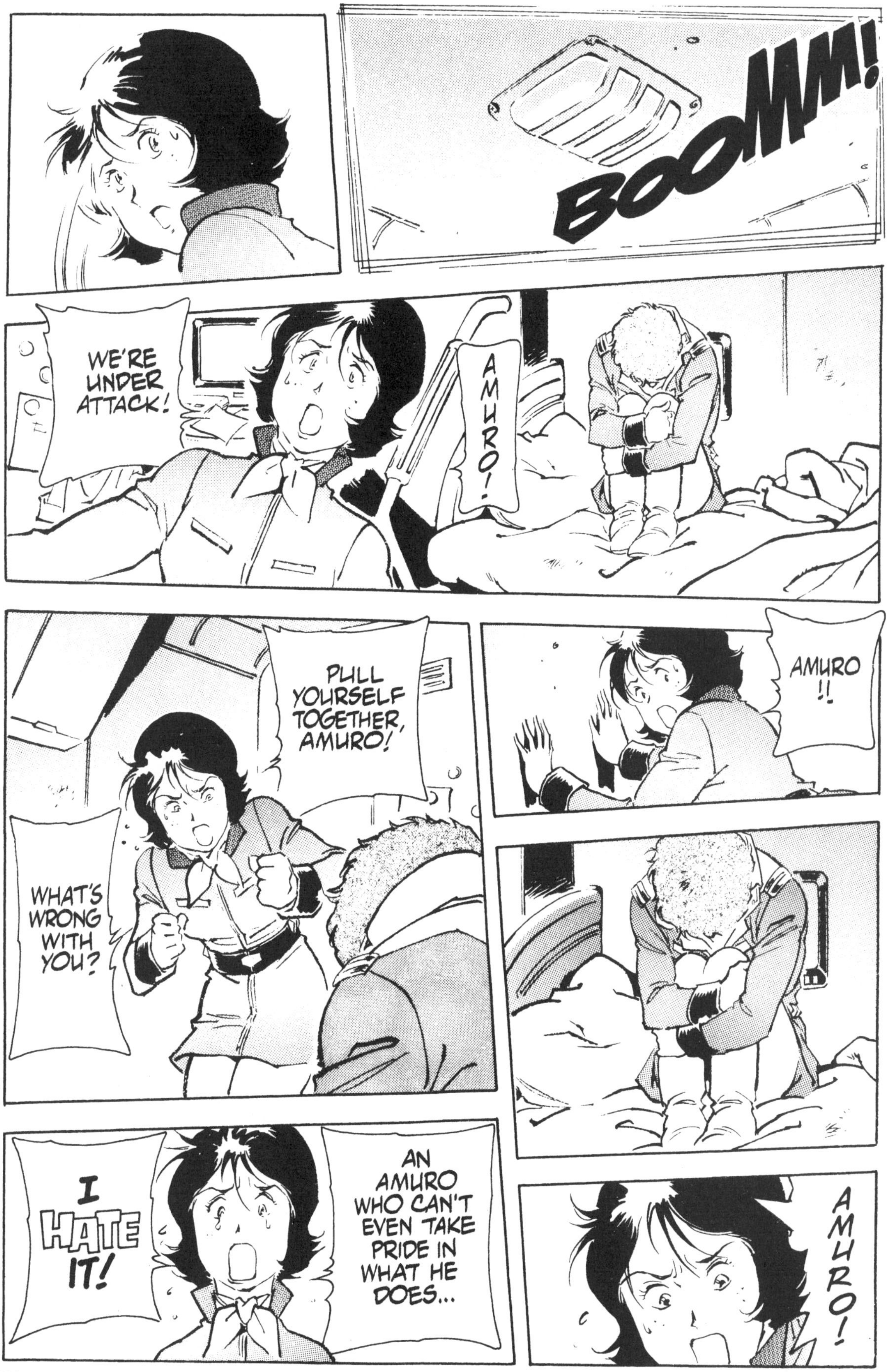
BOOMMM!
AMURO!
WE'RE UNDER ATTACK!
AMURO !!
PULL YOURSELF TOGETHER, AMURO!
WHAT'S WRONG WITH YOU?
AMURO!
AN AMURO WHO CAN'T EVEN TAKE PRIDE IN WHAT HE DOES...
I HATE IT!

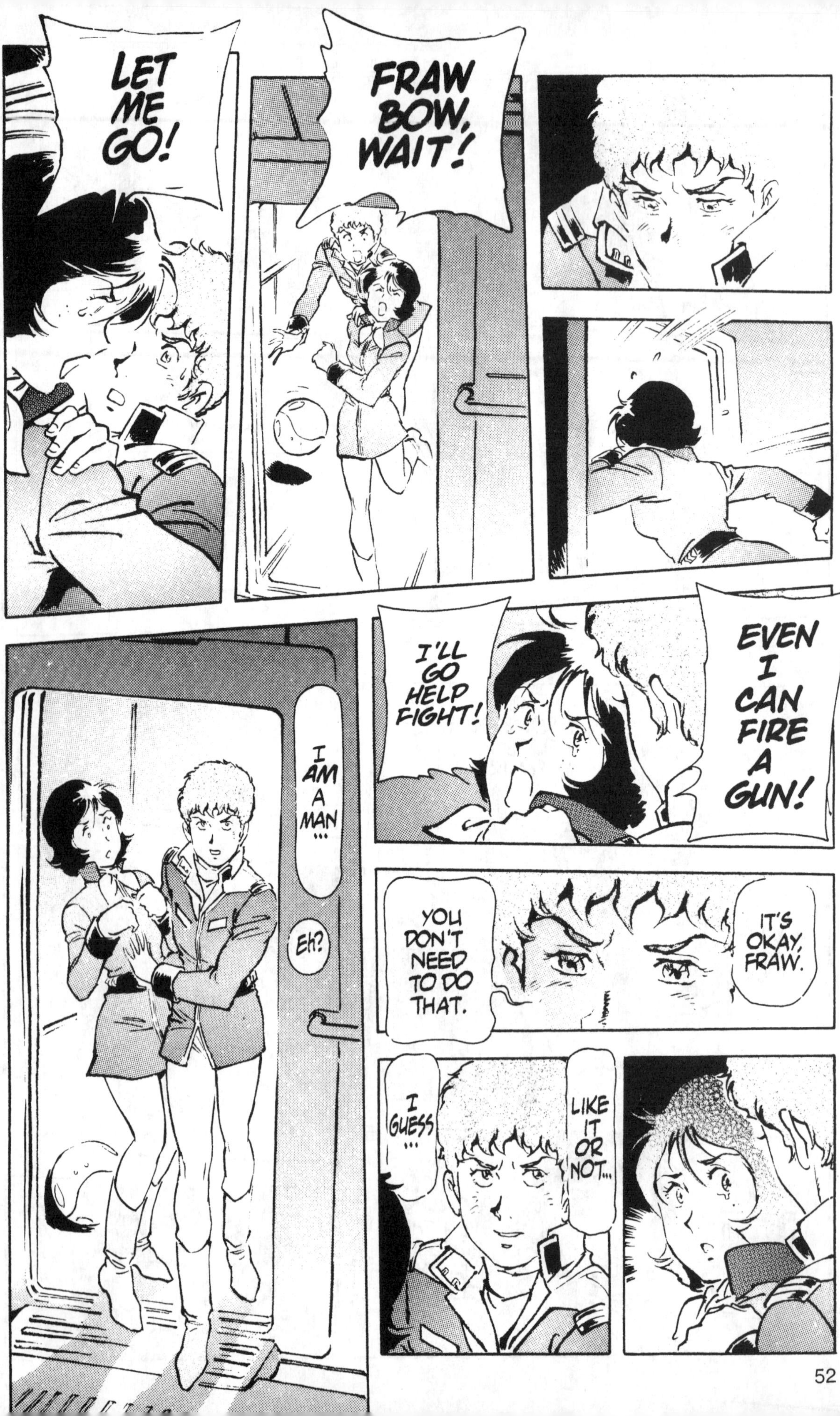
FRAW BOW, WAIT!
LET ME GO!
EVEN I CAN FIRE A GUN!
I'LL GO HELP FIGHT!
IT'S OKAY, FRAW.
YOU DON'T NEED TO DO THAT.
LIKE IT OR NOT...
I GUESS...
I AM A MAN...
Eh?

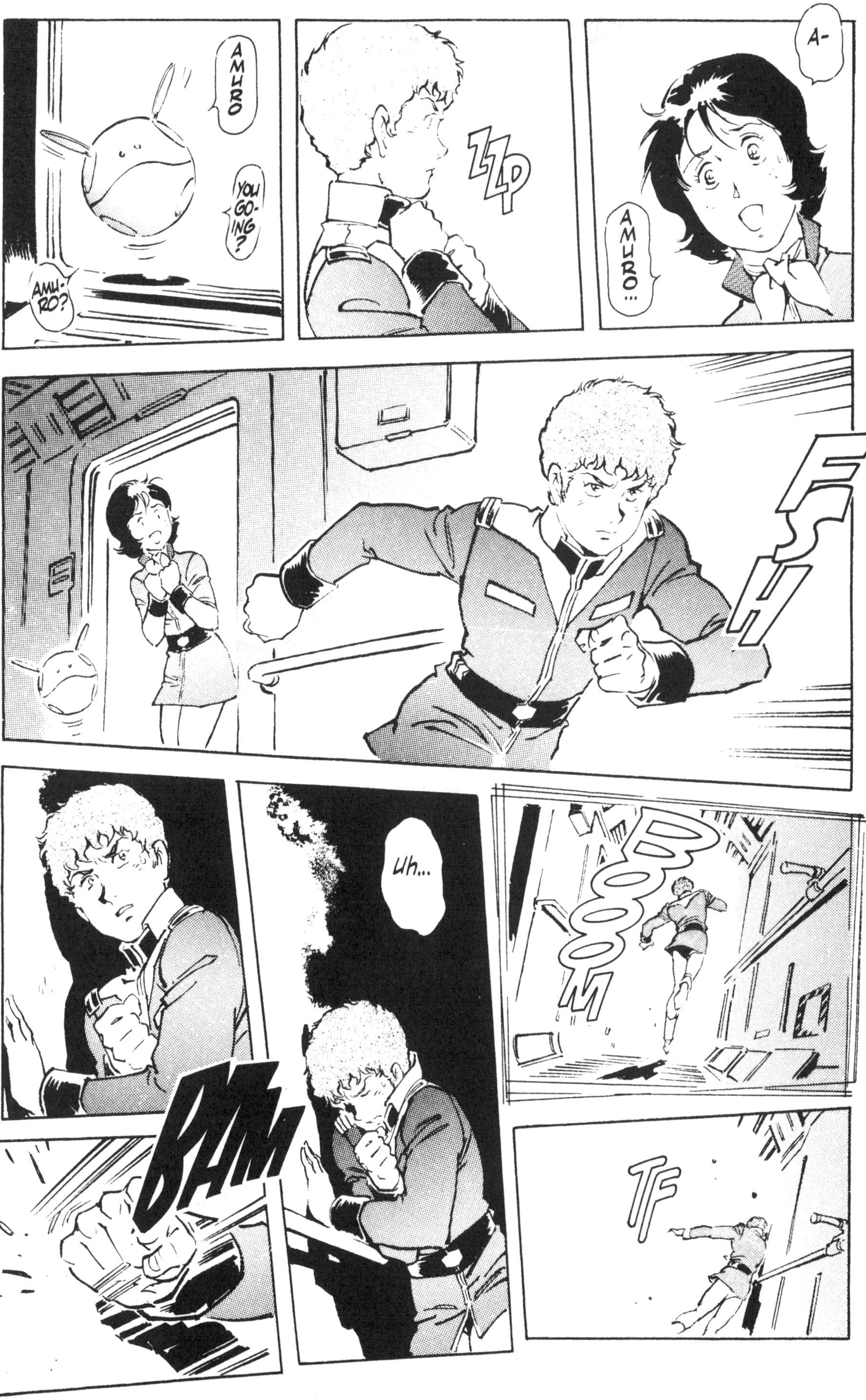
A-
AMURO...
ZZP
AMURO
YOU GO-ING?
AMU-RO?
FSH
BOOOOM
uh...
TF
BAM

GARMA

SECTION II

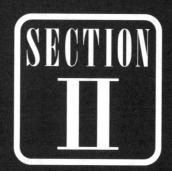

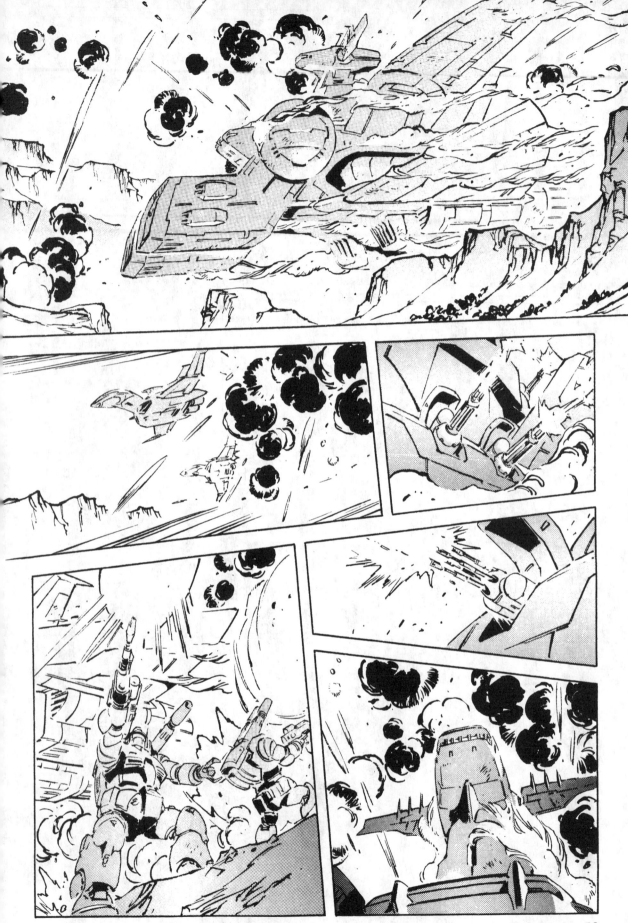

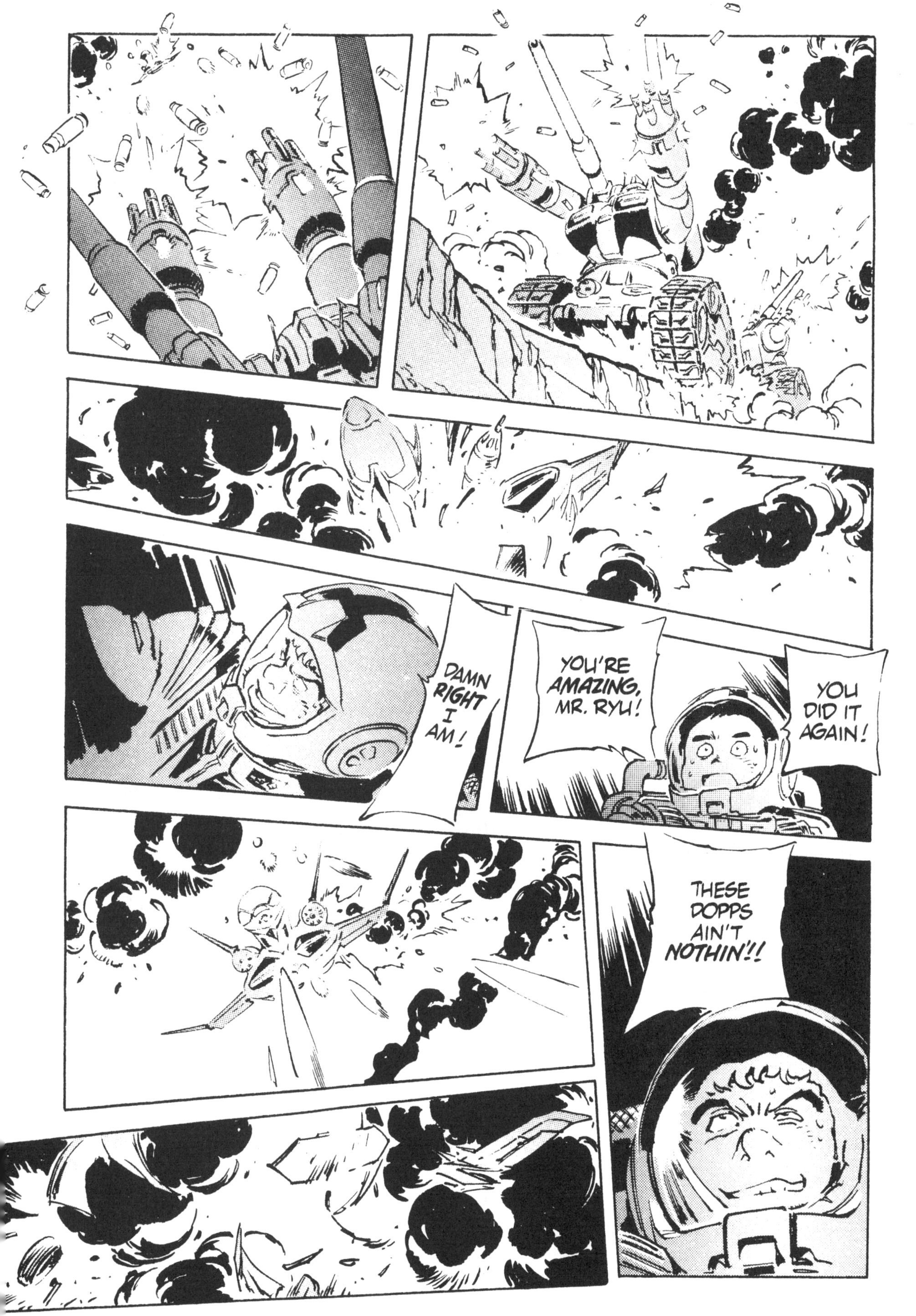
YOU DID IT AGAIN!
YOU'RE AMAZING, MR. RYU!
DAMN RIGHT I AM!
THESE DOPPS AIN'T NOTHIN'!!

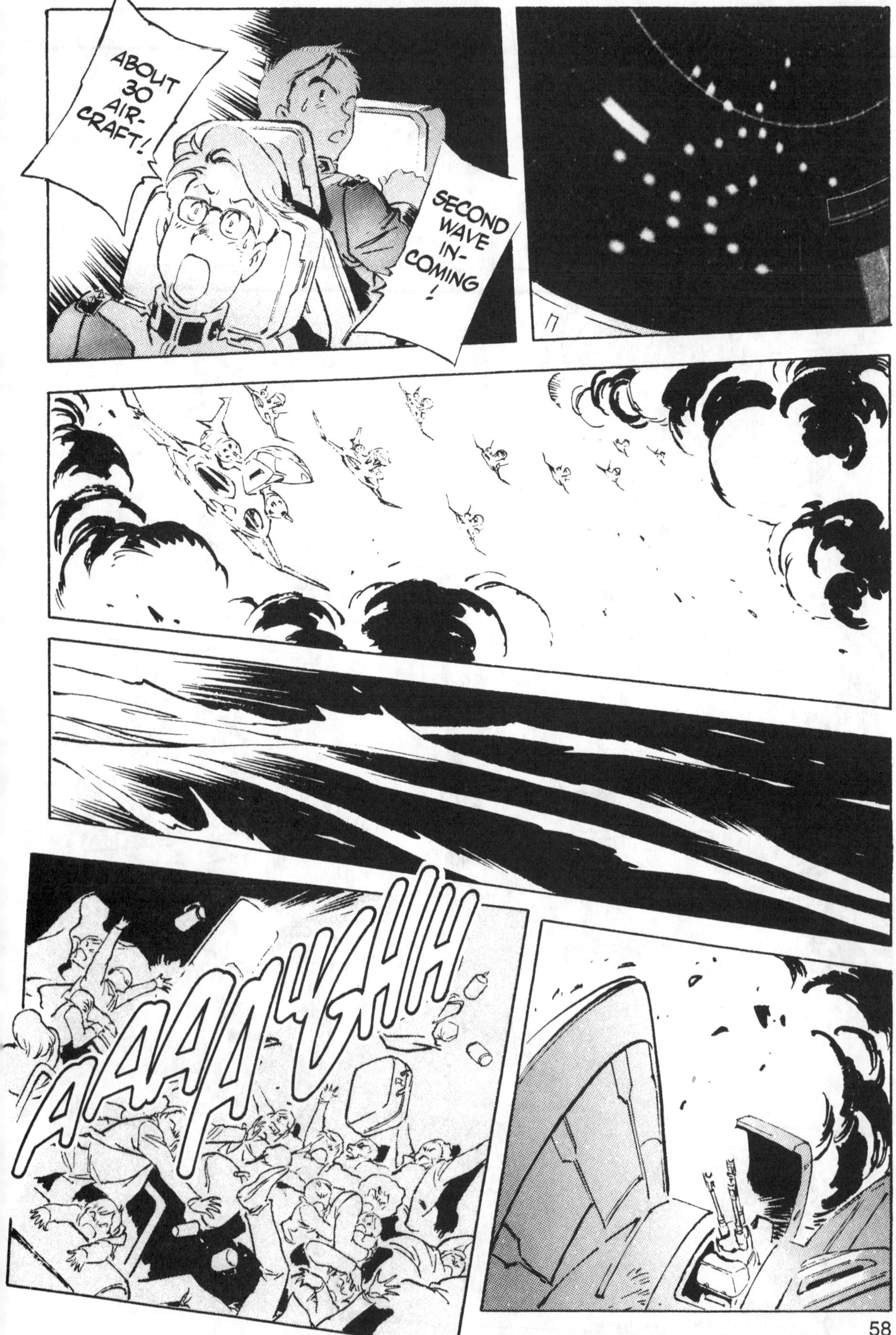
SECOND WAVE IN-COMING!
ABOUT 30 AIR-CRAFT!
AAAAUGHH

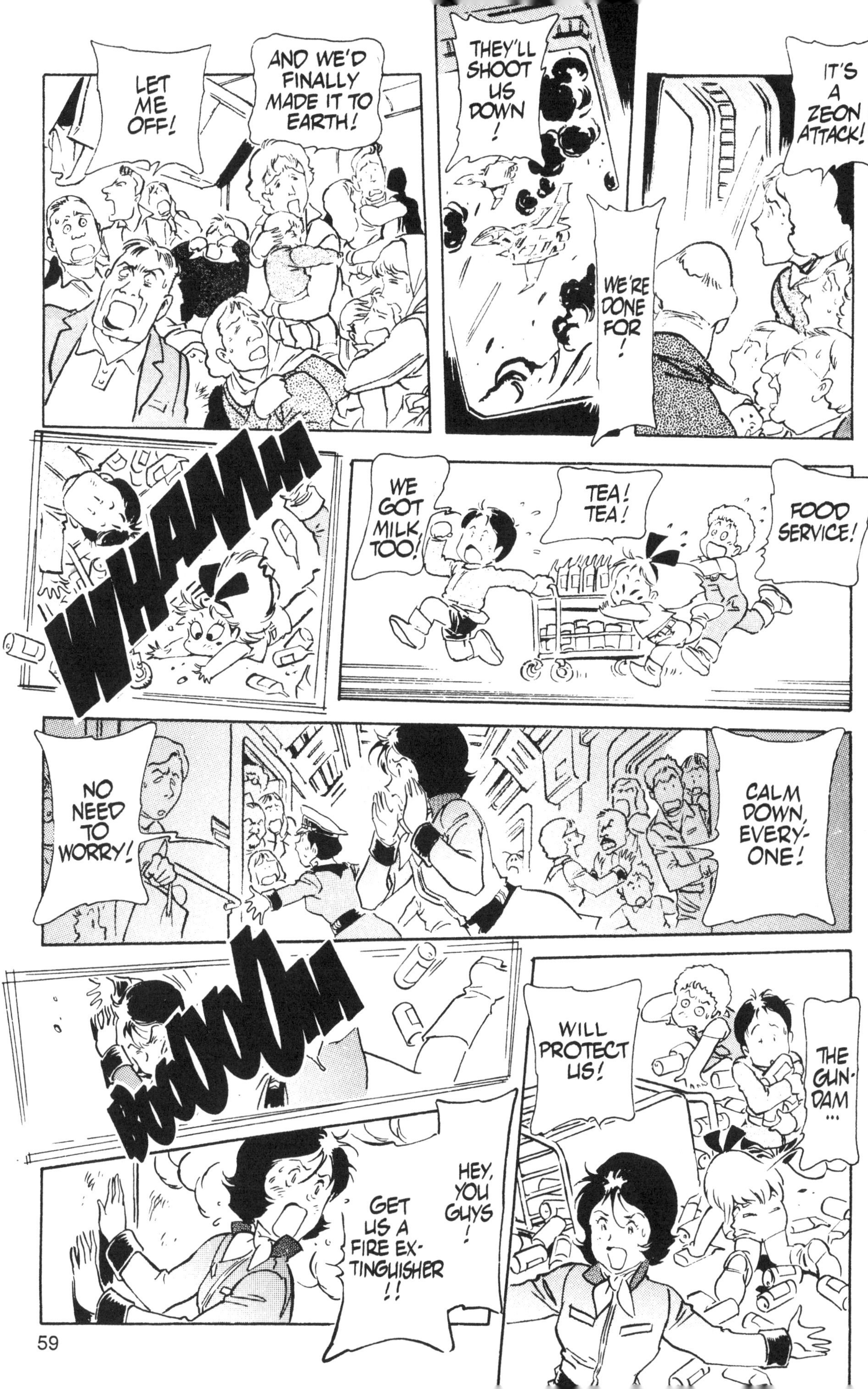
IT'S A ZEON ATTACK!
THEY'LL SHOOT US DOWN!
WE'RE DONE FOR!
AND WE'D FINALLY MADE IT TO EARTH!
LET ME OFF!
FOOD SERVICE!
TEA! TEA!
WE GOT MILK TOO!
WHAMM
CALM DOWN, EVERY-ONE!
NO NEED TO WORRY!
THE GUN-DAM...
WILL PROTECT US!
BOOOOM
HEY, YOU GUYS!
GET US A FIRE EX-TINGUISHER!!

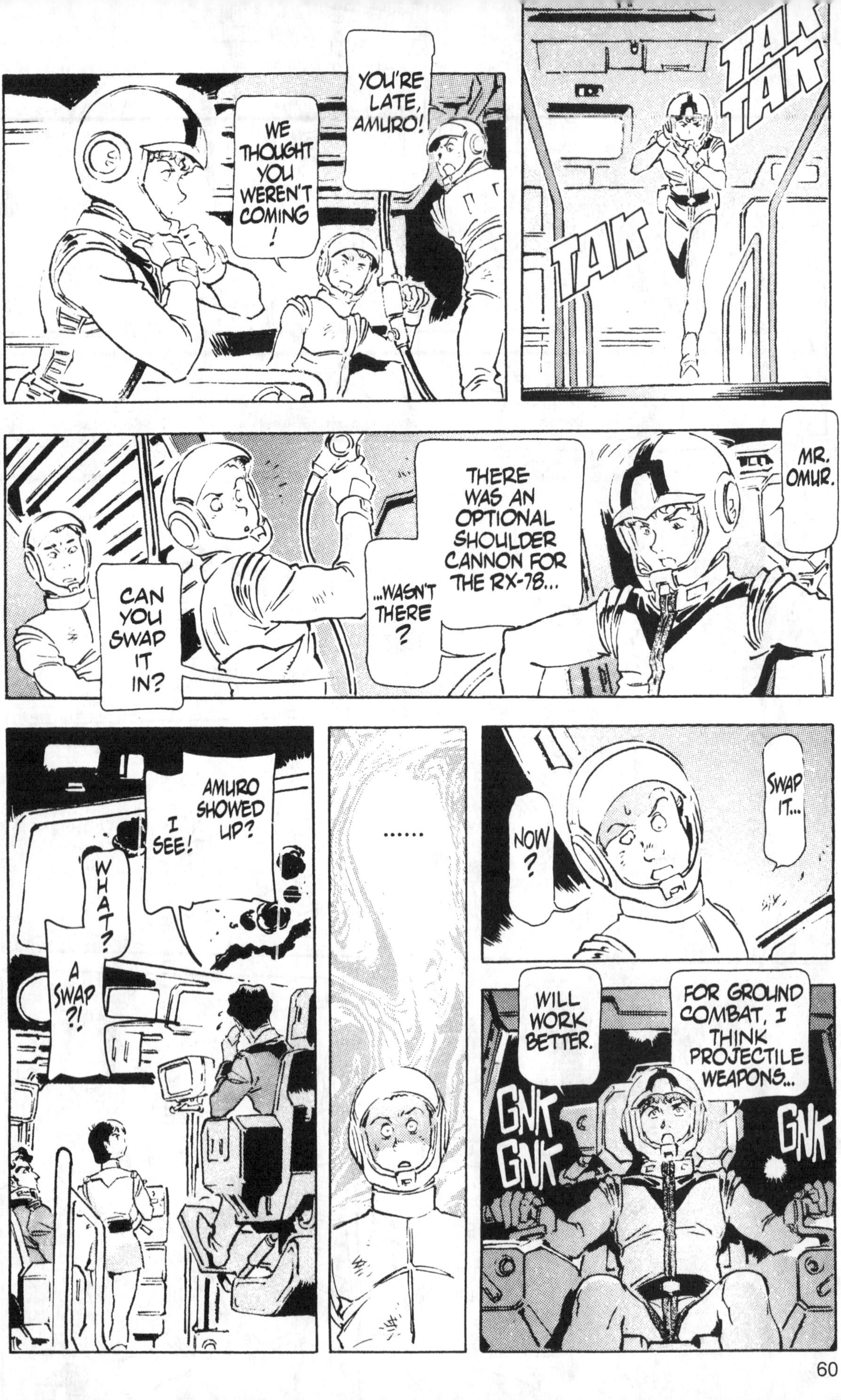
TAK TAK
TAK
YOU'RE LATE, AMURO!
WE THOUGHT YOU WEREN'T COMING!
MR. OMUR.
THERE WAS AN OPTIONAL SHOULDER CANNON FOR THE RX-78...
...WASN'T THERE?
CAN YOU SWAP IT IN?
SWAP IT...
NOW?
FOR GROUND COMBAT, I THINK PROJECTILE WEAPONS...
WILL WORK BETTER.
GNK
GNK GNK
......
AMURO SHOWED UP?
I SEE!
WHAT?
A SWAP?!

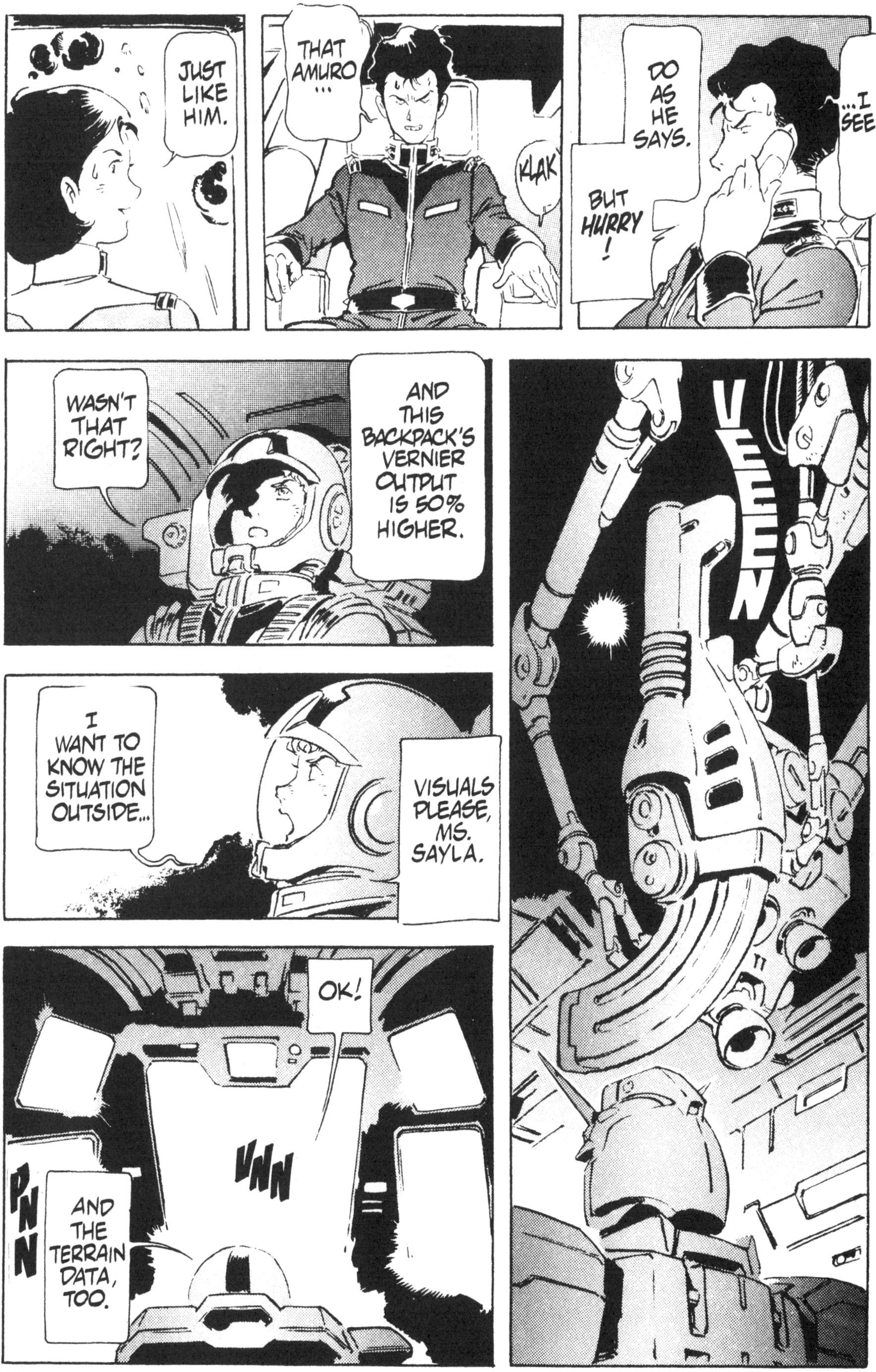
...I SEE.
DO AS HE SAYS.
BUT HURRY!
THAT AMURO...
KLAK
JUST LIKE HIM.
VEEEN
AND THIS BACKPACK'S VERNIER OUTPUT IS 50% HIGHER.
WASN'T THAT RIGHT?
VISUALS PLEASE, MS. SAYLA.
I WANT TO KNOW THE SITUATION OUTSIDE...
OK!
UNN
PNN
AND THE TERRAIN DATA, TOO.

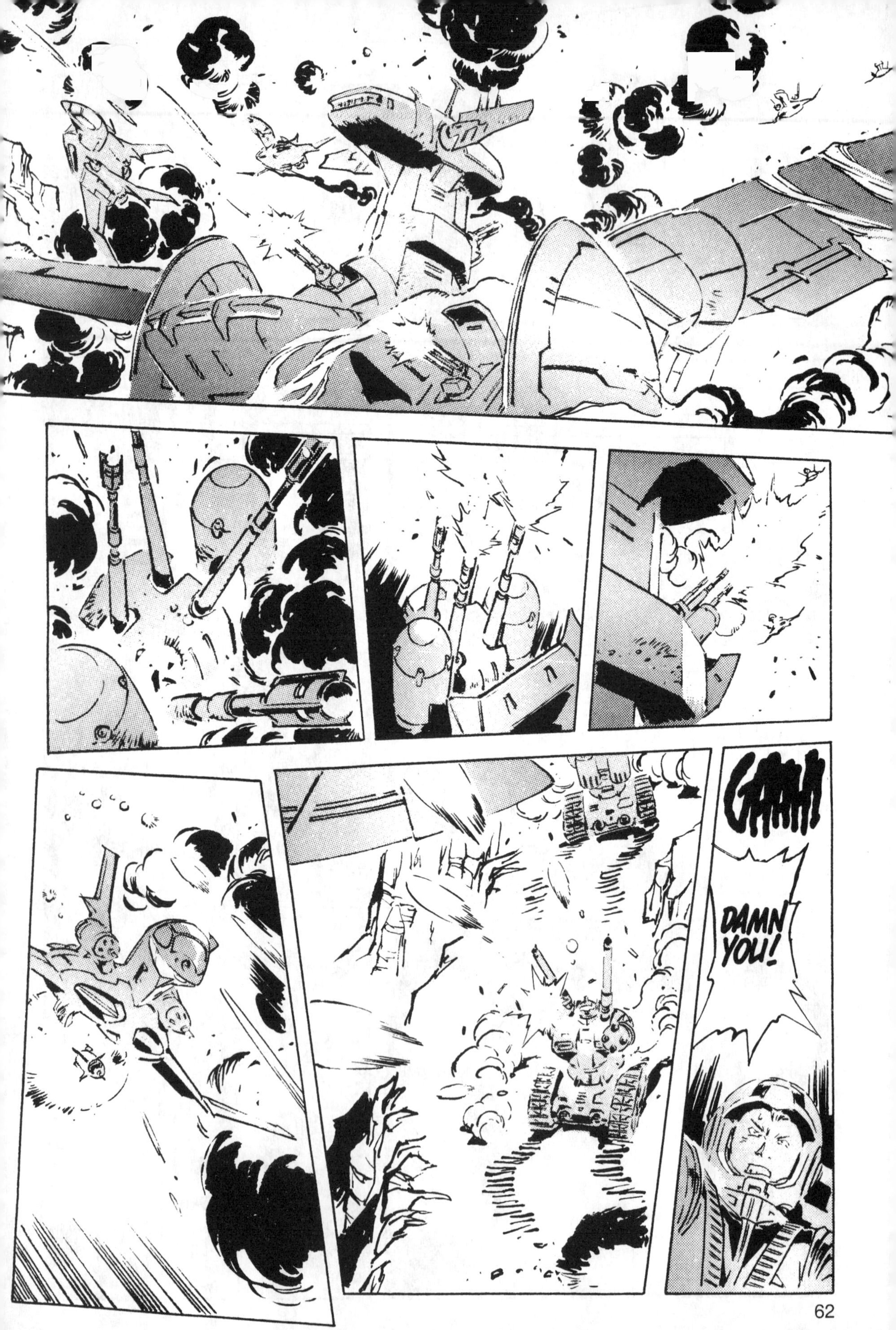
GAAH!
DAMN YOU!

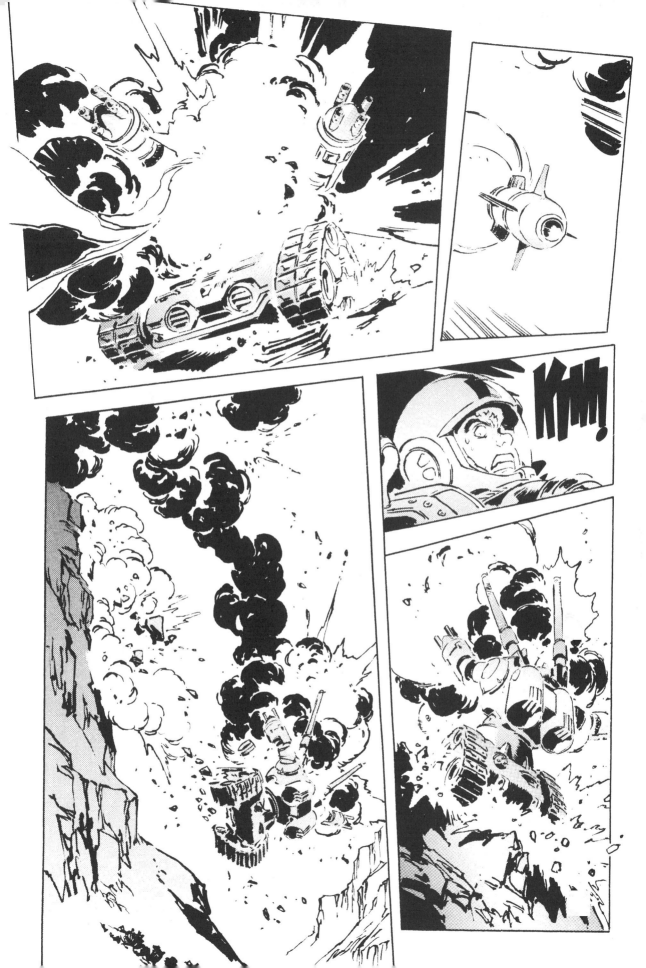

KMM!

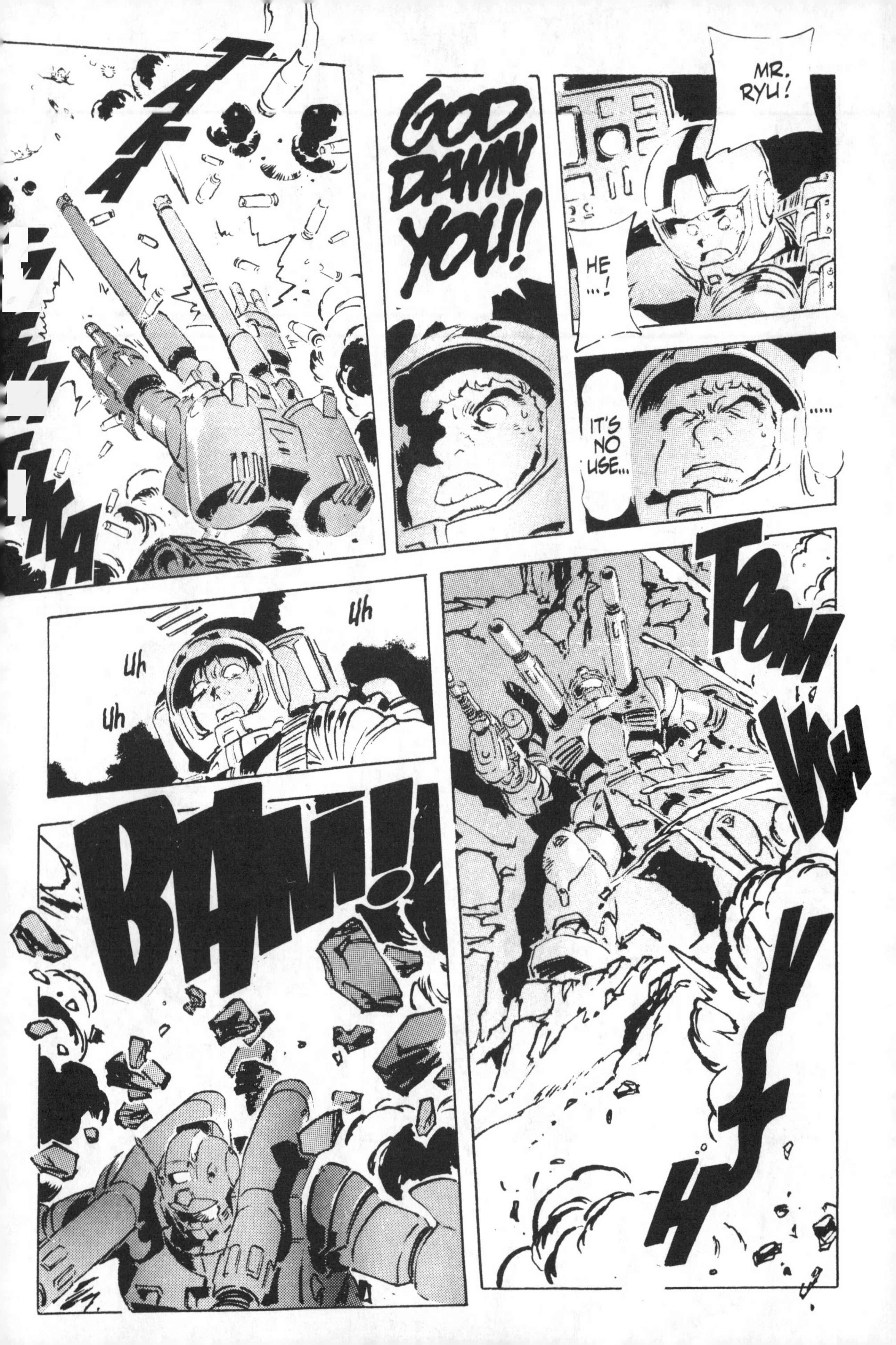

TATATA
GOD DAMN YOU!!
MR. RYU!
HE...!
IT'S NO USE...
......
uh
uh
uh
BAMM!!
TOOM
VSSSH

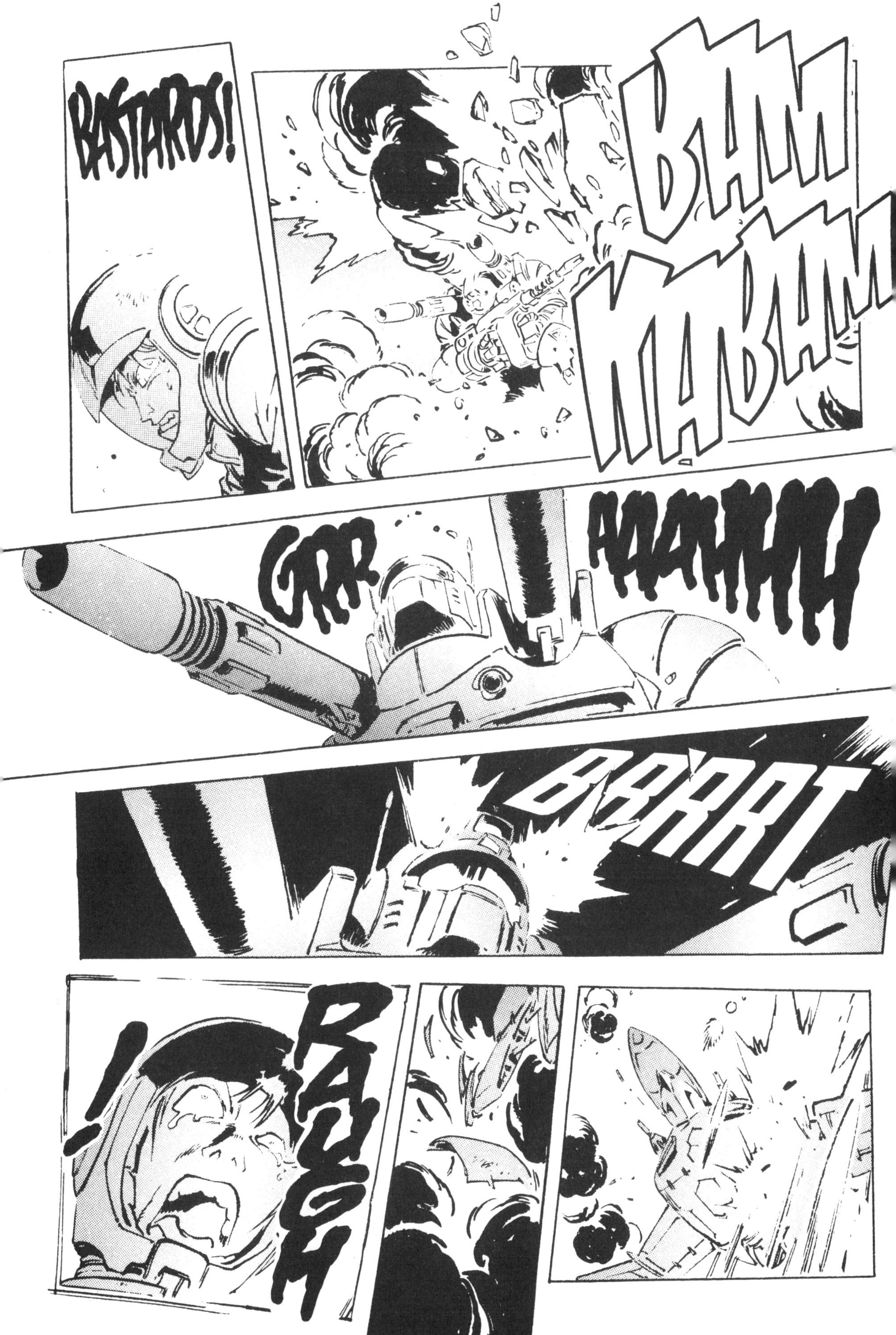
BAM
KABAM
BASTARDS!
AAAHHHH
GRR
BRRRT
RAUGH
!

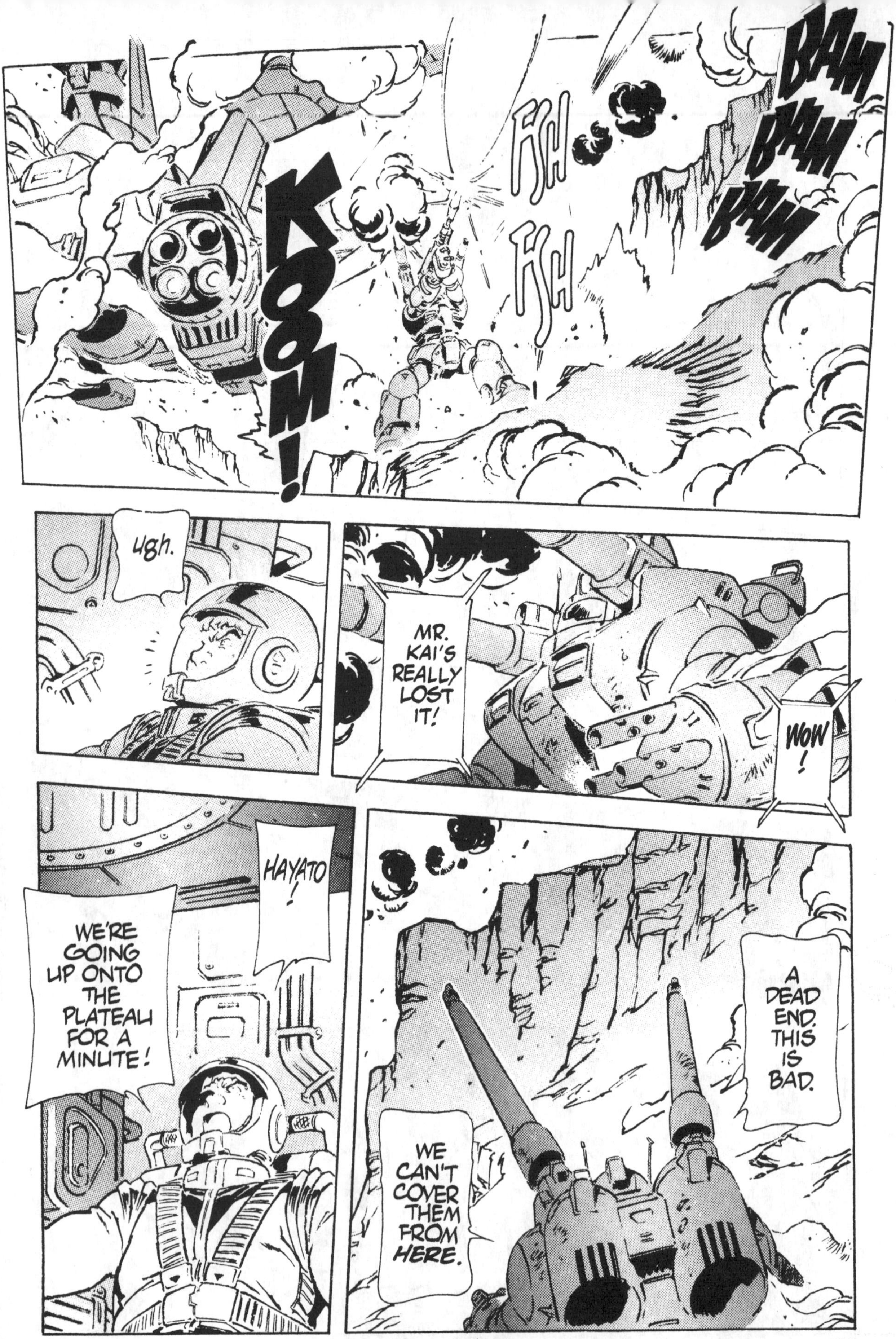
BAM BAM BAM BAM
FSH
FSH
KOOM!
WOW!
MR. KAI'S REALLY LOST IT!
ugh.
A DEAD END. THIS IS BAD.
WE CAN'T COVER THEM FROM HERE.
HAYATO!
WE'RE GOING UP ONTO THE PLATEAU FOR A MINUTE!

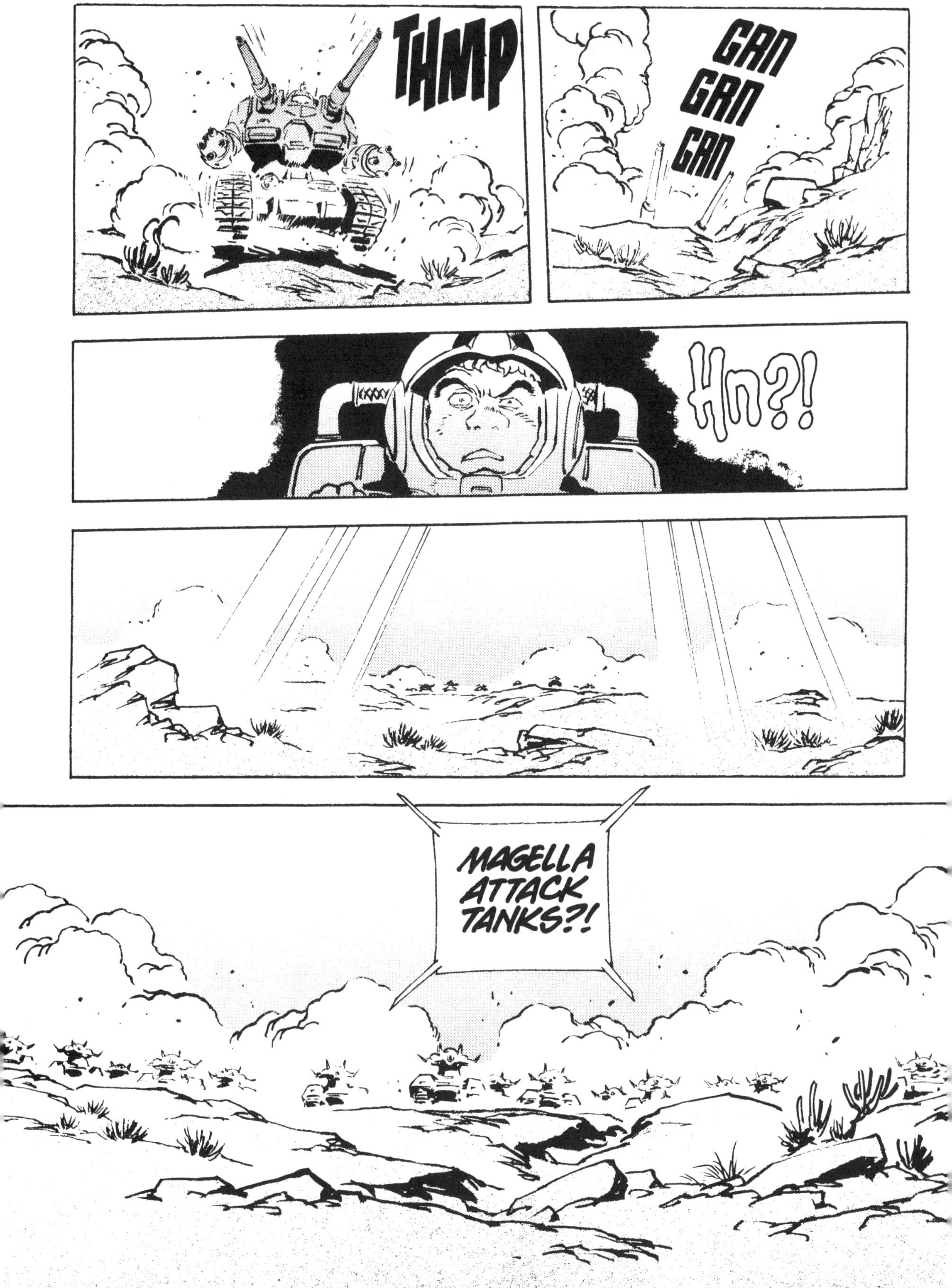
GRN
GRN
GRN
THMP
Hn?!
MAGELLA ATTACK TANKS?!

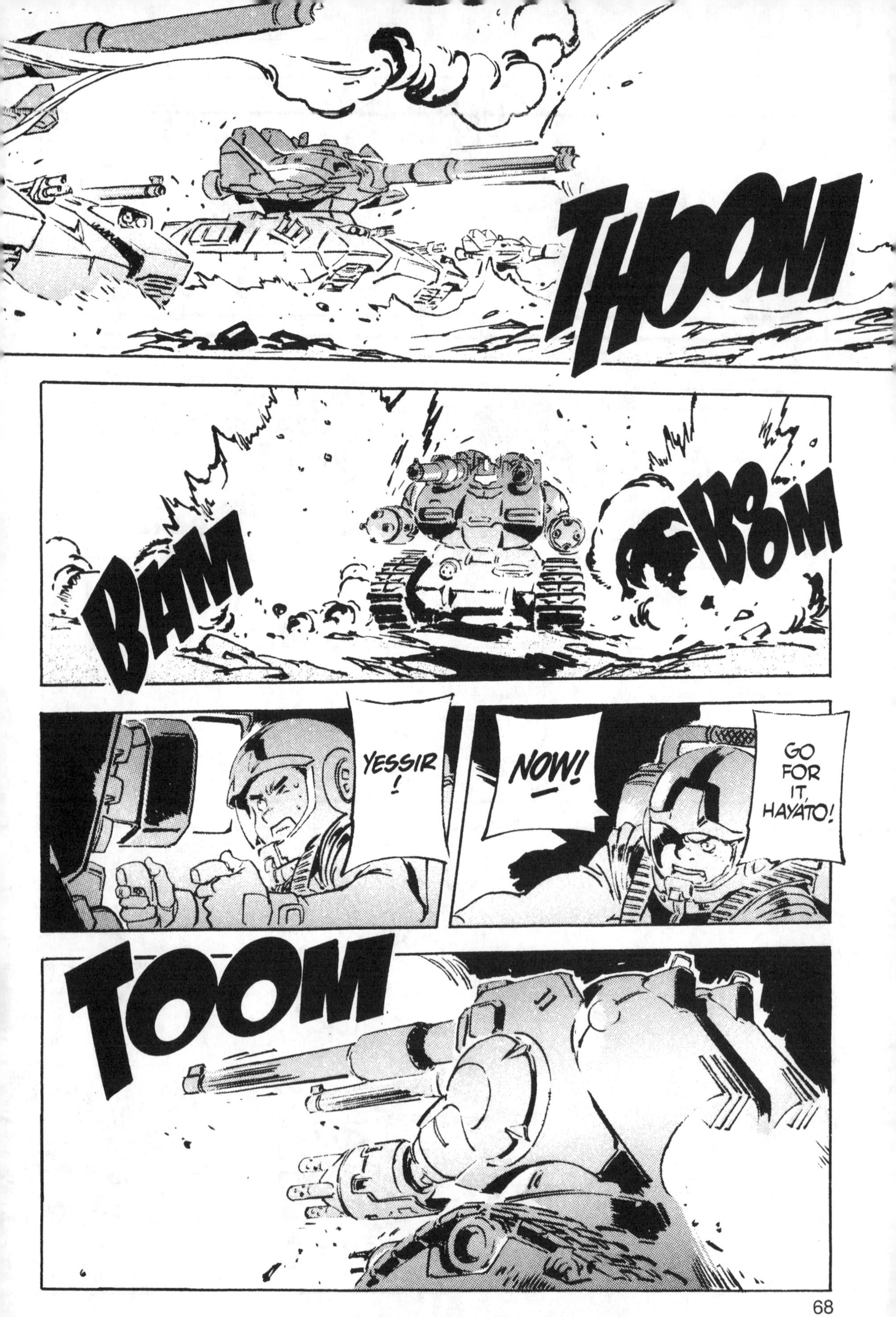
THOOM
BOOM
BAM
GO FOR IT, HAYATO!
NOW!
YESSIR!
TOOM

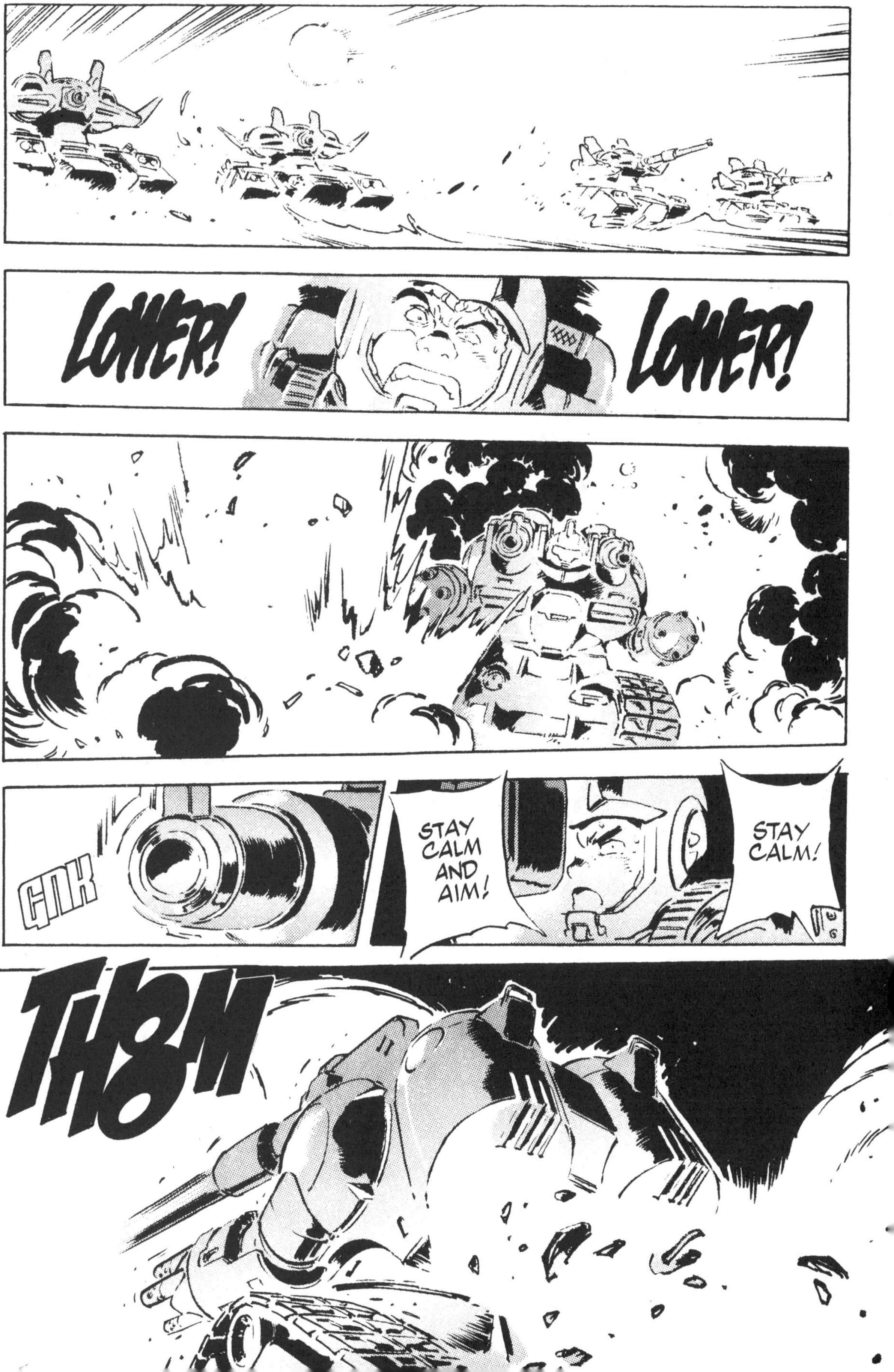
LOWER!
LOWER!
STAY CALM!
STAY CALM AND AIM!
GNK
THOOM

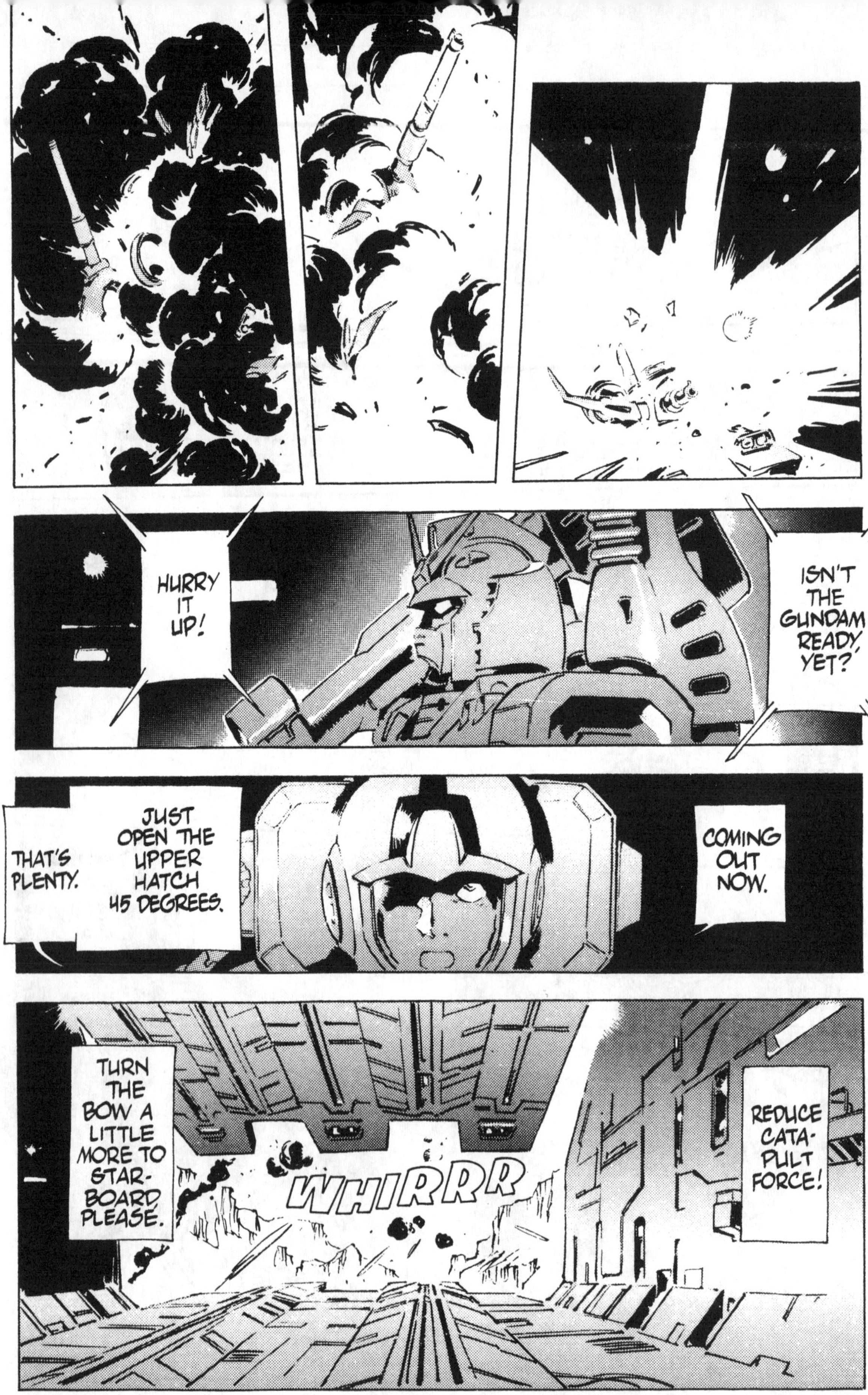
ISN'T THE GUNDAM READY, YET?
HURRY IT UP!
COMING OUT NOW.
JUST OPEN THE UPPER HATCH 45 DEGREES.
THAT'S PLENTY.
REDUCE CATA-PULT FORCE!
WHIRRR
TURN THE BOW A LITTLE MORE TO STAR-BOARD PLEASE.

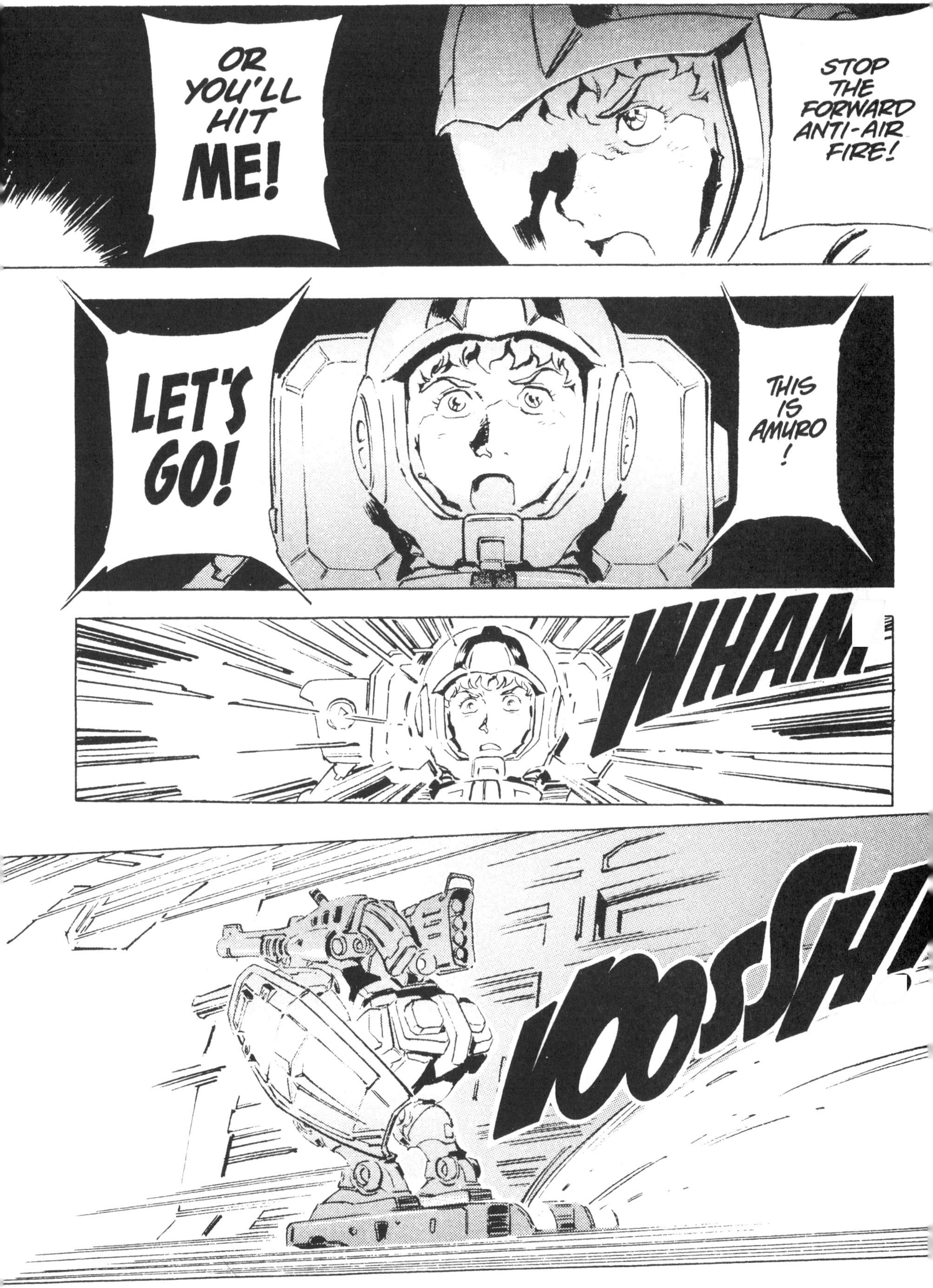
STOP THE FORWARD ANTI-AIR FIRE!
OR YOU'LL HIT ME!
THIS IS AMURO!
LET'S GO!
WHAM.
VOOSSH

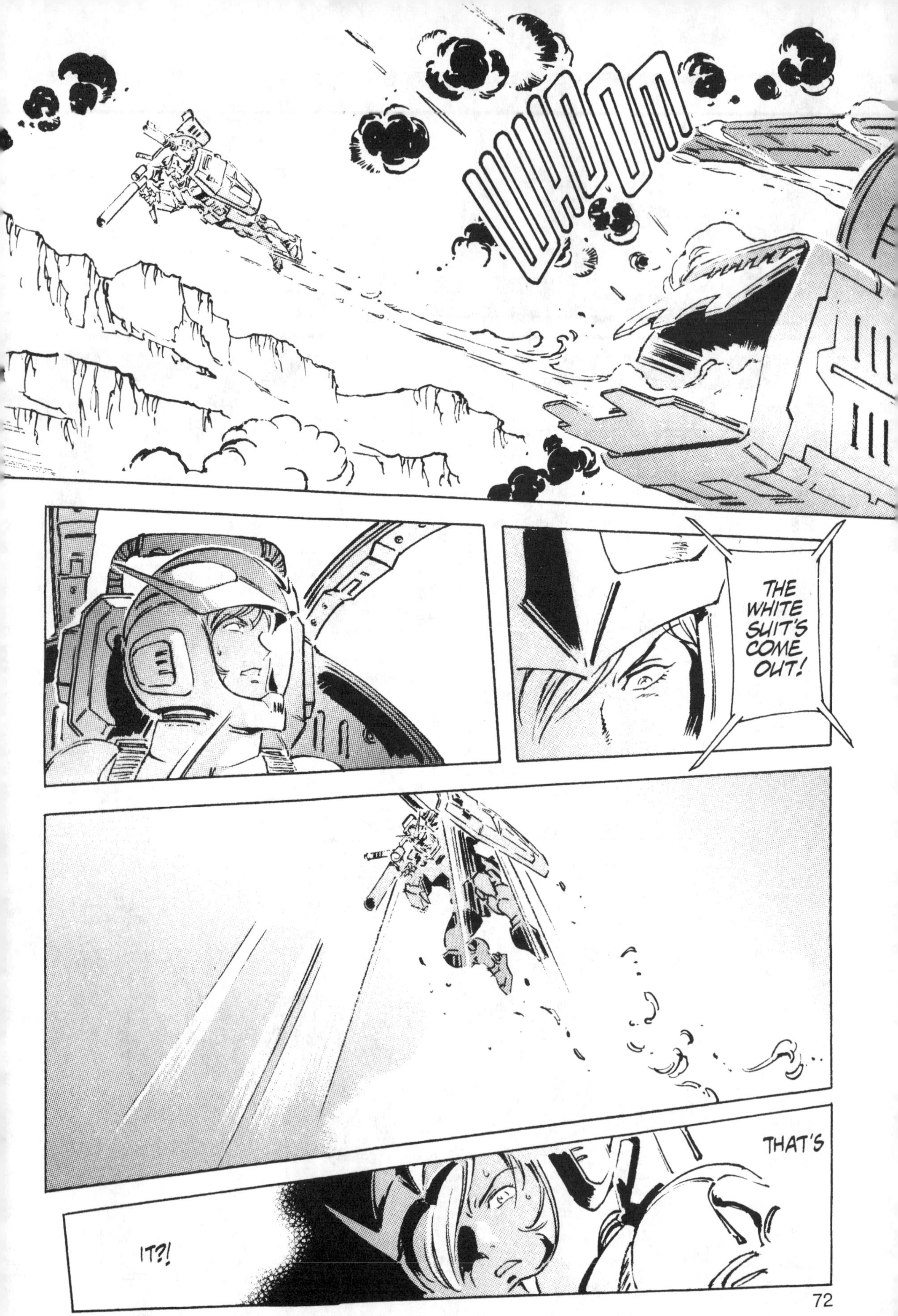
WHOOM
THE WHITE SUIT'S COME OUT!
THAT'S
IT?!

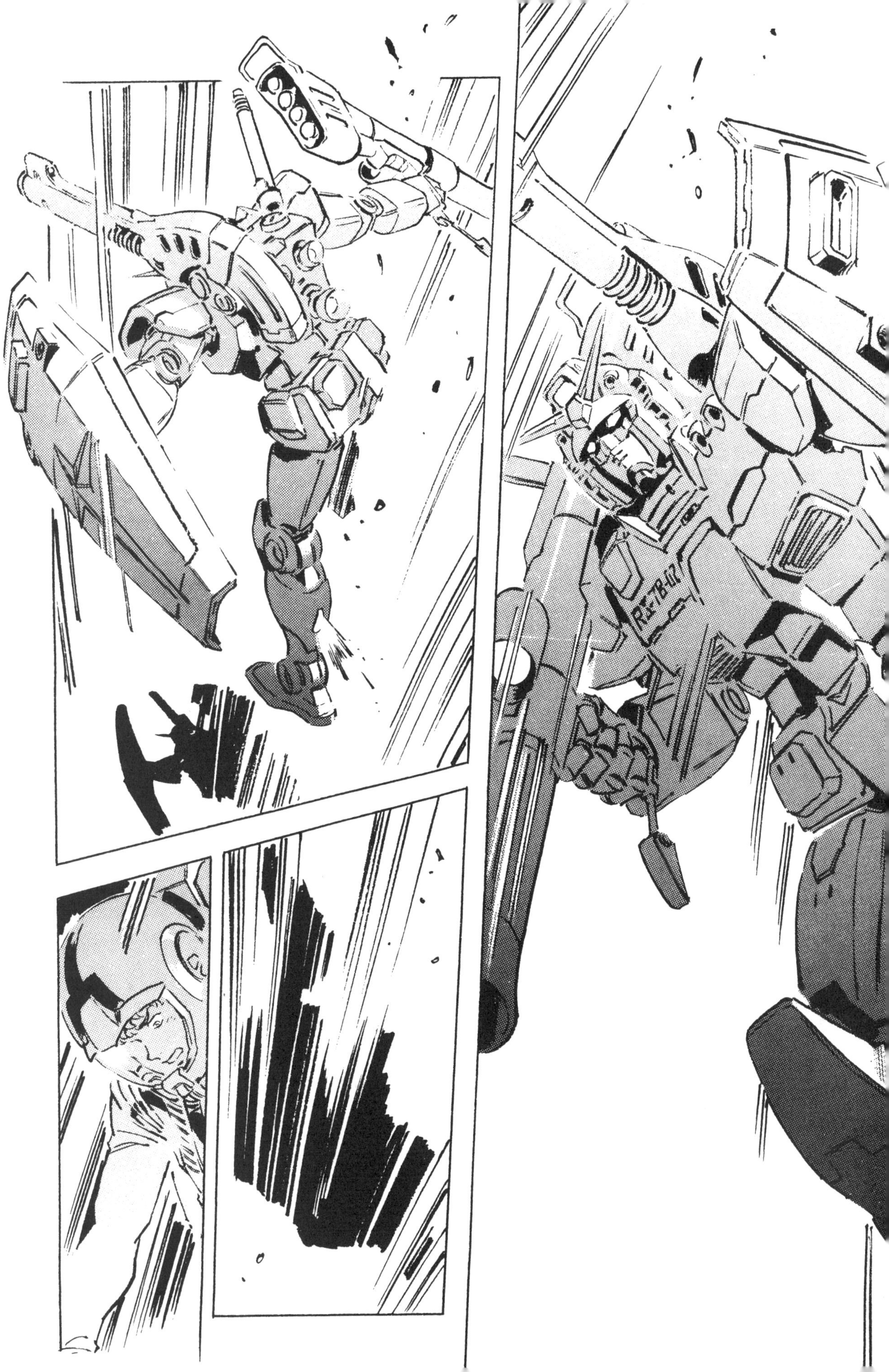
RX-78-02

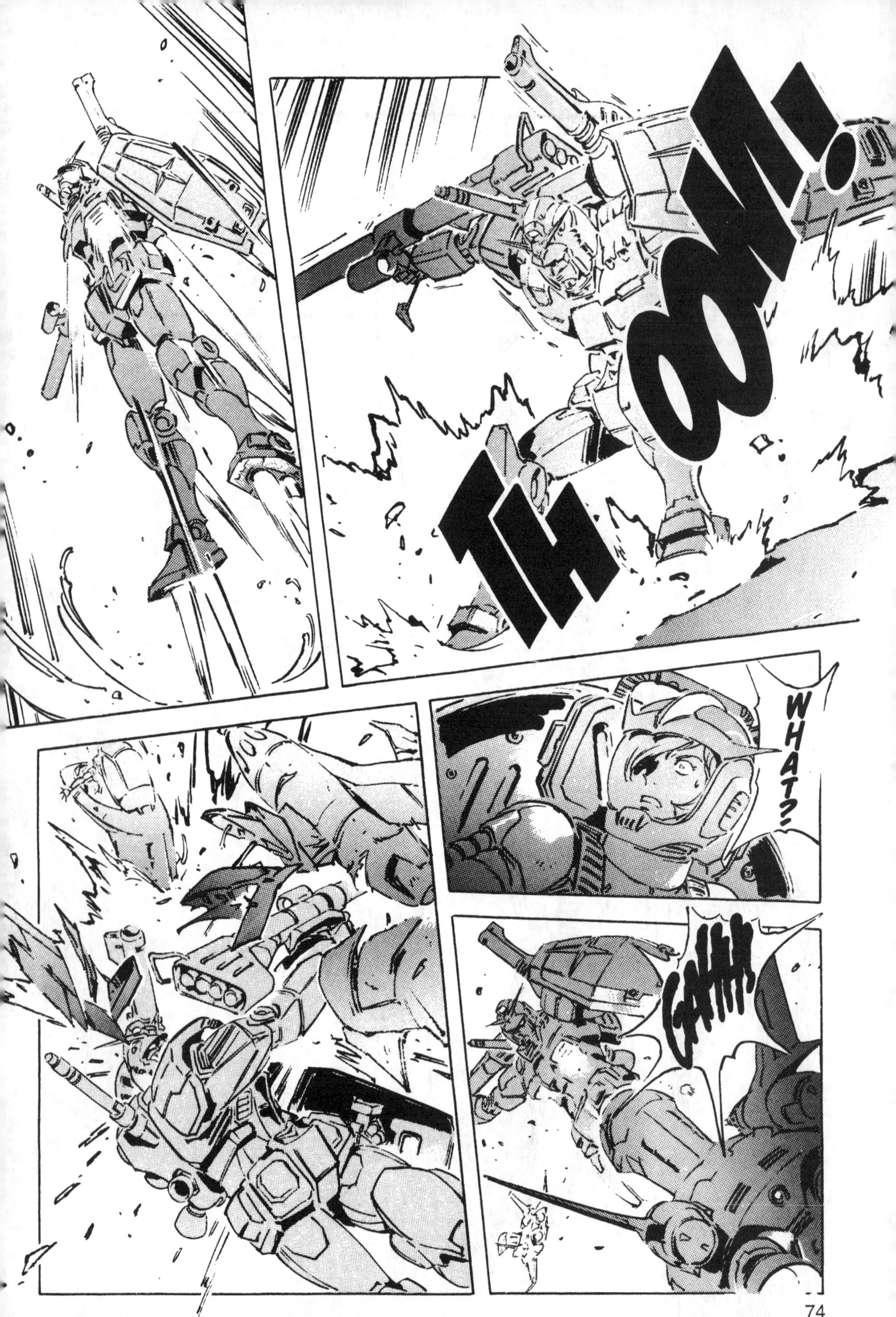
THOOM!!
WHAT?!
GAHH

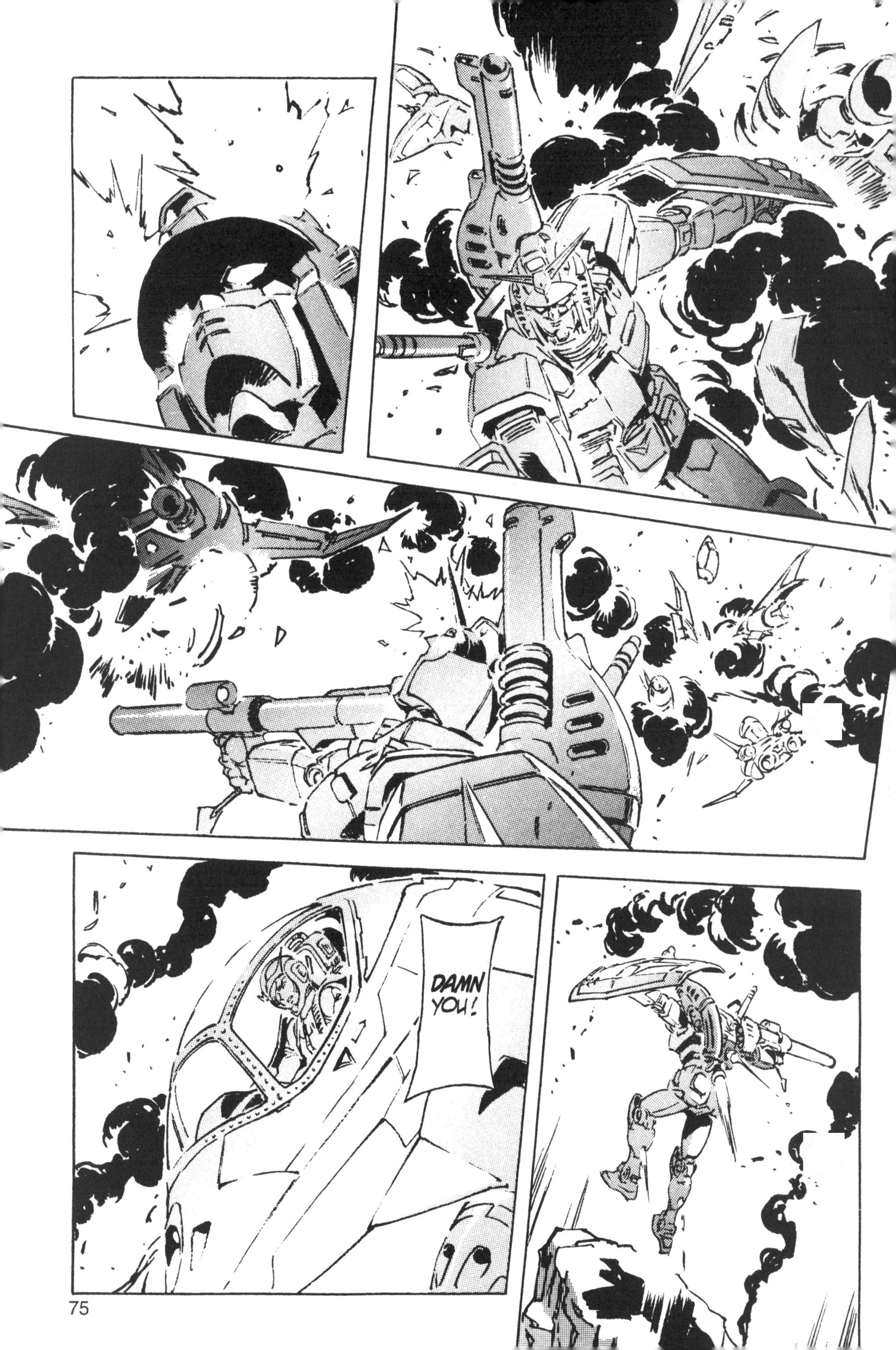
DAMN YOU!

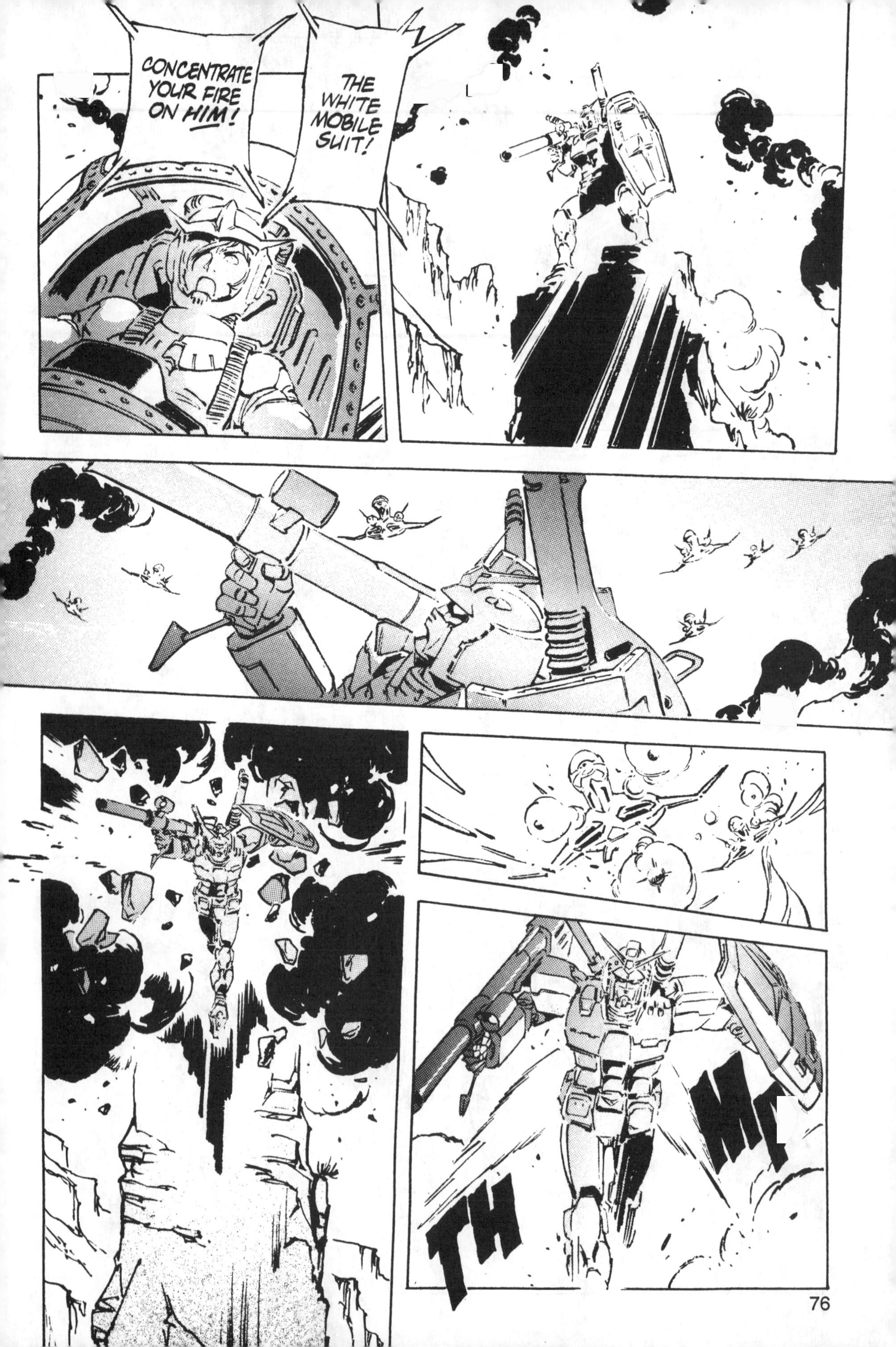
THE WHITE MOBILE SUIT!
CONCENTRATE YOUR FIRE ON HIM!
TH
M

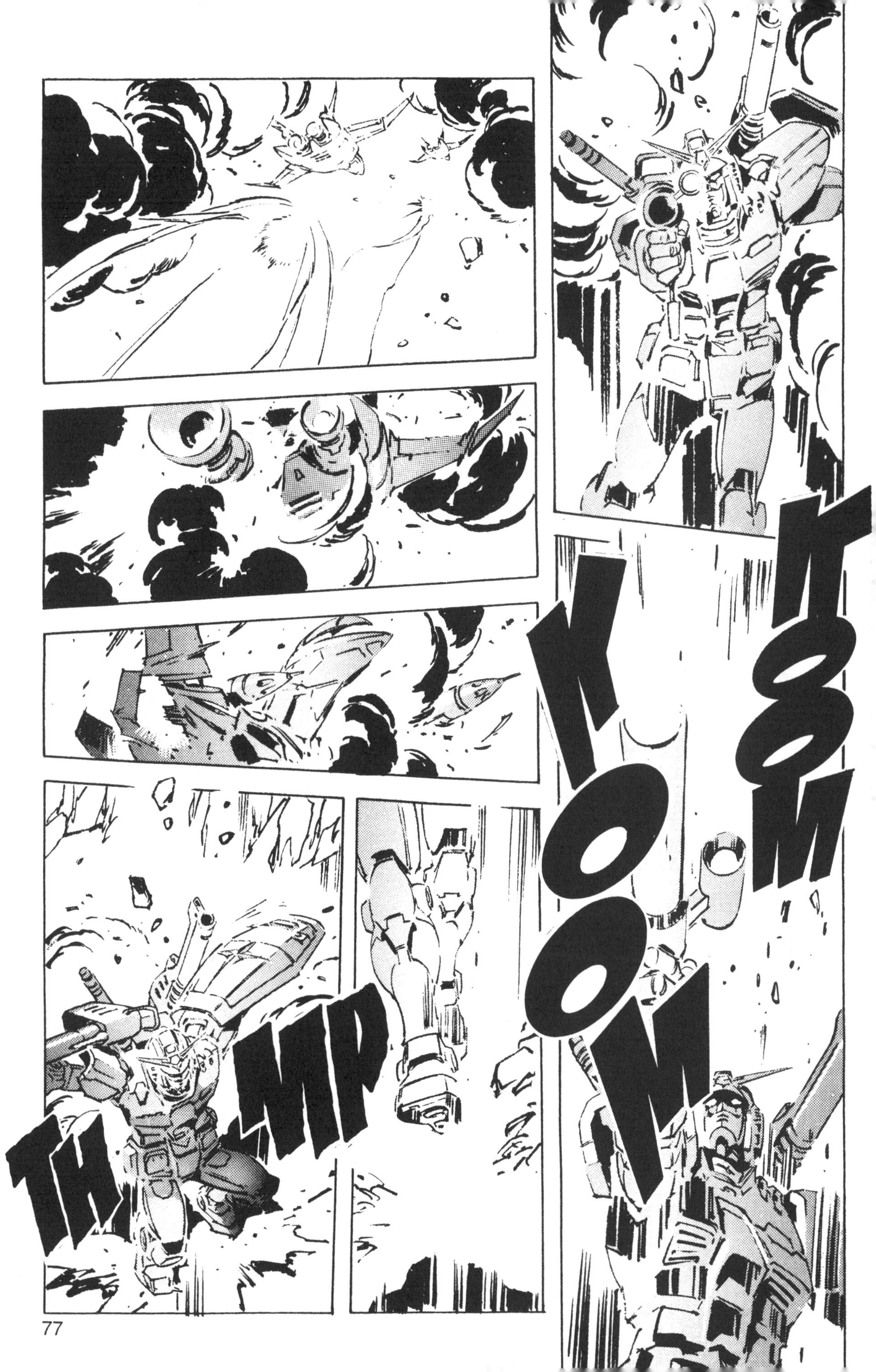
VOOM
VOOM
TH
MP

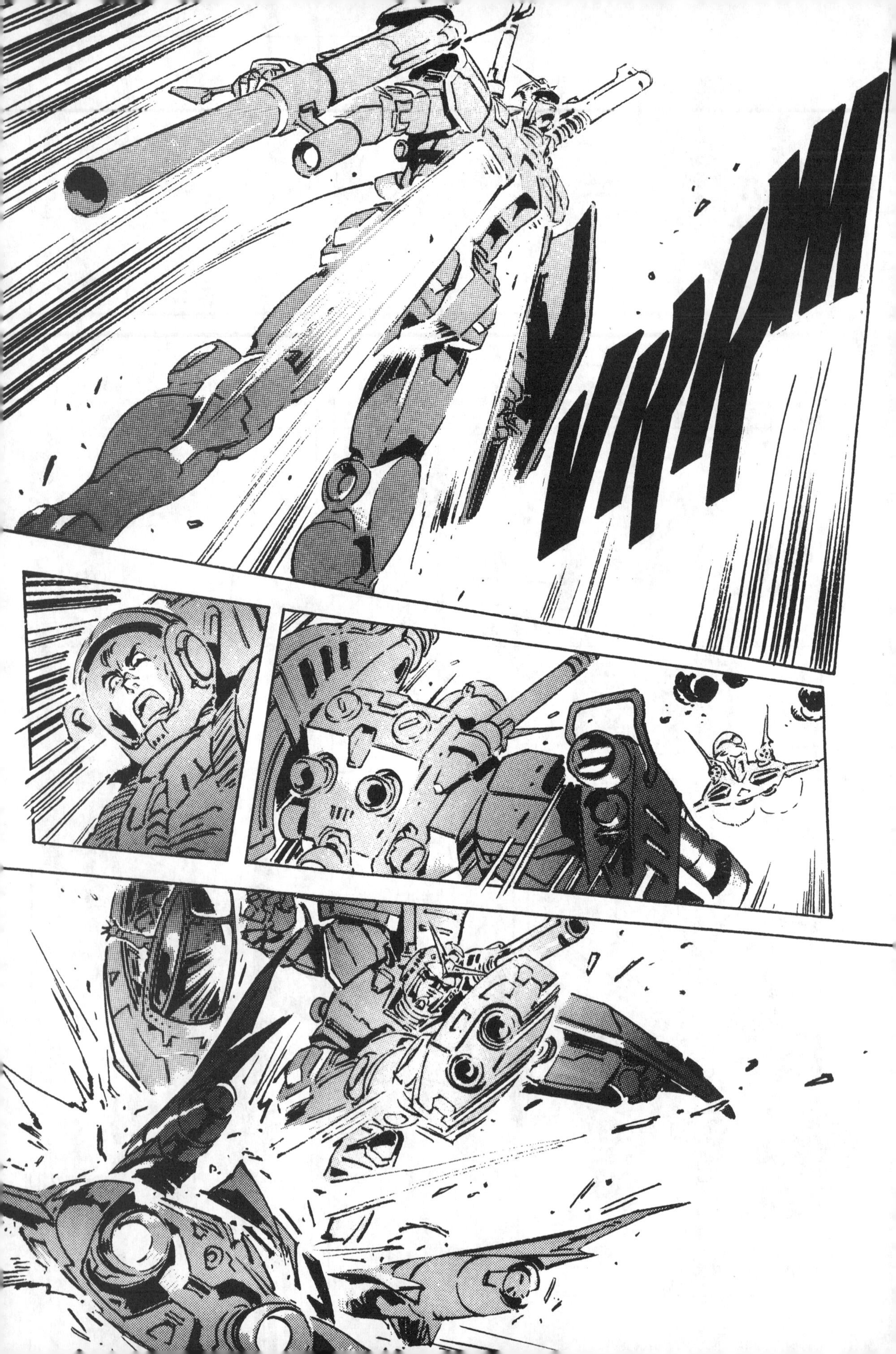

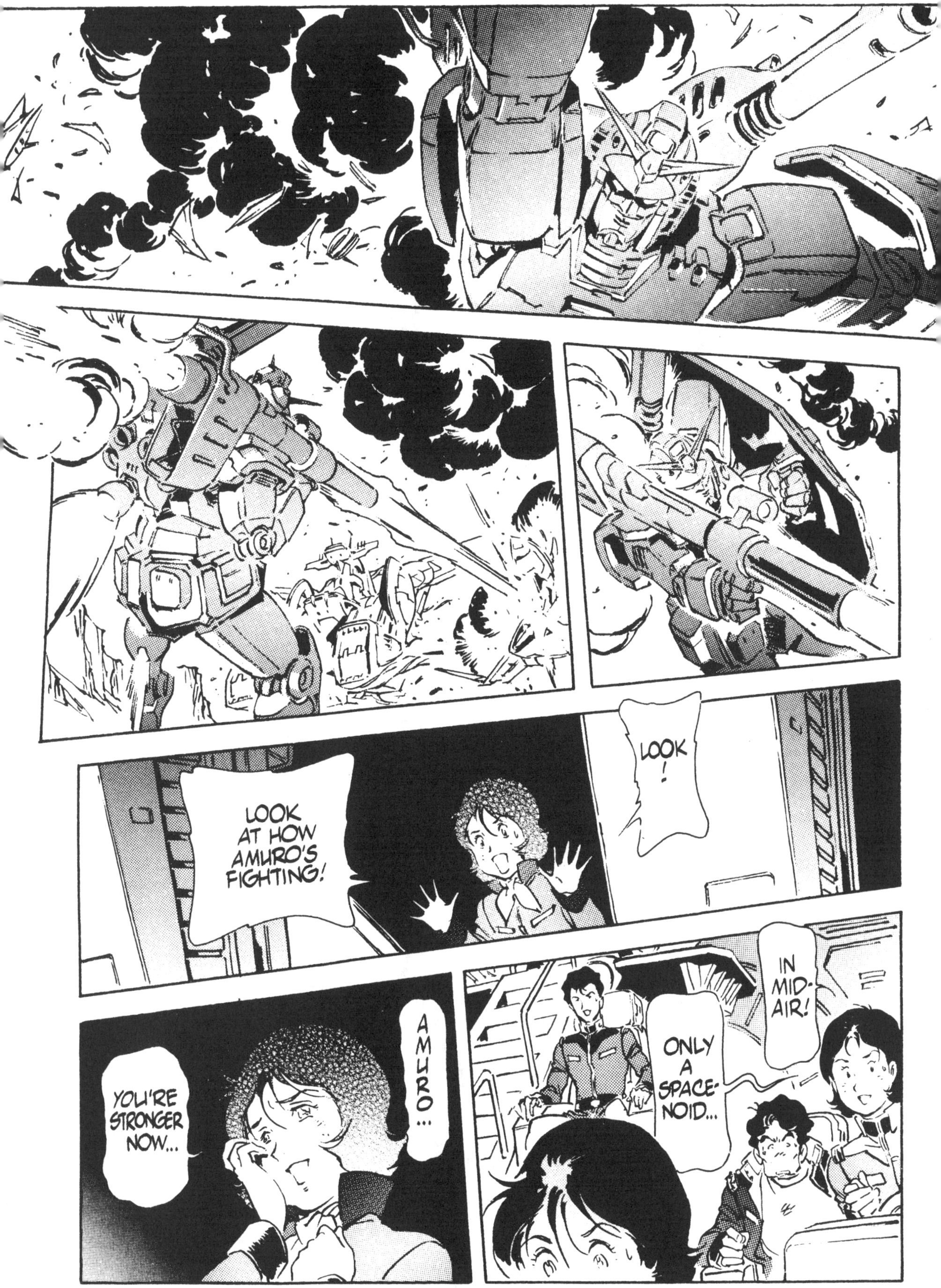
LOOK!
LOOK AT HOW AMURO'S FIGHTING!
IN MID-AIR!
ONLY A SPACE-NOID...
AMURO...
YOU'RE STRONGER NOW...

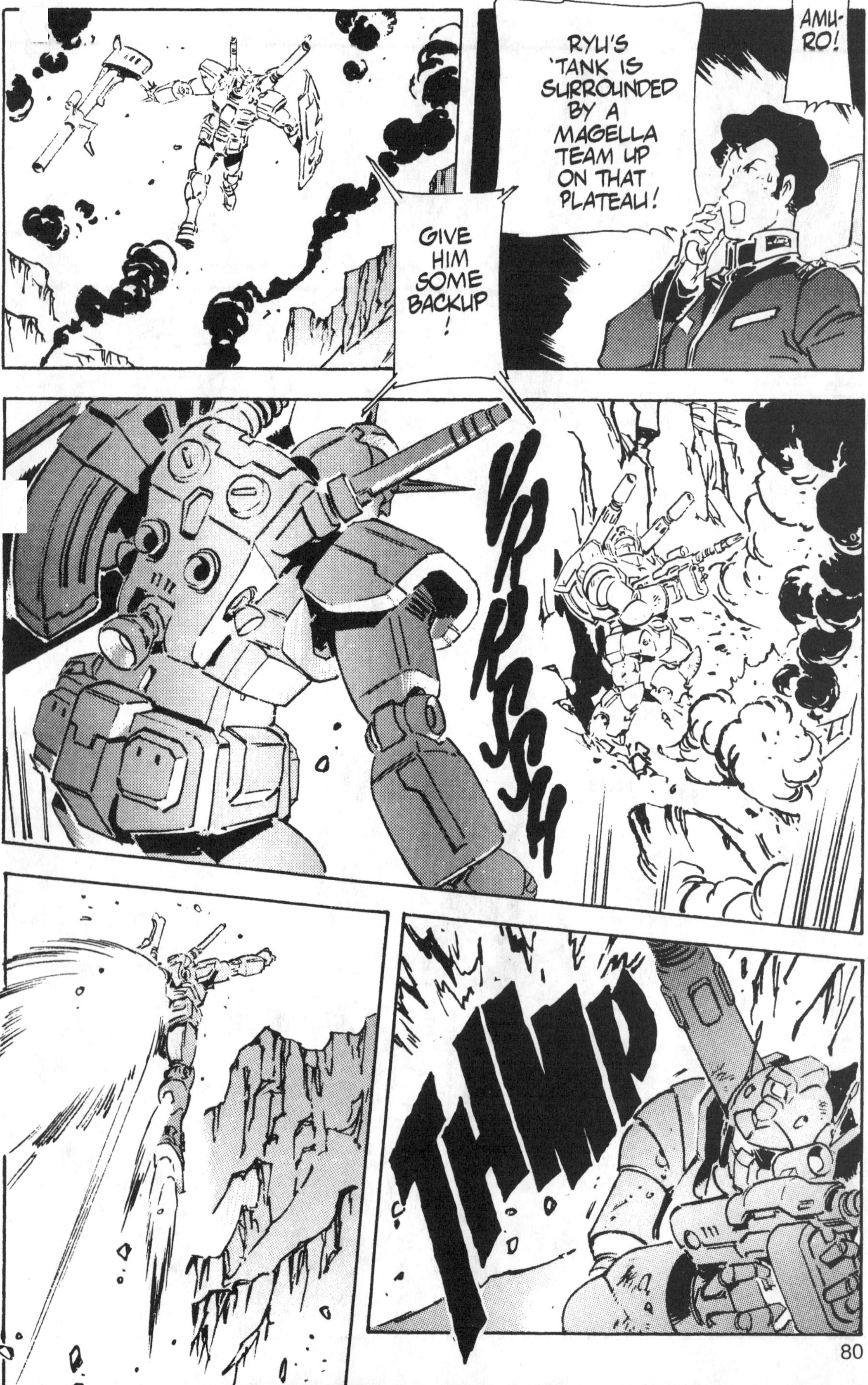
AMU-RO!
RYU'S 'TANK IS SURROUNDED BY A MAGELLA TEAM UP ON THAT PLATEAU!
GIVE HIM SOME BACKUP!
VRRRSSH
THMP

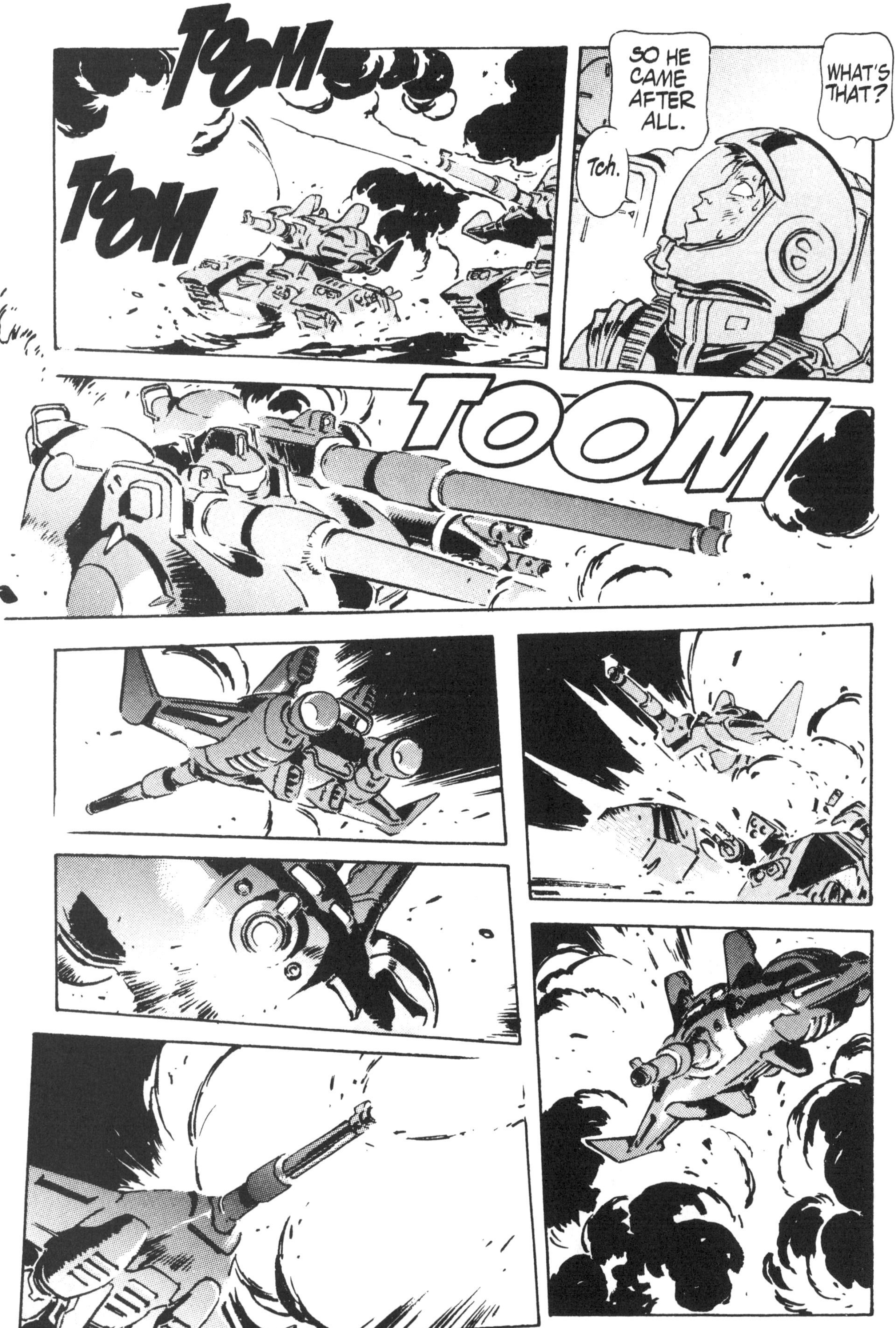
WHAT'S THAT?
SO HE CAME AFTER ALL.
Tch.
TOOM
TOOM
TOOM

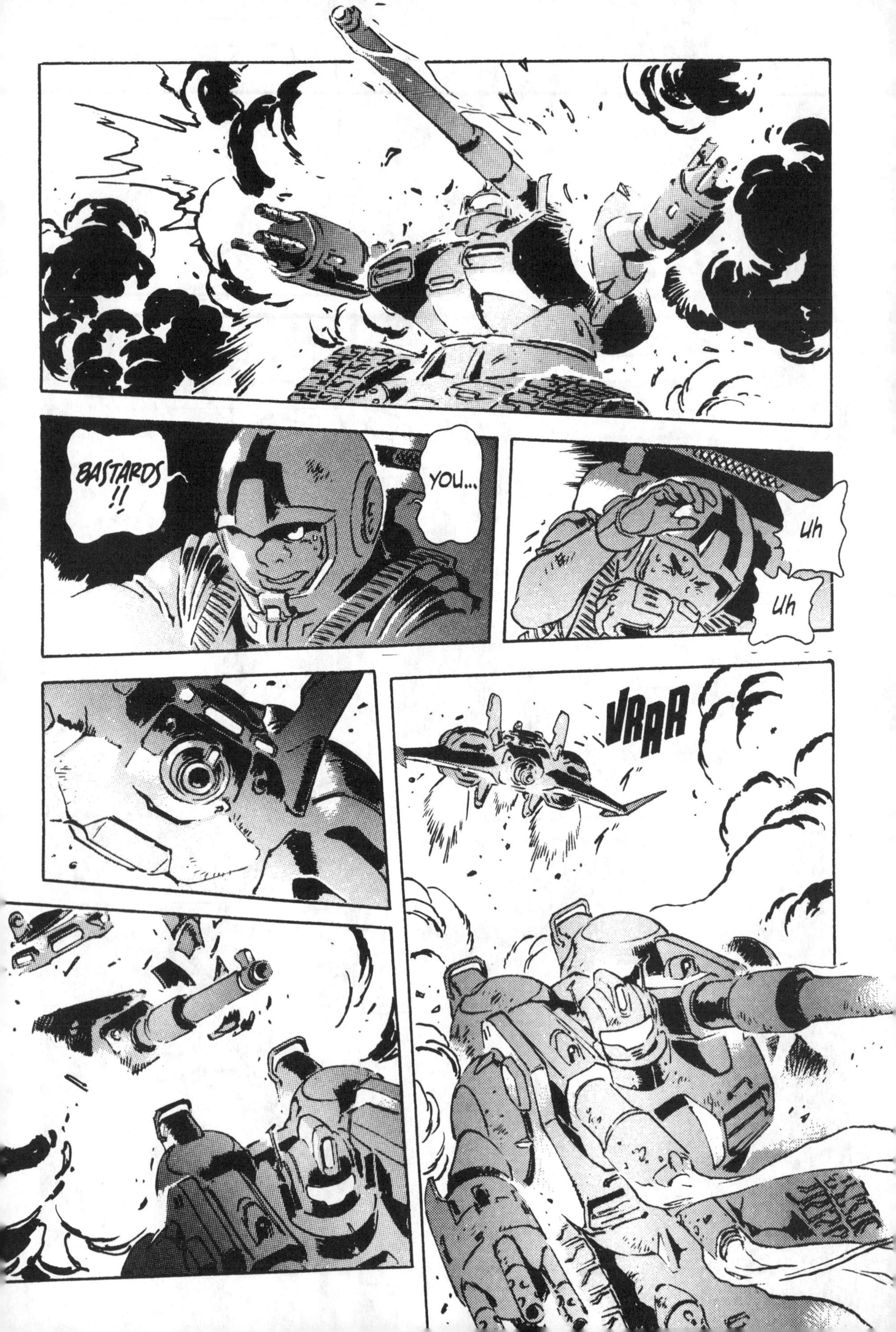
uh
uh
YOU...
BASTARDS !!
VRAA

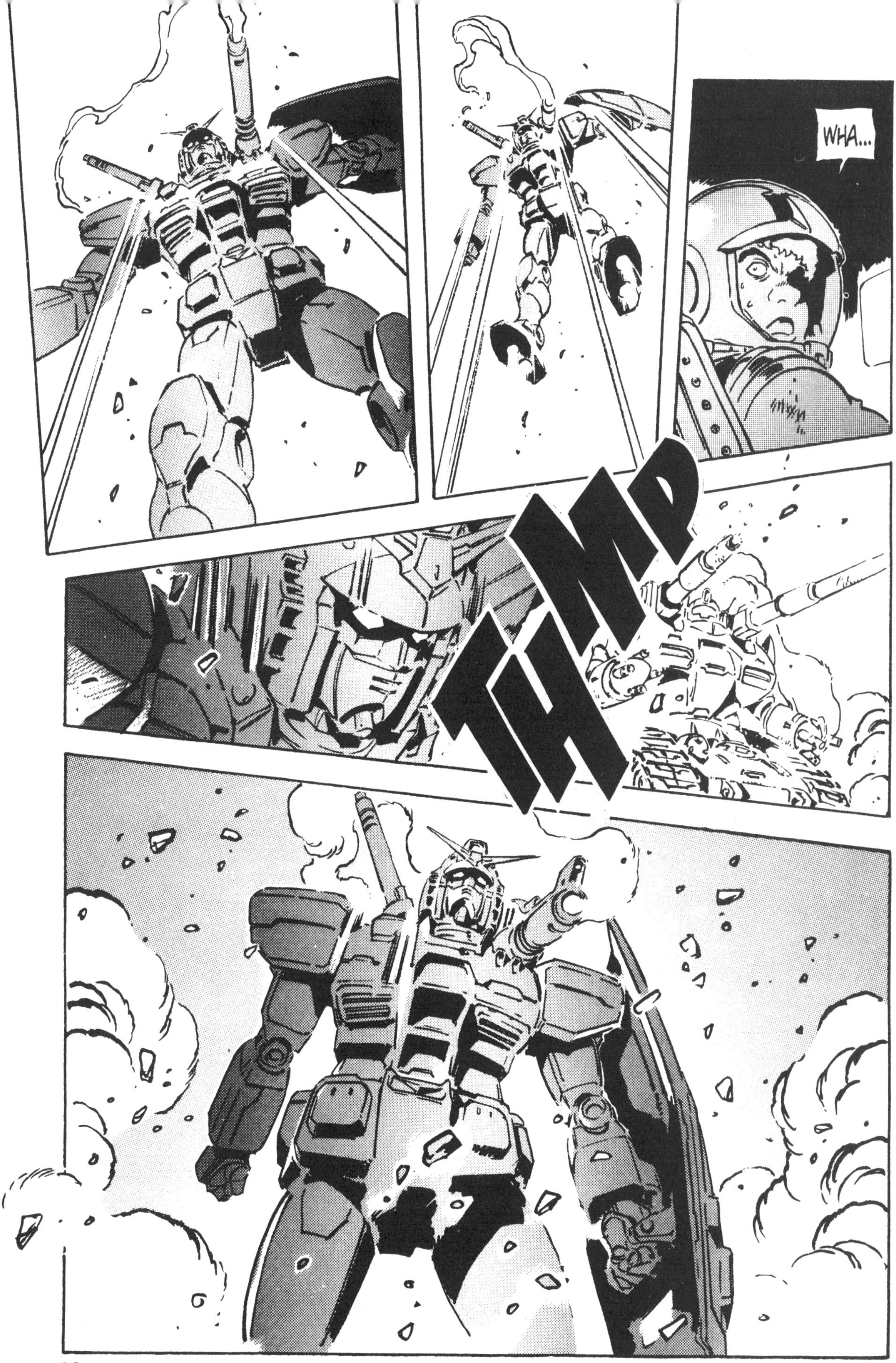
WHA...
THMP

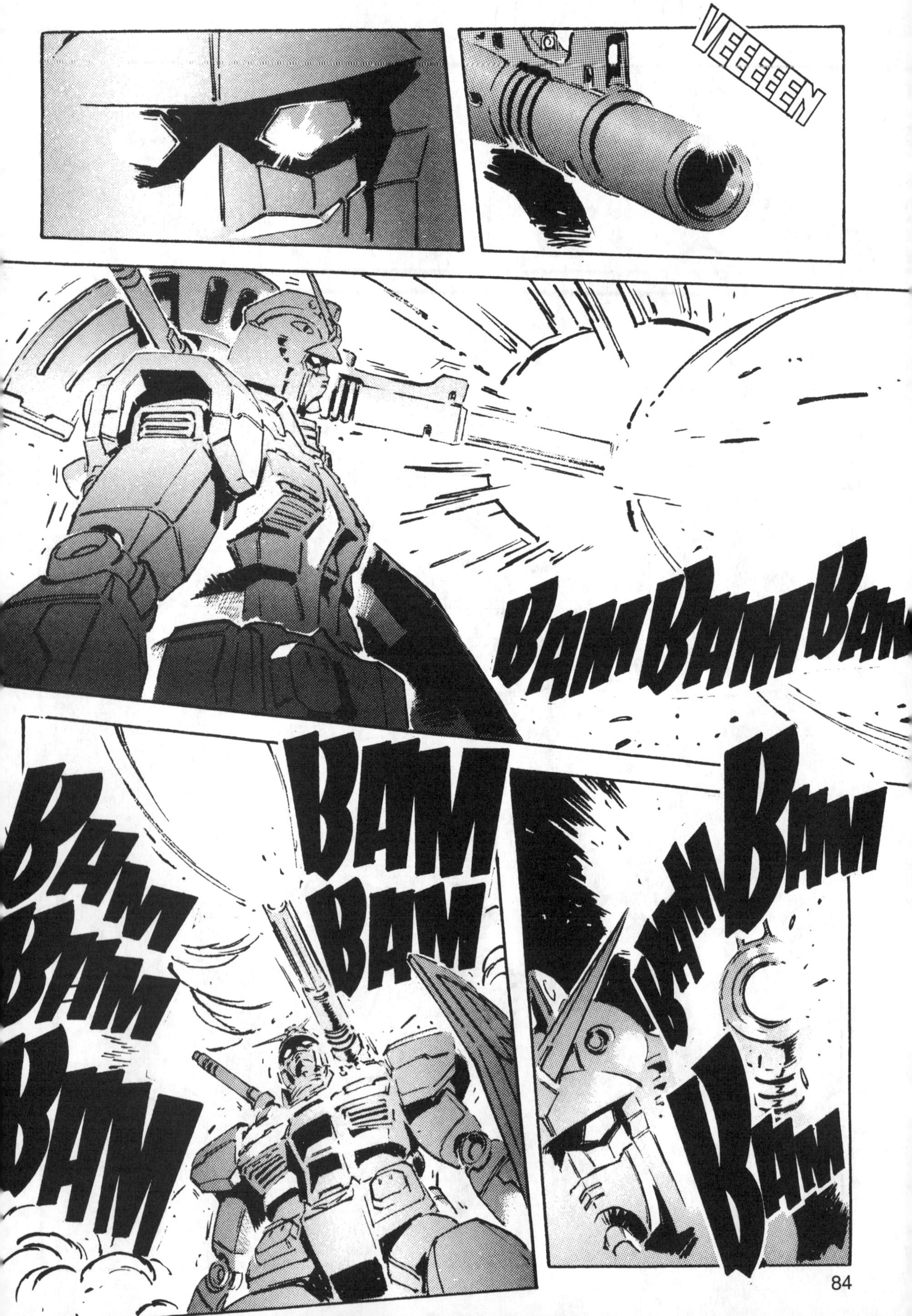
VEEEEEN
BAM BAM BAM BAM
BAM BAM BAM
BAM BAM
BAM BAM
BAM BAM BAM BAM
BAM BAM BAM BAM

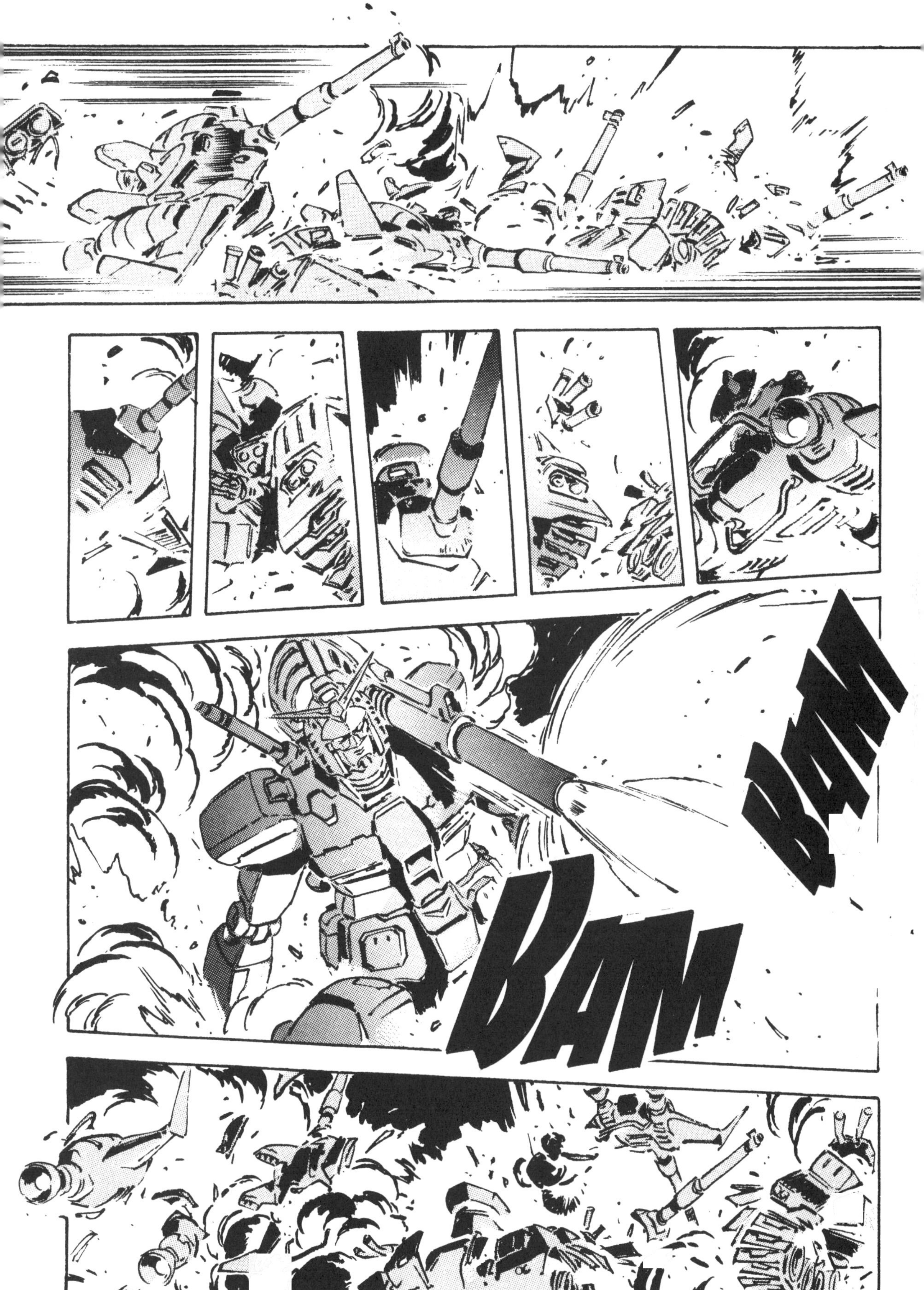
BAM
BAM

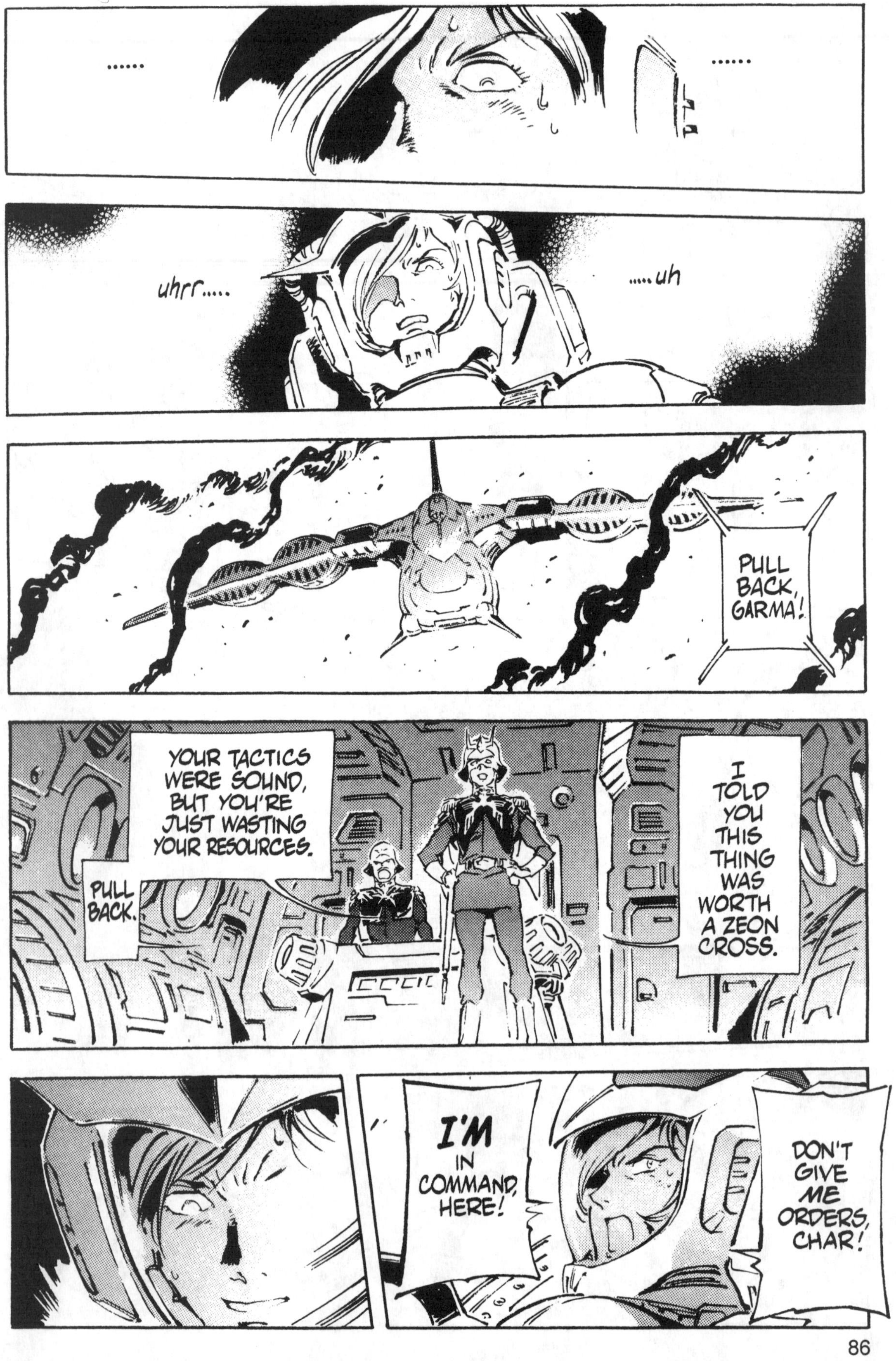
......
......
.....uh
uhrr.....
PULL BACK, GARMA!
I TOLD YOU THIS THING WAS WORTH A ZEON CROSS.
YOUR TACTICS WERE SOUND, BUT YOU'RE JUST WASTING YOUR RESOURCES.
PULL BACK.
DON'T GIVE *ME* ORDERS, CHAR!
I'M IN COMMAND, HERE!

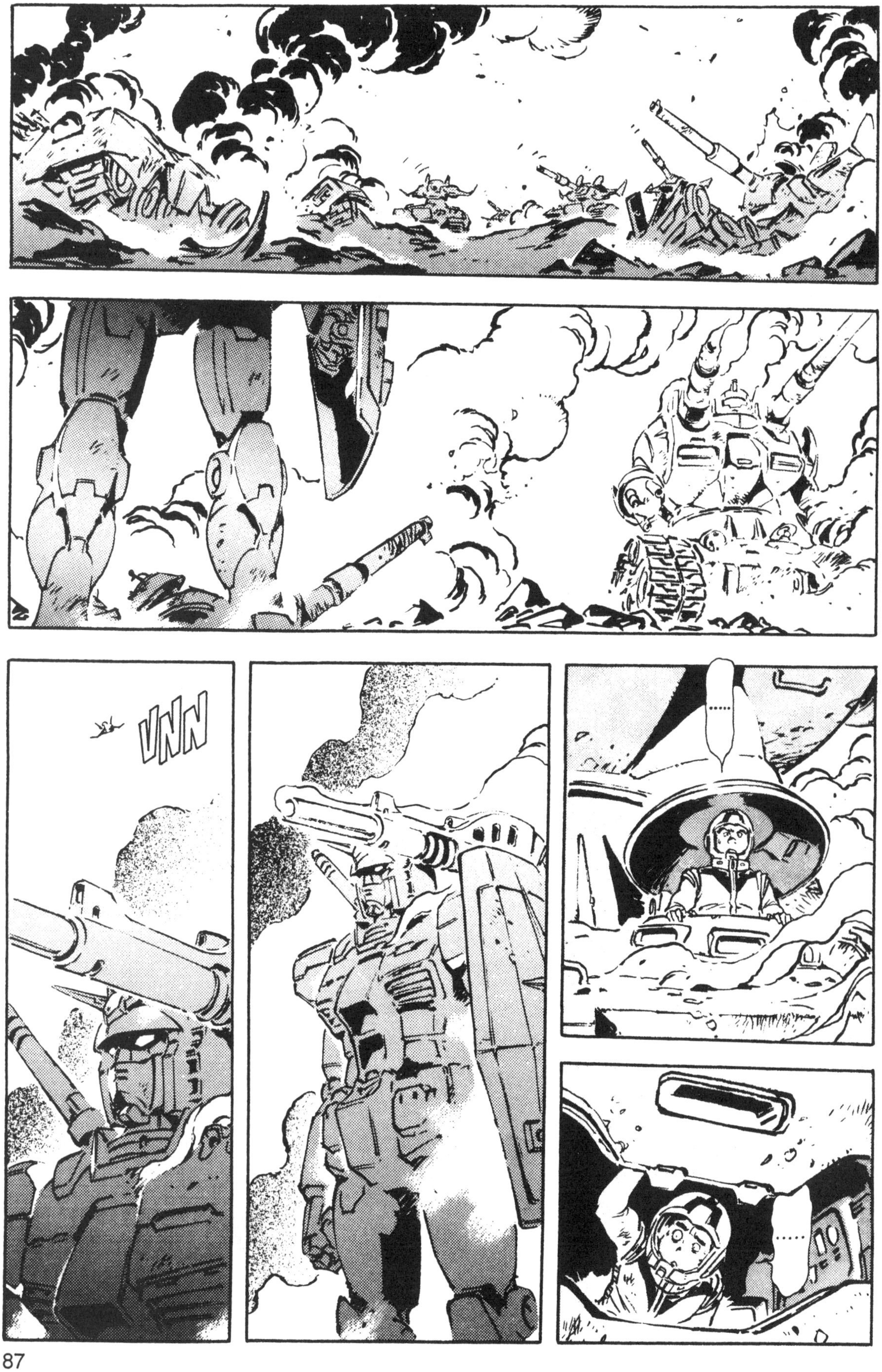
......
......
VNN

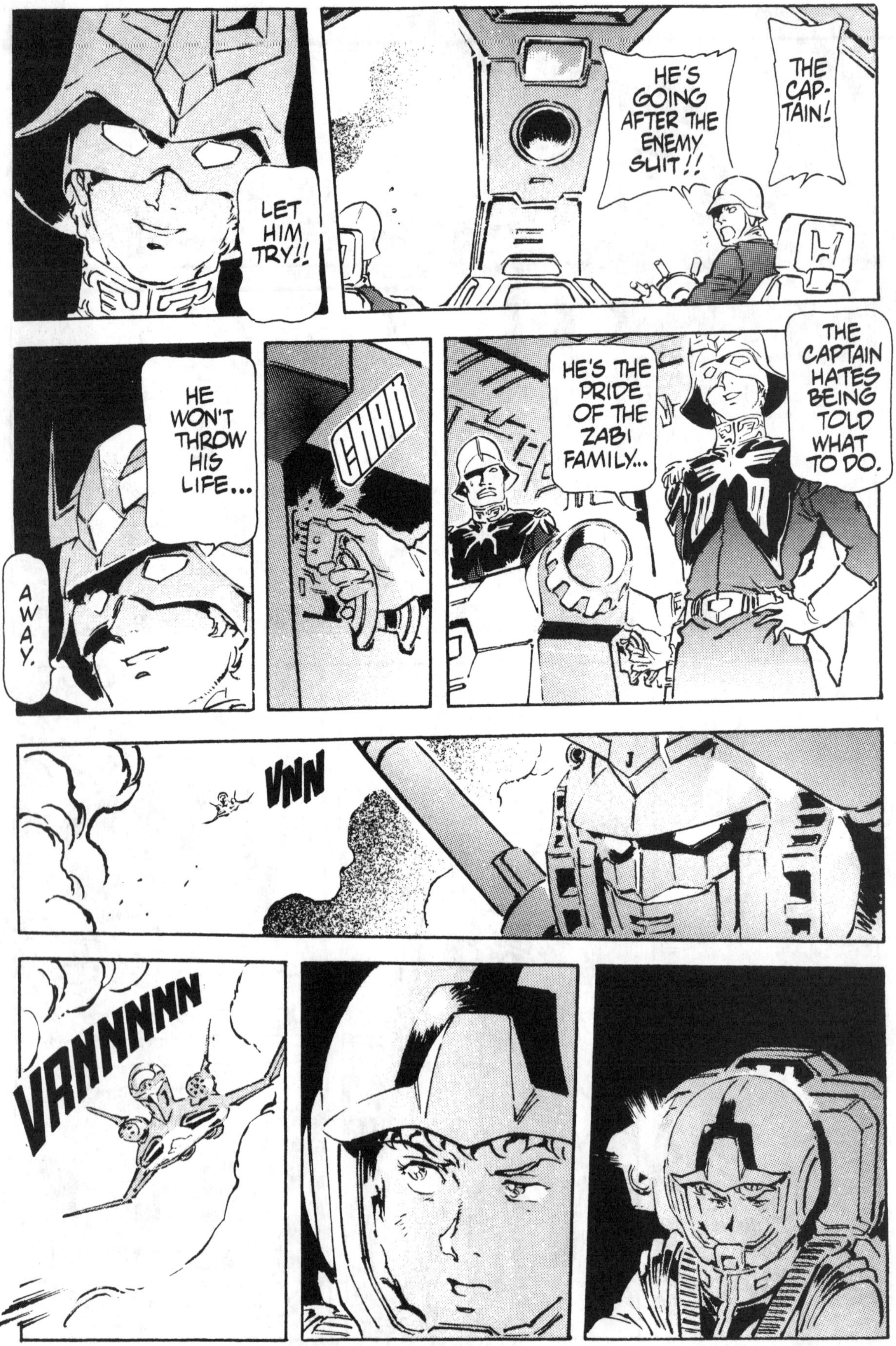
THE CAP-TAIN!
HE'S GOING AFTER THE ENEMY SUIT!!
LET HIM TRY!!
THE CAPTAIN HATES BEING TOLD WHAT TO DO.
HE'S THE PRIDE OF THE ZABI FAMILY...
CHAN
HE WON'T THROW HIS LIFE...
AWAY.
VNN
VRNNNNN

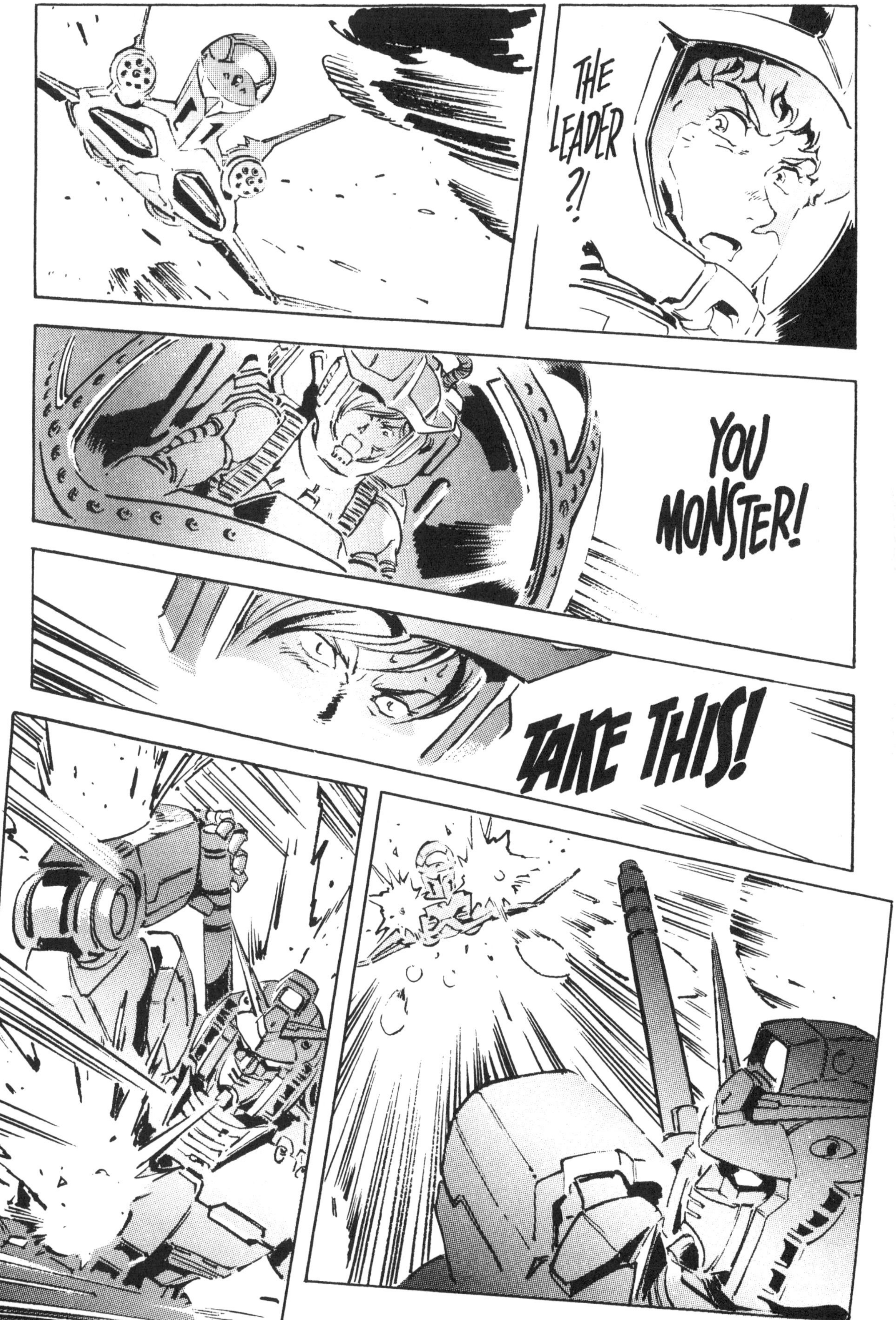
THE LEADER ?!
YOU MONSTER!
TAKE THIS!

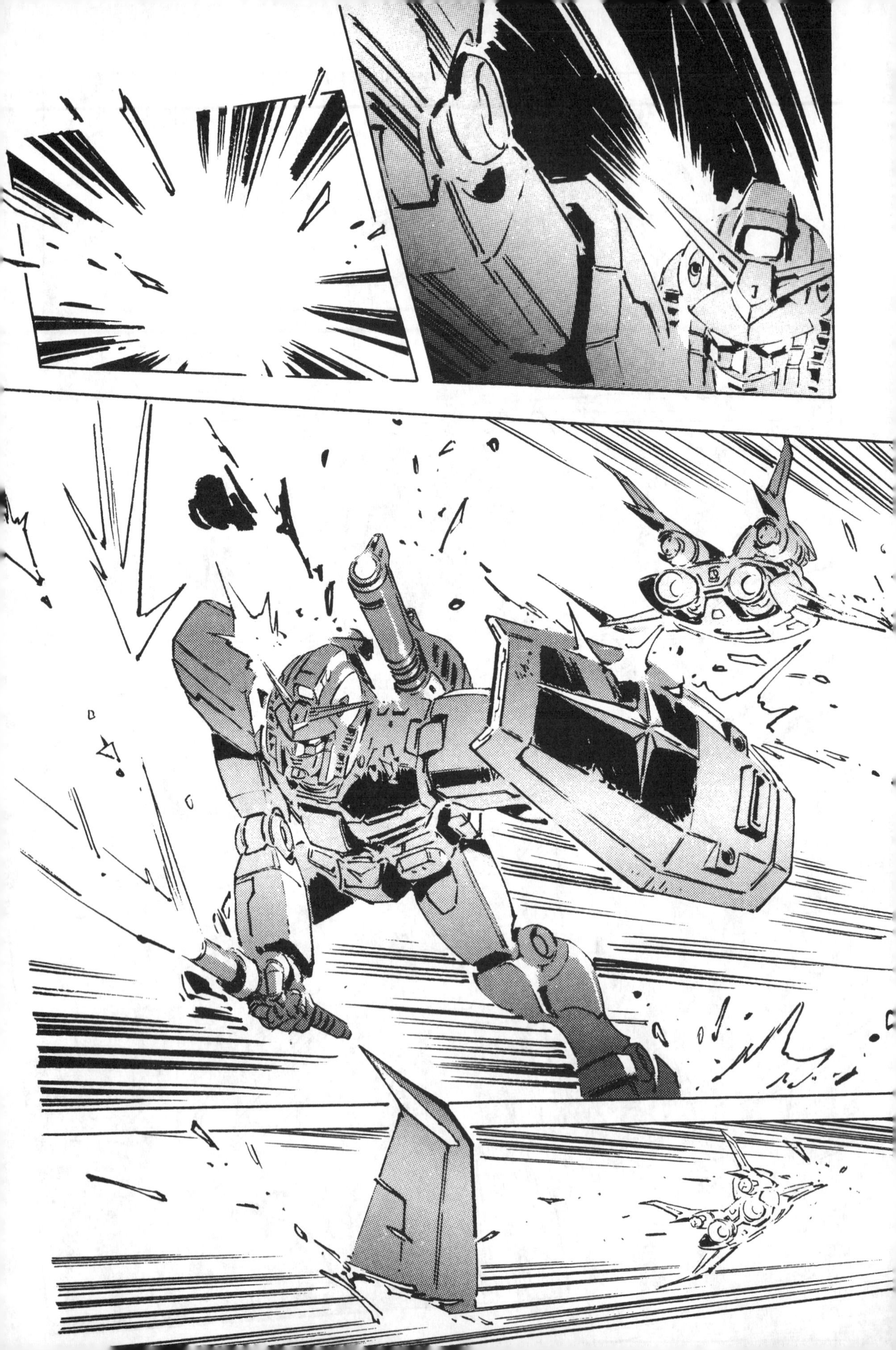

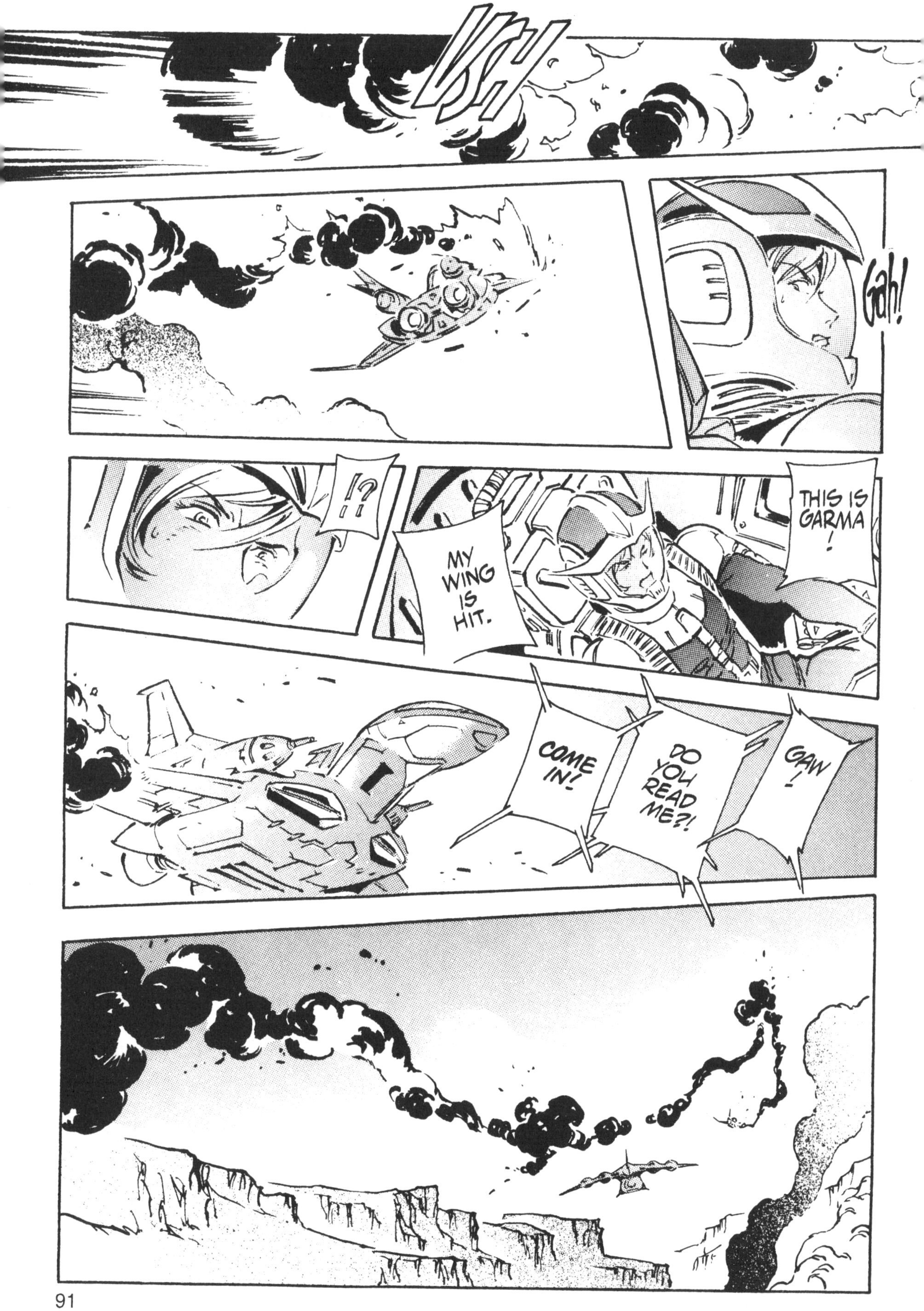
USH
Gah!
THIS IS GARMA!
MY WING IS HIT.
!?
GAW!
DO YOU READ ME?!
COME IN!

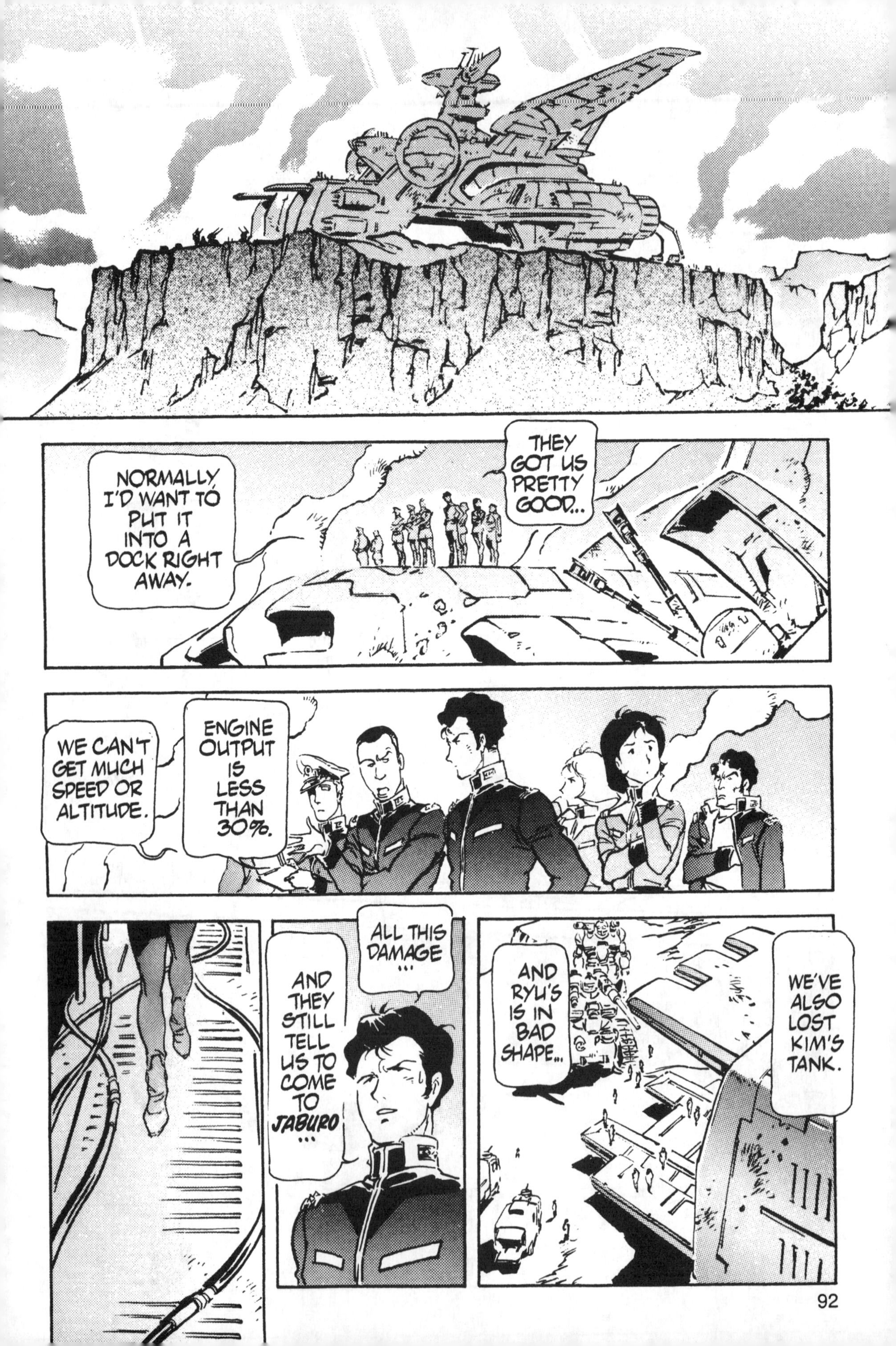
THEY GOT US PRETTY GOOD...
NORMALLY I'D WANT TO PUT IT INTO A DOCK RIGHT AWAY.
ENGINE OUTPUT IS LESS THAN 30%.
WE CAN'T GET MUCH SPEED OR ALTITUDE.
WE'VE ALSO LOST KIM'S TANK.
AND RYU'S IS IN BAD SHAPE...
ALL THIS DAMAGE...
AND THEY STILL TELL US TO COME TO JABURO...

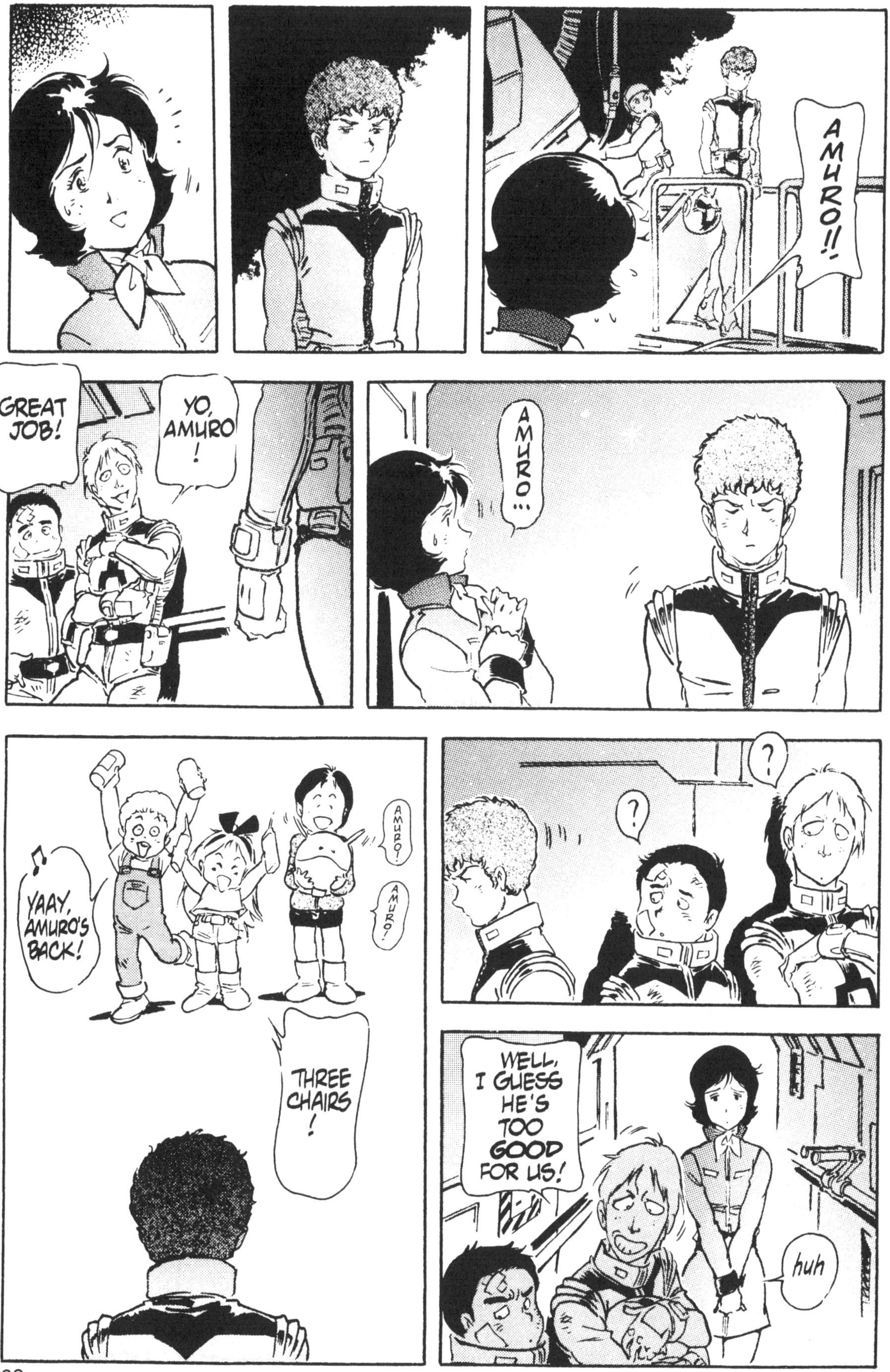
AMURO!!
AMURO...
YO, AMURO!
GREAT JOB!
?
?
WELL, I GUESS HE'S TOO GOOD FOR US!
huh
AMURO!
AMURO!
YAAY, AMURO'S BACK!
THREE CHAIRS!

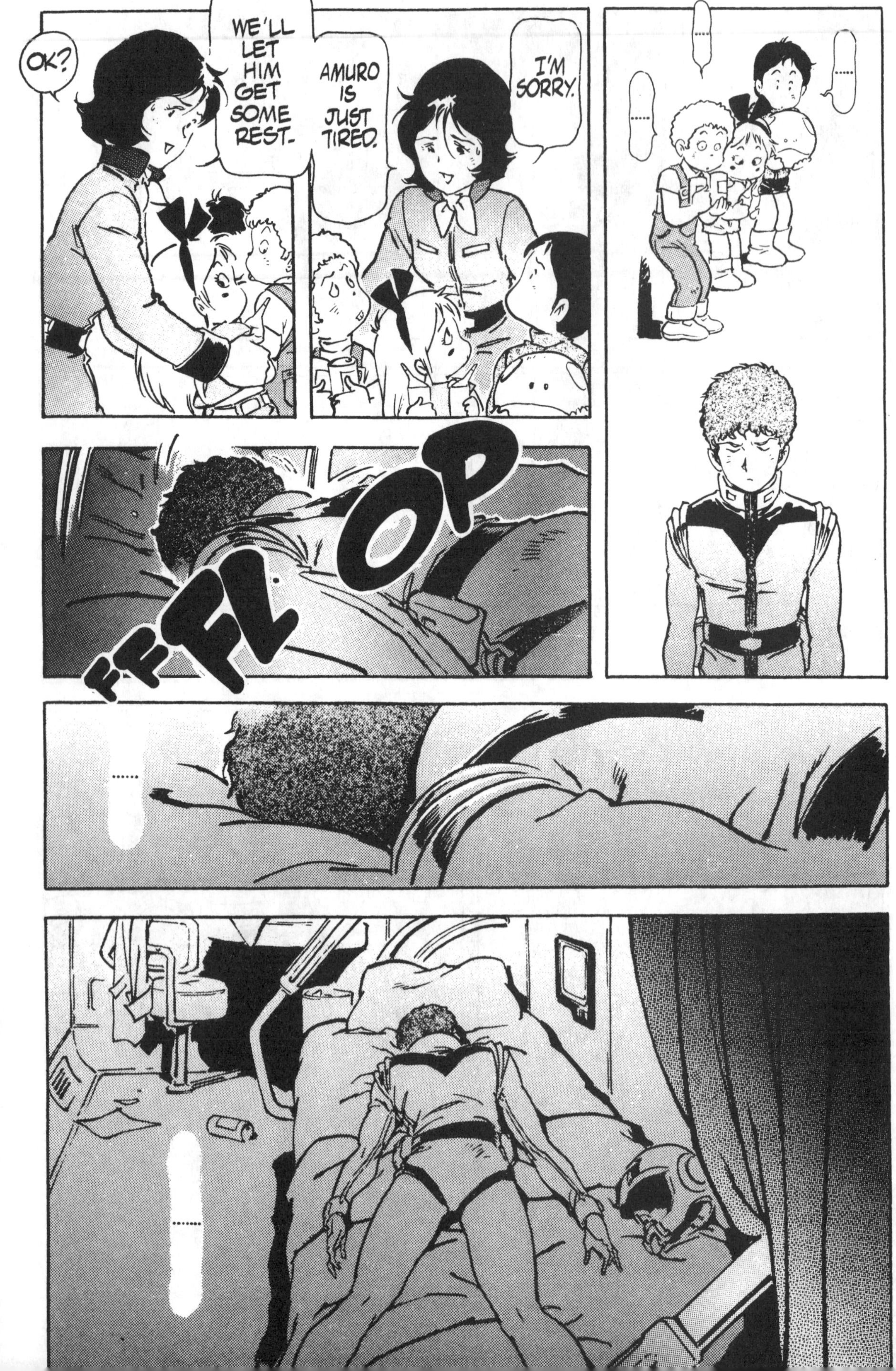
.....
.....
.....
I'M SORRY.
AMURO IS JUST TIRED.
WE'LL LET HIM GET SOME REST.
OK?
FFFLOP
.....
.....

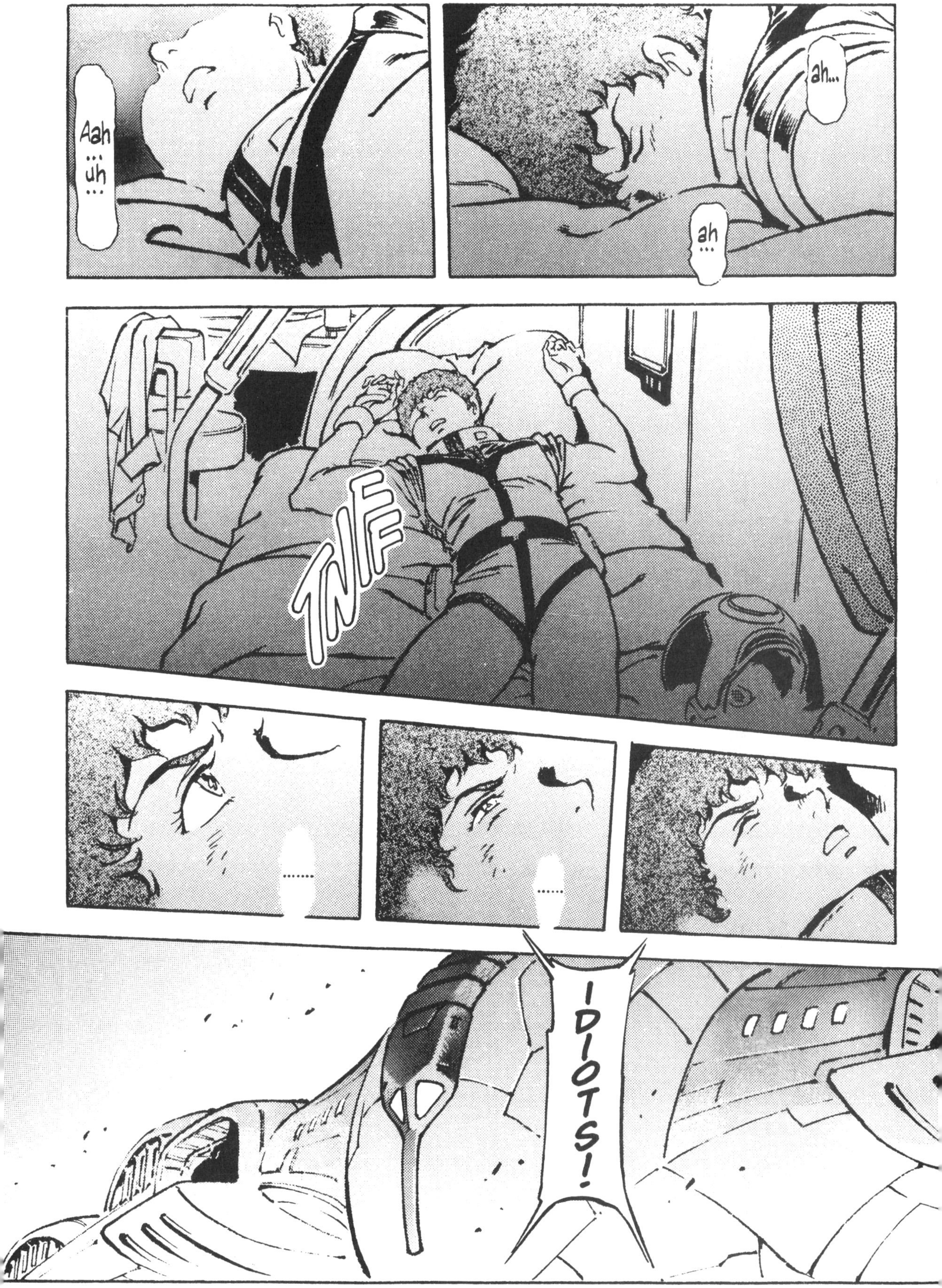
ah...
ah...
Aah... uh...
TWIFF
......
......
IDIOTS!

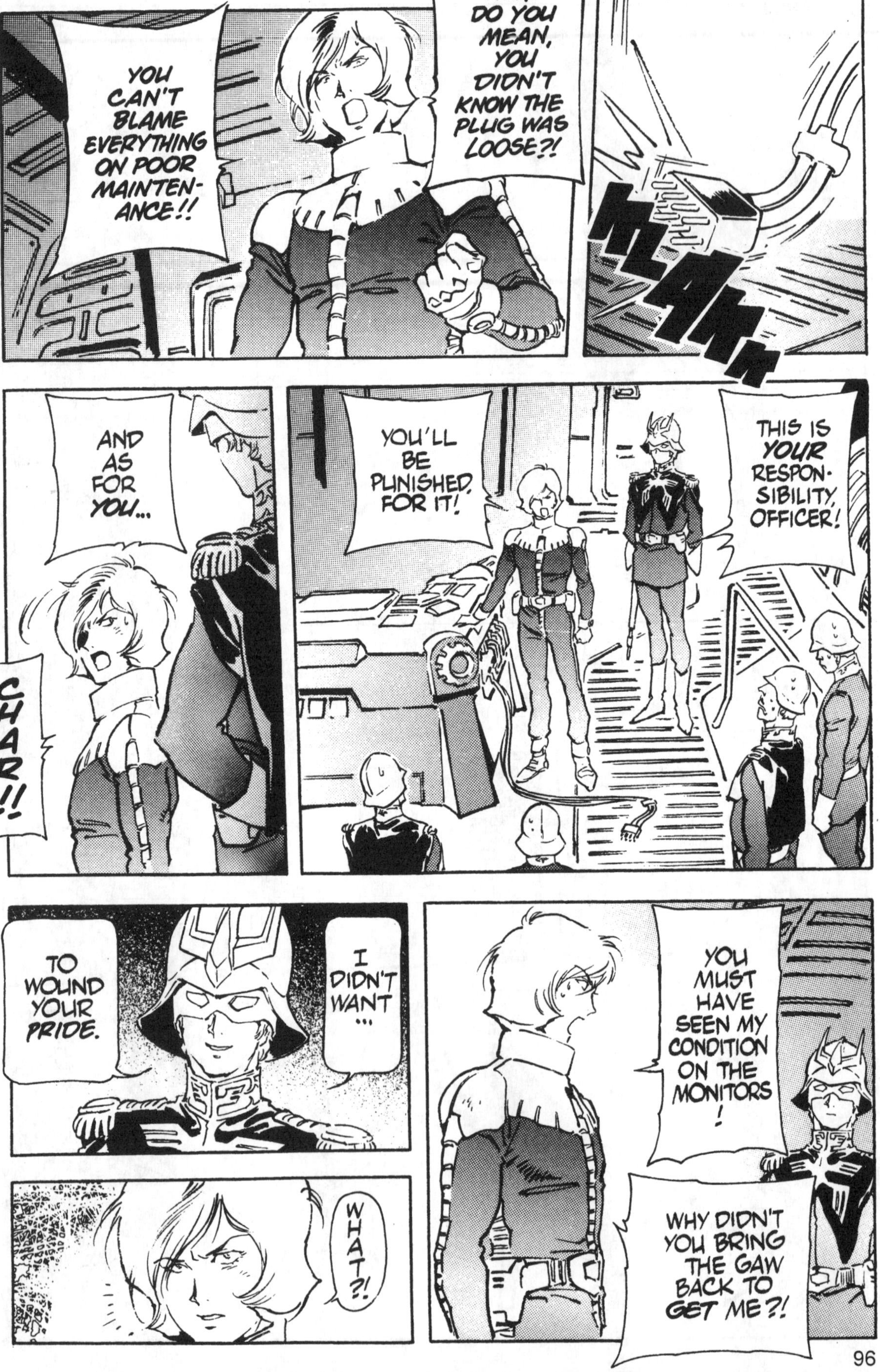
WHAT DO YOU MEAN, YOU DIDN'T KNOW THE PLUG WAS LOOSE?!
YOU CAN'T BLAME EVERYTHING ON POOR MAINTEN-ANCE!!
THIS IS YOUR RESPON-SIBILITY, OFFICER!
YOU'LL BE PUNISHED FOR IT!
AND AS FOR YOU...
CHAR!!
YOU MUST HAVE SEEN MY CONDITION ON THE MONITORS!
WHY DIDN'T YOU BRING THE GAW BACK TO GET ME?!
I DIDN'T WANT...
TO WOUND YOUR PRIDE.
WHAT?!

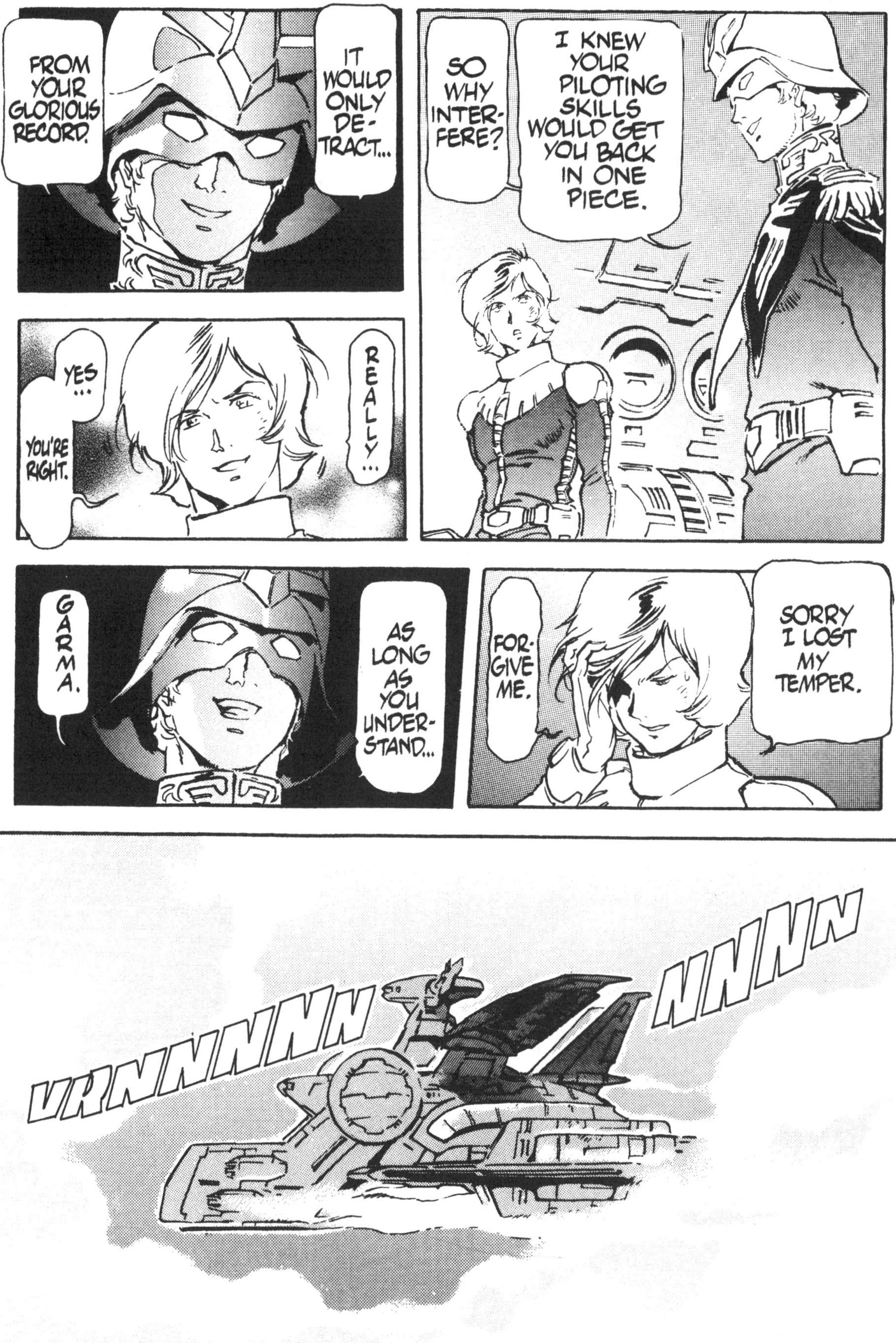
I KNEW YOUR PILOTING SKILLS WOULD GET YOU BACK IN ONE PIECE.
SO WHY INTER-FERE?
IT WOULD ONLY DE-TRACT...
FROM YOUR GLORIOUS RECORD.
REALLY...
YES... YOU'RE RIGHT.
SORRY I LOST MY TEMPER.
FOR-GIVE ME.
AS LONG AS YOU UNDER-STAND...
GARMA.
VRNNNNNN NNNN

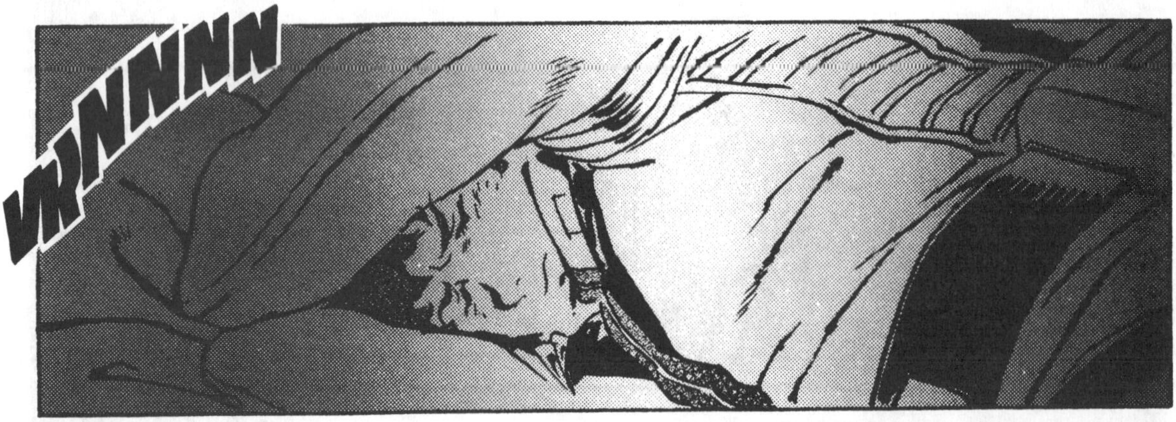
VRNNNNN

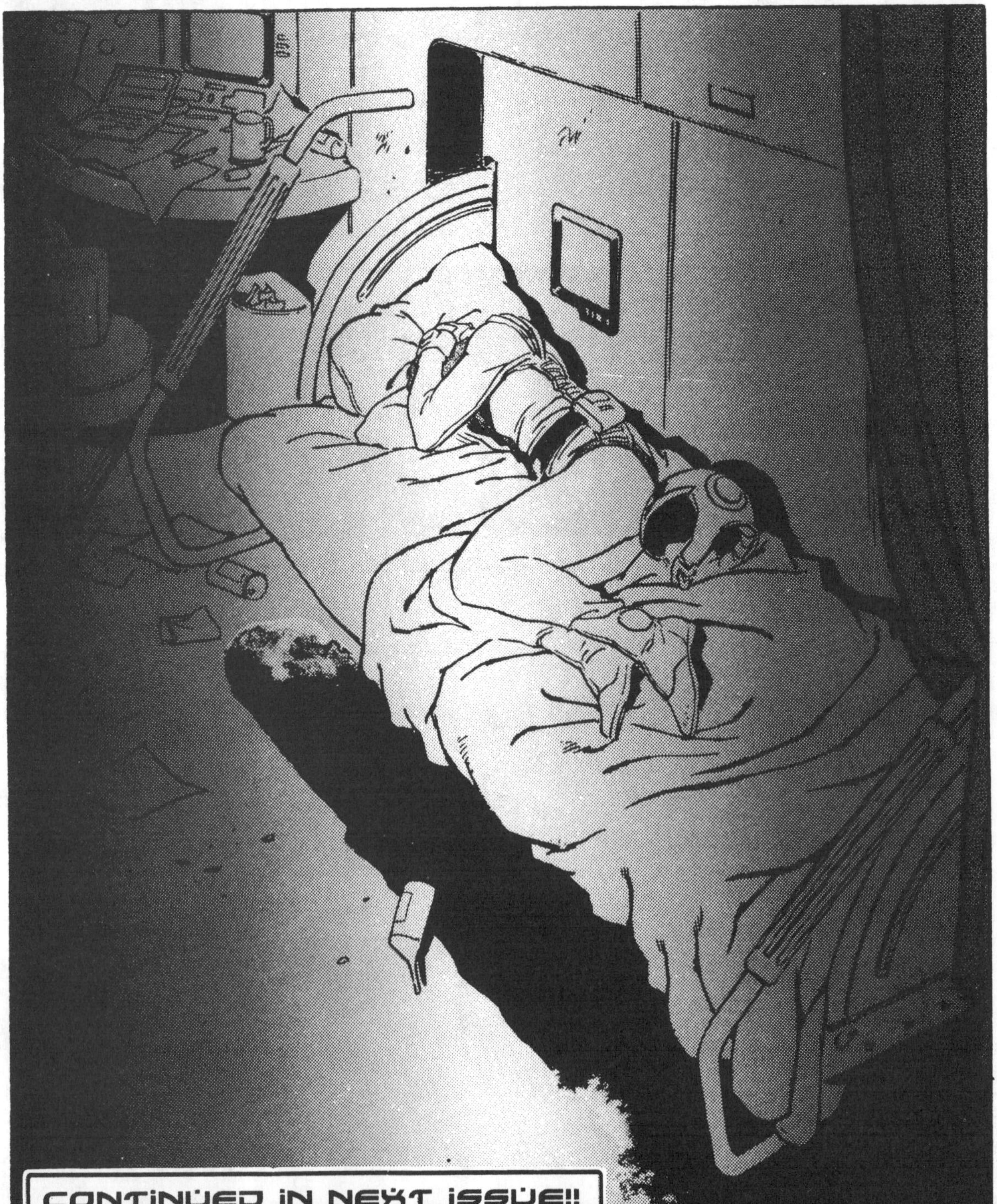
CONTINUED IN NEXT ISSUE!!

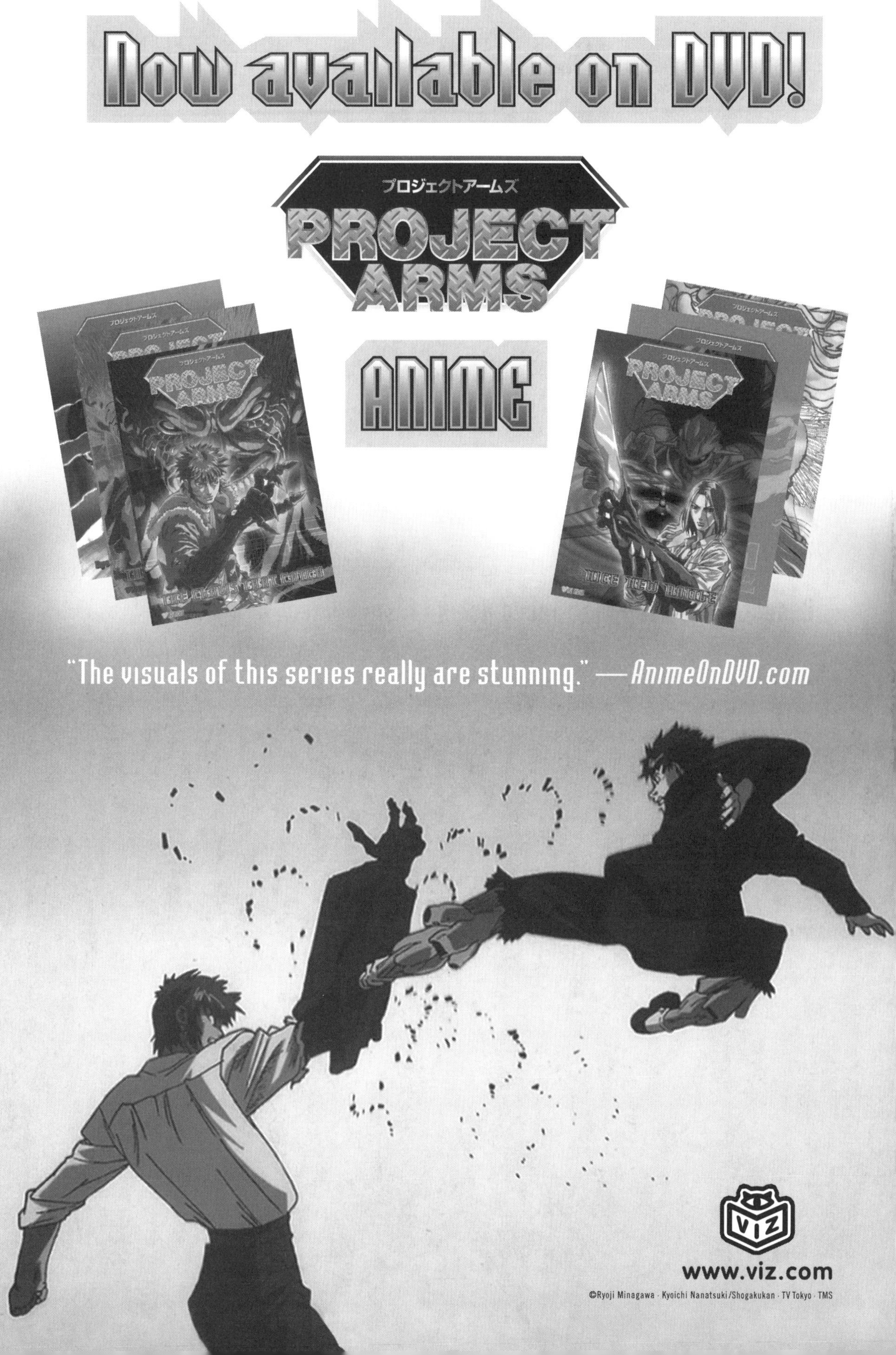
Now available on DVD!
プロジェクトアームズ
PROJECT ARMS
ANIME
"The visuals of this series really are stunning." —AnimeOnDVD.com
VIZ
www.viz.com
©Ryoji Minagawa · Kyoichi Nanatsuki/Shogakukan · TV Tokyo · TMS

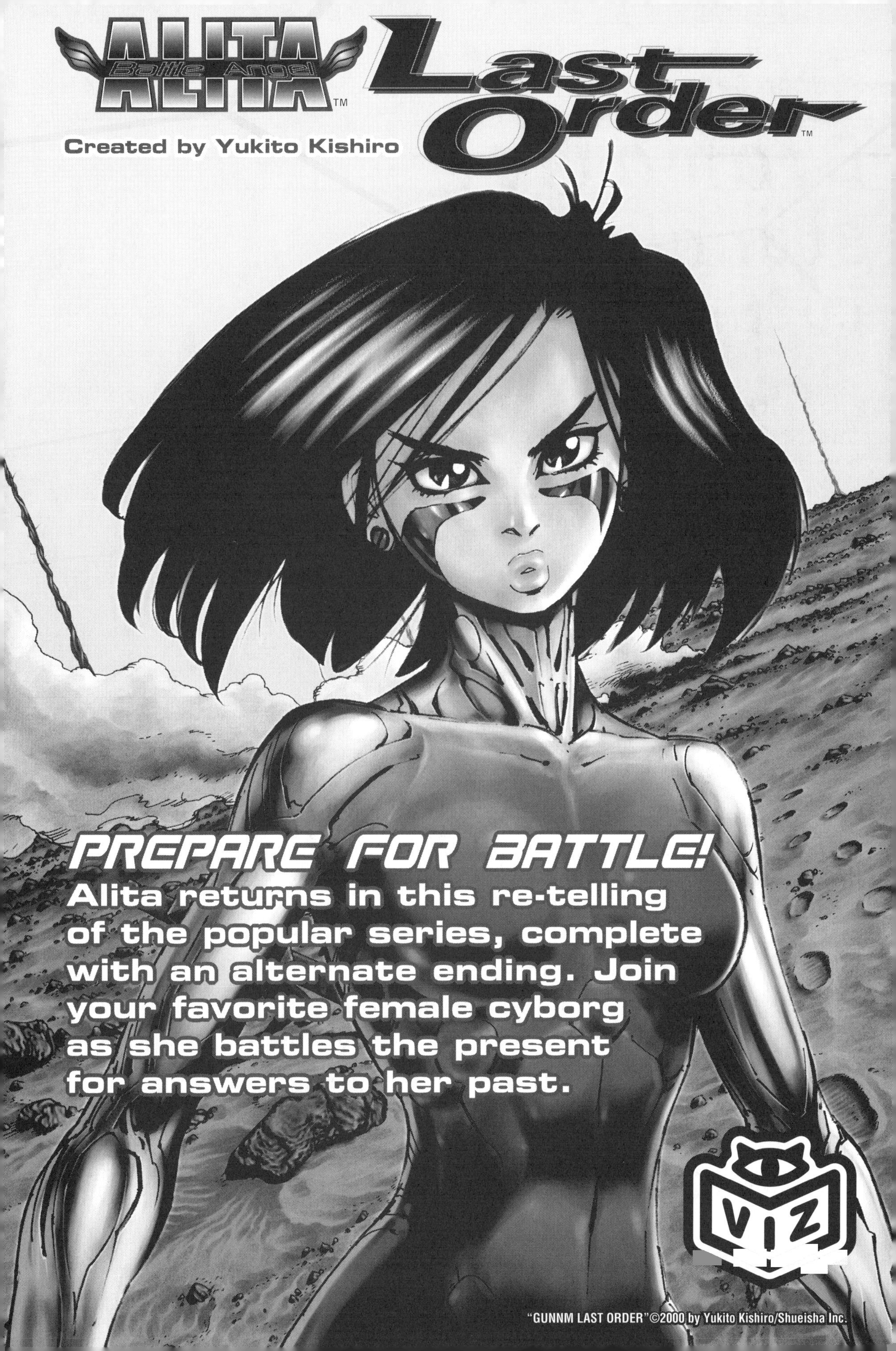
ALITA Battle Angel ALITA™
Last Order™
Created by Yukito Kishiro
PREPARE FOR BATTLE!
Alita returns in this re-telling of the popular series, complete with an alternate ending. Join your favorite female cyborg as she battles the present for answers to her past.
VIZ
"GUNNM LAST ORDER"©2000 by Yukito Kishiro/Shueisha Inc.

COMPLETE OUR SURVEY AND LET US KNOW WHAT YOU THINK!

☐ Please check here if you DO NOT wish to receive information or future offers from VIZ

Name: _____

Address: _____

City: _____ **State:** _____ **Zip:** _____

E-mail: _____

☐ **Male**   ☐ **Female**   **Date of Birth** (mm/dd/yyyy): ___ / ___ / _____ (Under 13? Parental consent required)

What race/ethnicity do you consider yourself? (please check one)

☐ Asian/Pacific Islander   ☐ Black/African American   ☐ Hispanic/Latino

☐ Native American/Alaskan Native ☐ White/Caucasian   ☐ Other: _____

What VIZ product did you purchase? (check all that apply and indicate title purchased)

☐ DVD/VHS _____

☐ Graphic Novel _____

☐ Magazines _____

☐ Merchandise _____

Reason for purchase: (check all that apply)

☐ Special offer   ☐ Favorite title   ☐ Gift

☐ Recommendation   ☐ Other _____

Where did you make your purchase? (please check one)

☐ Comic store   ☐ Bookstore   ☐ Mass/Grocery Store

☐ Newsstand   ☐ Video/Video Game Store   ☐ Other: _____

☐ Online (site: _____)

What other VIZ properties have you purchased/own? _____

_____

How many anime and/or manga titles have you purchased in the last year? How many were VIZ titles? (please check one from each column)

ANIME
☐ None
☐ 1-4
☐ 5-10
☐ 11+

MANGA
☐ None
☐ 1-4
☐ 5-10
☐ 11+

VIZ
☐ None
☐ 1-4
☐ 5-10
☐ 11+

I find the pricing of VIZ products to be: (please check one)
☐ Cheap   ☐ Reasonable   ☐ Expensive

What genre of manga and anime would you like to see from VIZ? (please check two)
☐ Adventure   ☐ Comic Strip   ☐ Detective   ☐ Fighting
☐ Horror   ☐ Romance   ☐ Sci-Fi/Fantasy   ☐ Sports

What do you think of VIZ's new look?
☐ Love It   ☐ It's OK   ☐ Hate It   ☐ Didn't Notice   ☐ No Opinion

THANK YOU! Please send the completed form to:

VIZ

NJW Research
42 Catharine St.
Poughkeepsie, NY 12601

All information provided will be used for internal purposes only. We promise not to sell or otherwise divulge your information.